Ballina in the days that have been . .

THIS booklet, although intended as a reference for descendants of Ballina families wishing to explore their origins, is also aimed at stimulating an interest locally in the towns past, and provides a lot of material for Mayo descendents to digest. 44 million Americans claimed Irish ancestry in the last U.S. census, and the Australian-Irish connection where forty per cent of the population have Irish roots. Not forgetting the millions in Britain, Canada and elsewhere in the world. During the Famine in Ireland, Co. Mayo's population in 1841 was 390,000 and by the year 1851 the population was down to 274,000. Mayo was badly affected where an estimated 50,000 people died between 1845 and 1850, with over 25,000 more emigrating in the years 1850/55.

The reason for my interest is as follows, not only is genealogy part of our heritage it is also very much in demand. Looking for information concerning your family origins is very time consuming and labourious. I realised how difficult and time consuming it is to do even a simple search for your roots. I wasn't long discovering the futility of even a visit to local or national centres where so much raw material is contained. It's important that a basic research is done beforehand so that you know the names and dates which are the keys to these literary storehouses. This is why I decided to do all the hard work for you so that you can put your feet up and study this book at your own ease. Ballina is a fine looking town, and Mary Robinson, one of our brilliant ex-presidents of Ireland, hails from Ballina.

(2004) Noel Farrell.

CO

All r

The town of Ballina and 50 surrounding townlands

THANKS . . .I wish to take this opportunity to express my sincere thanks to the National Archives for their permission to reproduce material for this publication, the National Library for their facilities and all other offices I had occasion to visit seeking Ballina material. Not forgetting the locals, I would like to thank Terry Reilly, Patrick John Bourke, and Ed Gaughans Bar, O'Rahilly St. for their warm friendly welcome.

1901 Census for Ballina

THE 1901 CENSUS is the earliest full census returns available for the entire country and can be inspected at the National Archives in Dublin. Mayo's County Library, in Castlebar, has the 1901 and 1911 census returns for the county on microfilm. The official return for each household lists the occupants, their relationship to householder, name, age, occupation, religion, ability (or otherwise) to speak English/Irish. It also gives details of the house, but absentees are not listed. The extracts below include townland or street, house number (in towns) and the names of all occupants, including lodgers and even servants in some cases. A photocopy of the original return for any household may be arranged from the National Archives for 3.00 euro incl. postage. Some townlands are divided into rural and urban.or else where they cross different parishes.

The majority of all people in the parishes of Ardagh, Kilmoremoy & Ballynahaglish (Backs) worked on the land as farmers. Any job other than farming is listed

ARDBUCKLE ROW

1. vacant
2. O'DEA - Anna, Georgina Crean, Ada Crean, Louisa Crean.
3. CONNOLLY - Michael and Mary, Michael, Annie, (tailor).
4. vacant
5. WADE - Martin and Norah, Lucinda, Norah, Martin, William, Christina, Amelia, William Fergus, (coachbuilder).
6. MORAN - William and Maria, John, Peter, Robert, Kate, Joseph, (painter).
7. EAKINS - William and Jane, Willie, Daisy, Isabella, George, John, Elizabeth, (ex RIC).
8. AHEARN - Louisa, Agnes.
9. EGAN - Daniel and Bridget, John, John McEvoy.
10. O'HARA - James and Rebecca, Henry, William, Annie, Edith, Amy.
11. DEVERS - Terence and Mary, Annie, Kathleen, Frederick, Ernest, Maud, Vincent, (printer).

ARRAN PLACE

1. PETRIE - Peter and Susanna, Elizabeth, Jessie, Peter, Frederick, Myra, (fish mcht
2. TUOHY - Malachy, Bridget Brogan, (organist).

ARRAN STREET

1. STRONG - James and Margaret, William, Alice, Margaret, Mary, James Murphy, Daniel O'Neill, James Agnew, Essie Howe, Ella Barr, Minnie Armstrong, Eliza Weir, Mary Walsh, Catherine O'Malley, (general draper).
2. FLEMING - Michael, George, Kate, John, George.
3. GALLAGHER - Hugh, John Quigley, Edward McHale, Edward O'Hara, Edward McLoughlin, Myles Tempanny, Bridget Dolan, Maria Forde, Mary Grehan, (shop asst.).
4. DAVIS - Michael, William McIntyre, William Hanley, Thomas Kelly, Thomas Ruddy, Francis Gilboy, Thomas Foy, (shop asst.).
5. HUME - Samuel, Rebecca, Susan, Elizabeth Patterson, Delia Lynch, Kate Daly, (flour agent).
6. BEIRNE - May, JOhn, Francis, Gertrude, Marie, Louise, Lilly, Annie, (publican).
7. GRIMES - John and Sarah, Belinda, Sarah, Lucinda, Michael Foody.
8. MURRAY - John and Margaret, Mary, Teresa, Louisa, John, Alfred, Hubert, Constantine, (comm. agent).
9. McCONN - James and Teresa, Eugene, Michael Connolly, Thomas Boland, Michael Gavaghan, Patrick Mulhearn, Kate Davis, Anne Duffy, (hardware mcht.).
10. FRAZER - William, Henry, (hairdresser).
11. CARR - Patrick and Maria, Edward, Patrick, (ex head Const. RIC).
12. McDONAGH - Patrick, Patrick, Bridget McPherson, Grieck McPherson, (grocer & publican).
13. TIMLIN - John and Bridget, Patrick, Kate, Sarah, Bridget, John, Joseph, Patrick McHugh, Michael Crean, (smith
14. Saw Mill 15. Mineral water Factory
16. CONNELL - Thomas and Bridget, David, Gilbert, Connie, Eliza, Joseph, Sarah Tuohy, (printer).
17. CORCORAN - Anne, Annie, Julia, Martin Jordan, Joseph Beatty, William Campbell, Robert Gordan, (lodging hse)
18. vacant
19. HEFFRON - Bridget, Michael, Bridget, William Brennan.
20. BRODERICK - Patrick and Marie, Patrick, Mary, John, Mary, (baker).
21. GORDAN - James, Sarah Shaw, Mary Shaw, Victor Shaw, John Geraghty, (boat maker).
22. O'HARA - Patrick and Lizzie, Mary Kelly, James Golden, Maria Clarke, Aggie Beirne, Mary O'Hara, Peter O'Hara, Ellen O'Hara, Patrick O'Hara, (draper).
23. WALSH - Thomas and Frances, Barbara Forde, (newspaper proprietor).
24. McNULTY - Patrick and Anne, John Gallagher, Michael Kearney, Mary Skally, (shopkeeper).
25. FITZGERALD - Michael and Nannie, Eva, Eily, Gerald, Frank Maher, (tailor).
26. vacant
27. ARMSTRONG - Thomas and Lizzie, Thomas, George, Francis, Nannie Magee, (watchmaker).

ARTHUR STREET

1. KERR - John and Helen, Mary Clince, Elizabeth Quinn, Thomas Crozier, (land agent).
2. JOYNT - George and Annie, May, Ellen Conway, Norah Walsh, (civil engineer).
3. FAIR - Wesley and Mary, (clerk).
4. JOYNT - Noulda, Amelia.
5. KELLY - Thomas and Mary, Patrick, Charles, Alice, Marke, Joseph, (comm. traveller).
6. KERR - Robert and Elizabeth,Margaret, John, Muriel, Bridget Ferguson, (solicitors clerk).
7. JOYNT - Margaret, Essie, Margaret Howley.
8. NILAN - John and Jenny, Jack, Bridget Tolan, (inland rev. officer).
9. vacant 11. vacant
10. Town Hall
12. PORT - George, (watchmaker).
13. SMYTH - Bartholomew, Margaret, Catherine.
14. GALLAGHER - Lizzie, Robert, Dan, Patrick, Lizzie, Kate, Mary McNally
15. COYLE - Margaret, Celia, Agnes, John O'Horo, Catherine Kavanagh, Patrick O'Horo.
16. MELVIN - Patrick and Catherine, Mary, Bridget, Patrick, John, Michael.
17. McNALLY - Michael and Catherine, John, Patrick.
18. SWEENEY - Martin, Mary, Martin, Bartholomew, Michael, Bridget Kelly, Bridget Quinn, (corn mcht.).
19. National School.

ARDNAREE OR SHANAGHY (URBAN)

GILMARTIN - Mark and Anne.
KEATING - Anne, Anne, Bridget Furey, Winifred Tigue.
KEANE - Patrick and Mary, John, Bridget, Ellen.
O'HALLORAN - Bee, (shop).
LEIGHTON - Richard and Mary, Anne, Alice, John, Lilly, Lucinda, Esther, Maryanne, (tailor).
JACKSON - Michael and Anne, Patrick, Michael, James, Anne, Bridget, Maggie, (horse dler.).
JORDAN - John and Jane, Mary.
JUDGE - Bridget, Ellie, Martin, (shop).
STEPHENSON - Catherine.
JORDAN - Thomas and Bridget, John, James, Kate, Thomas, Edward.
McLOUGHLIN - John and Maria, Patrick, Michael.
McLOUGHLIN - Anthony and Ellen, Michael, Mary, Martin.
NOONE - James and Mary, Michael, Ellen, John, Patrick, Bridget, (carpenter)
FOSTER - Catherine, Annie, Mary, Sarah Cuffe.
MELVIN - Patrick, Bridget Feeney, Martin Harte.
CASEY - John and Ellen, Patrick, Jane, John, Luke, Ellie, Agnes, (tinsmith).
JORDAN - Patrick and Mary, John, Patrick, Martin, Anthony, Nellie, Michael.
MAYOCK - Catherine, Annie, Bridget, Patrick, Hannah, Teresa.

This great photo was taken the 1930s from King Street, which is now called O'Rahilly St. after The O'Rahilly, who died in the 1916 rising. The picture also looks down over Knox Street (now Pearse St.) also. Henry Ford was popular in Ballina.

JORDAN - Anne, (shop).
SCANLAN - William, John Battle, Patrick O'Hora.
MULOWNEY - William and Catherine, Richard, Mary, William, John, (ex army)
HOWLEY - Peter and Winifred, James, Patrick, Winifred, Martin.
CARROLL - Thomas and Bridget, James, John, Mary, Patrick, Thomas, Bridget, (shoemaker).
TULLY - James and Maggie, Mary, James, Maggie, Patrick.
REGAN - John and Maggie, Bridget, Maggie, John, Michael.
DURKAN - Mary, Maria, Ellen.
MANGAN - Michael and Bridget, Peter, John, Michael.
MULLARKEY - Bridget, Mary, Teresa.
CUFF - James, Patrick, William and Mary, (clerk).
SWEENEY - Ellen, Fanny, Harry, James, May.
GORDON - Michael and Mary, John, Michael, William, James, Bridget, (jarvey).
GILMARTIN - Charles and Anne, Michael, Charles, Bridget, Martin, Mark, Sarah, Barbara Culkin.
McLOUGHLIN - John, ROBINSON: Pat and Mary, Michael.
FLEMING - Patrick and Catherine, Michael, Mary, Jane, Martin, James.
MOLLOY - Bridget.
MOLONEY - Elizabeth, Norah, Elizabeth, Christopher.
MONAGHAN - Peter and Mary, Michael, William, Bridget Rafter, (cellar man).
COSTELLO - Charles, Anne, Mary, (baker).
McGOWAN - Anthony and Mary, Catherine Mulrooney, (jarvey).
SCANLAN - James and Mary, Mary, Michael, William, John Sweeney.
STOCK - William and Elizabeth, Frederick, Henry, Isabella, Alfred, George, Valentine, Florence, (clerk).
LALLY - James and Mary, Maryellen, Margaret, Patrick, Edward, Bridget, James, Michael, Martin.
KAVANAGH - Patrick, (ex army).
NIXON - John and Maria, Kate, Maggie, Mary, Jenny, John, Patrick, James, Bridget, Alice, Josephine, Thomas, Patrick, Patrick Forbes, (bootmaker).
LEWIS - Samuel and Mary, George, Arthur, Emily, Charles, Mabel, Stephen, (church sexton).
McMUNN - William and Annie, Rose, Annie, John, Edward.
WILSON - John and Margaret, Annie Brice, (corn miller & fishery lessee).

ARDNAREE OR SHANAGHY (RURAL)

DOHERTY - Michael and Jane, Patrick, Anthony, Bridget, Helly.
MEERS - Edward and Anne, John, Patrick, Michael.
CORCORAN - John and Mary, Patrick, James, Patrick.
GORMAN - Mary.
MYLES - Thomas and Bridget.
HARTE - James and Bridget, James, John, Mary, Patrick.
LYNCH - Patrick and Ailisha , Tom, George, James, Mary, Maggy, Bridget, Alice.
KILGALLON - John, John, Mary, Thomas Quinn.
DEMPSEY - John and Bridget, Lackey, John, John Grehan, Michael Ferguson, (tailor).
KING - Catherine, Joseph, George, Richard, Henry.

ABBEY STREET

ARDNAREE

1. LAING - Sarah, Mary, Anne, Sarah, Mary Mulderrig, (publican).
2. DURCAN - Celia, Patrick, Kathleen, Mary, Michael Lynn, (shop & pub).
3. CALLAGHAN - Thomas and Mary, Mary Kelly, (shop & pub).
4. McMULLEN - Nathaniel and Mary, Susanna, Lucinda, Mary, John Dournie, (publican).
5. MONSON - Thomas and Sarah, Violet, James, Sela Leary, Daniel Collins, (RIC inspector).
6. FAIR - William and Cecelia, Anna, Olive, (fishery clerk).
7. WALSHE - John and Sarah, Henry, John, Albert, Charles, Maud, (RIC).
7. RIC Barracks - J.W. P.W., P.S., T.W., W.M., J.M., (all constables).
8. McLOUGHLIN - Michael, Mary, Hannah, Michael, James, Edward, (publican).
9. DURCAN - Margaret, FLANNERY: Robert and Jessie, Pat English, Maggie Durcan, Ellen Lowe, May Brennan, Kate Murley, (hotel owner).
10. McTAGGART - Robert and Anne, Anne Doyle, John Doyle, FRAIN: Dominick, Michael, TUOHY: Hugh, James, Thomas Cowley,MichaelCowley, McDONNELL: Mark, James.
11. WHITE - Richard and Mary.

Bridge st.

12. COWMY - John, Katie Deane,(Bishop)
13. McCOURT - Margaret, Katie, Adelaide, Elizabeth, Alice.
14. BARRETT - Anne, Maggie, Robert, William, Thomas.
15. SWEENEY - James and Margaret, Michael Walsh, Patrick Gillard, (tailor).
16. LYNCH - Thomas and Kate, Mary, Alice, John, Kate, Bridget, Maggie.
17. KENNEDY - James and Catherine, Bridget, Thomas, Mary, James, Michael, Kate, Timothy, Edward, Martin,(mason)
18. CLARKE - Michael and Maryanne, O'HORO: John and Mary, John.
19. MURRAY - Bridget, Rose, Joseph, Mary, Patrick Meehan.
20. HOWLEY - Michael and Anne, John, Maria, John, Michael, Bridget, James, William, (shoemaker).
21. HANICK - Anne, John, Mary, (publican).
22. McGUINNESS - Mary, Luke, Patrick, Mary, WALSH: Sarah, Joseph, John, May, (victualler).
23. REID - John, Frederick Spearman, (painter).
24. QUINN - Anne, William, William Armstrong, Alfred Stansfield, James Daly.
25. ARMSTRONG - Thomas and Emily, Edward, Patrick, Charlotte, (carpenter).
26. RUSHE - Mary, Henry, May, Maud, Agnes, Christina, John, KELLY: Michael and Anne.

27/28. vacant

29. KEEFE - Mary, John, Maggie Hannon.
30. MELODY - James, John Gaughan, (carpenter).
31. KERRIGAN - Annie, Gertrude, James, Esther, Ellen Gallagher, Mary Ormsby.
32. MULLEN - John, Pat, Margaret, (shop & pub).
33. MURPHY - Patrick and Anne, Patrick, John, Anne Conmy, Mary Cawley, (shop).
34. DONEGAN - John and Anne, Owen, MURRAY: James, Richard, Anne Gorman, Michael Dempsey, Michael Geraghty, DONEGAN: James, William, O'Brien: Martin, Patrick, (shop).
35. GINTY - John and Mary, Edward, Patrick, Mary, James, John, Michael, Mary Melody, (shop).
36. GANNON - John and Mary, Cecelia, Patrick, Annie, Thomas, Winefred, Frederick, William, (ex RIC).
37. O'BOYLE - Michael and Kate, John, Patrick, Hugh, Mary, John, McLOUGHLIN: Mary, Michael, Michael Flynn, John Durkan, (shipping agent).

ABBEYHALFQUARTER

BURKE - John and Bridget, MaryKate, John, Ellen, (bottler in water factory).

McDONNELL - Mark and Bridget, Mary, Eugene, (slater).

HOWLEY - Michael and Mary, Bridget, Patrick, Mary, Michael, William,(mason

McHALE - William and Mary, John, Catherine, Mary, Patrick, DALY: Mary, Michael, Annie, (baker).

CABRY - John and Anne, Hugh, John, Anne, Mary, Michael.

McLOUGHLIN - Michael and Anne, James, Winifred, William, BURKE: William, Bridget.

QUINN - Patrick and Margaret, Maria.

CASEY - Patrick and Anne, Mary, Patrick, Bridget,. Thomas, Mark, Michael, Anne, (tinsmith).

COAN - Michael and Winnie, Winnie, Thomas.

MELODY - Michael and Bridget, Michael, Kate, John, James, Patrick Banks.

MALLEY - Patt and Margaret, John.

HENIGAN - Kate, John and Maggie.

SHERIDAN - Celia, Maggie.

LACKEY - Patrick and Mary, May, Patrick, Patrick Rutledge.

DAVITT - Anthony and Margaret, Annie, Michael, James, Bridget, Alice, Teresa, Anthony, John.

CONLON - Catherine, Mary, Kate.

CASEY - John and Bridget, Anne.

McDERMOTT - John, John, Mary, William, James, Annie, Annie, (bootmaker).

KANE - Patrick and Mary.

McLOUGHLIN - Thomas and Mary, Teresa, Maggie, (ex RIC).

NAUGHTON - Thomas and Catherine, Mary, Bridget, Catherine.

JUDGE - William and Anne, John, Mary.

FORDE - Henry and Maria, John, Henry, Richard, Patrick, Denis.

GORMAN - Mathew and Catherine, Owen, Michael, Mathew, Annie, Mary Croghan, (carpenter).

DEVANEY - Mary, Martin.

IRWIN - Samuel and Arabella, John, Ethel, Lucinda, L.G.Lionel, J.K. Bertram, D.R. Russell, F. Edith, John McLean, (shop asst.).

HOPE - John.

CAULEY - Ellen.

FLEMING - Michael and Bridget, Jane, Ellie, James, Michael, John, Thomas, Anne, Patrick, Edward.

DEVANY - Catherine, Mary Horlon, Bridget Murray.

LOFTUS - John and Mary, Mary, Bridget, Martin, Anne, John, (butcher).

NAUGHTON - Mary, (spinner).

LOFTUS - Daniel and Sarah, Mary, Margaret, Sarah.

ANDERSON - Thomas and Maria, Mary, Eanas, (RIC).

JUDGE - Michael and Margaret, Margaret, Patrick, Catherine, Ellen, Michael, James, William.

O'BOYLE - Patrick and Catherine, Michael, James, Hugh, Stephen, Norah, John, Marykate.

HEALY - Anthony and Anne, Michael, Anthony, Mary, (carpenter).

CLARKE - Bridget, Anne, Patrick, Thomas.

SWEENEY - Thomas and Honoria, John, Margaret, James, Thomas.

MORRISSON - Anne, Maggie, Mary, John, Michael.

WARD - Thomas and Ellen, Patrick, Ellen, (tinsmith).

JACKSON - Bridget, Maggie Barrett.

MARSHALL - John and Bridget, Bridget, John, Maggie, Thomas, Anne, Robert, Mary.

LOFTUS - Mary, Maggie, Norah, Bridget Ralph.

WARD - Bridget, Bridget, Mary, MURRAY; Thomas, Thomas, Martin.

McDONNELL - Owen and Mary, Norah, (slater).

CONLAN - James and Mary, Michael, James.

ARDOUGHAN

GALLAGHER - John, James, Patrick, Anne, Catherine, Thomas.

HUNTER - Bridget, James, Michael, Bridget, John Quinn.

O'HORA - John and Bridget, Anne, Pat, (carpenter).

LAVIN - James and Mary, John, Ellen, Michael, James, Thomas, Sabina, William, Owen.

O'HORA - Thomas, Mary, Ellen.

KENNEDY - John and Bridget, Bridget, Michael, Thomas, Stephen, James, William.

GINTY - Michael and Mary, Bridget, John.

ROBINSON - John and Mary, Michael, Katie, Agnes.

QUINN - Thomas and Annie, Maggie, Anne, Patrick, Agnes, Lizzie, Michael.

LAVIN - Patt and Anne, Michael, Patt, Sarah.

MOORE - Edward, Maggie, John.

MELVIN - Patrick and Anne.

HANAHOE - Honora, Michael, Edward, Bridget, Thomas.

BALLINA (PART OF URBAN).

1. RUANE - Patrick and Mary, Patrick, Anthony, John, William, Martin.
2. QUINN - Peter, Bridget.
3. Convent of Mercy.
3. DILLON - Mary, Mary Lyons, Mary Molloy, Mary Aloysius Scally, Mary Madden, Mary Molloy, MaryO'Connell, Mary O'Donnell, Mary O'Connell, Mary Boyle, Mary Delaney, Mary Clare Egan, Mary McCarrick, Mary Henegan, Mary Scally, Mary Garrick, Lizzie D'Arcy, Mary Neville, Mary O'Donnell, Mary Greely, Mary Higgans, Mary Holmes, Mary A. Holmes, (sisters of mercy).
3. Kate Munnelly, Margaret Golden, Lucy McCarthy, (servants).
3. Gertrude McCarthy, Maud Madden, Nora McCarthy, Eva Madden,(orphans)
4. CORCORAN - Martin and Mary, John, Andrew, Maria, Elizabeth, William, (coachman).
5. FINERTY - Michael and Catherine, Michael, John, James.
6. DONNELLY - Patrick and Maria, Eamon, Patrick, (customs clerk).
7. BROWNE - Thomas and Annie, Hanora.
8. HANLEY - Margaret, Arabella, Margaret, John, Andrew.
9. McMAHON - John and Elizabeth, Isaac, John, Annie McAndrew, Bridget McHale, Mary McLoughrie, (teacher).
10. TIMLIN - Patrick and Elizabeth, Elizabeth, John, Michael, Anne Frein.
11. CLARKE - Mary, Michael Kelly.
12. KILKER - Anthony and Mary, Gertrude, Anthony, James, John, Albin, Adelene.
13. DEVLIN - Charles and Catherine,

Michael, Mary, Joseph, Patrick, Charles, Robert, Teresa, Sarah, (blacksmith).
14. MORRELL - William and Ellen, Bridget, Joseph, John, Francis, Michael, Thomas, (blacksmith).
15. CONVEY - James and Marsella, Arthur, Ethal, Mary, (clerk).
16. ROACHE - Edward and Catherine, Annie, Bridget, Mary.
17. O'HARA - John and Delia, Mary, Kathleeen, Peter, (master of workhouse)
17. MURRAY - Susan, Annie, (teacher).
17. McLOUGHLIN - Margaret, Johanna Campion, (nurse).
17. McELVENY - Anne, Annie Campbell, Mary Murphy, (nurse).
17. MOHAN - Mary, Annie Clyns, Susan Scanlon, Annie Hallinane.
17. REALE - William.
17. Workhouse - 137 enlisted,-initials only
17. Mental Asylum - 25 enlisted, (initials only)
18. Dispensary
18. McLOUGHLIN - Bridget, Thomas, Thomas Boshell.
19. Convent National School.

BALLALLEY LANE

1. HOLMES - Margaret.
2. LOFTUS - Thomas and Catherine, Michael, Patrick, Peter, (butcher).
3. O'NEILL - Thomas and Jane, Michael, Thomas.
4. CONNOLLY - Bridget, (seamstress).
5. DOHERTY - Thomas and Anne, John, Katie, Winnifred, Patrick, (smith).

BOHERNASUP

1. KILGALLON - Anthony and Annie, James, Brdiget Devanny.
2. vacant
3. MICHAEL - John and Mary, Edward, Annie, Martin, Mary, Patrick.
4. GILBOY - William and Sydney, William, William Wade, (shoemaker).
5. CARDEN - Michael and Bridget, Honor O'Horo, (butcher).
6. GILLIGAN - Francis and Margaret, James, Kate, Michael, Francis.
7. CASEY - James and Susan, John, Michael, Bridget, (plasterer).
8. McNULTY - Maria, Ellen Judge.
9. McLOUGHLIN - Patrick and Bridget, Jane, Michael, Ellen, Margaret, Patrick, Bridget McDonnell.
10. WADE - Timothy and Mary, Thomas, Timothy, Henry, (coach builder).
11. DURKAN - Michael and Winifred, Martin, Elizabeth, (fish dler.).
12. MAYBERRY - Thomas.
13. WALSH - Mary, Thomas.
14. JOYCE - Catherine, Patrick, John, Bridget.
15. ALLEN - Judy, (knitter).
16. McGINTY - Anthony and Anne, Thomas, Ellen.
17. JOYCE - Bridget, Martin Mitchell, Annie Mitchell.
18. BECKETT - Honor.
19. McNAMARA - Michael and Anne, Mary, Alice, Margaret, Nora, Michael, Patrick, Annie, (butcher).
20. GALLAGHER - Hugh and Bridget, John, Henry.
21. COX - John and Bridget, Michael Walsh, (dealer).
22. DEVANNY - Anthony and Anne.
23. REILLY - Sarah.
24. MURPHY - Mary, Kate, Thomas, John, Mary, Annie, Michael, (fish dler.).
25. COX - Catherine, Patrick, Mary Conlon, Henry Keane.
26. MANLEY - Bridget.
27. McNULTY - John, James, Maggie, Bridget.
28. SYMES - William and Mary, Bridget, (bill poster).
29. MURPHY - Bridget, Bridget, (hardware dealer).
30. BARRETT - Anne, Margaret, Jane.
31. LALLY - Anthony and Mary.
32. McNAMARA - Darby and Catherine, (bacon curer).
33. REILLY - Patt and Maria, Joseph, William, Thomas, (soldier).
34. MURPHY - Mary, Martin, Thomas, Patrick, James, (fish dealer).
35. TIGHE - Patrick, Ellen, James.
36. GALLAGHER - Anne, Ellen Barrett.
37. DURKAN - John and Bridget, Annie, Katie, Patrick, Michael, John, Anthony, Martin, (thatcher).
38. DEVERS - John and Mary, James, MORAN: Mary, John, Bridget, Martin, Sarah, Maggie.
39. FALLON - Catherine, Kate, (fish dler.)
40. DEVERS - Mary.
41. CAULEY - Patrick and Annie, Mary, Michael, Patrick, Annie, Martin, Bridget, John.
42. O'NEILL - Kate.
43. ORMSBY - Thomas and Mary, William, Lizzie, John, Thomas, (shoemaker).
44. McNALLY - Peter and Anne, (shoemaker).
46. McDONNELL - Mary, Norah, (dressmaker).

BRIDGE STREET

1. SULLIVAN - Martin, Minnie, Edward, Margaret Beirne, (shop asst.).
2./3. Pub & Butchers Stall.
4. GARRETT - John and Lavinia, Lavinia, Frances, Beatrice, Eileen, George, Bridget O'Connor, Bernard O'Dowd, Dick Winters, Samuel Walker, John Sheridan, Anne Juage, (grocer,publican)
5. PATTERSON - John, O'Soar, (boot mcht.).
6. Pub
7. COOLICAN - Francis, Anthony Scott, Pat McHoock, John Boland, George Brown, Pat Walshe, Lizzie Gallagher, (merchant).
8. CHAMBERS - Edward and Elizabeth, John Brown, (gen. grocer).
9. Shop
10. CHAMBERS - Patrick and Ellen, Nora, Maria, John Hegerty, Mary McHale, Annie McHale, Patrick McHale, John McHale, (shopkeeper).
11. DEVANEY - Henry, John, Josephine, May, Michael, Patrick Clarke, Andrew Kilcullen, Mary Harrison, Bridget Gallagher, James Keane, (grocer & pub).
12. DODD - Andrew and Margaret, Ellen, Andrew, John, Bridget, Mary Tully, James Jackson, Michael Melvin, (merchant).
14. BROWNE - John and Bridget, John, George, Matthew, Anthony, James.
15. O'HARA - Edward and Margaret, Gerald, (boat maker).
16. MELVIN - Martin and Nannie, Patrick, Maggie, Mary, Jane, Jane Duffy, (shopkeeper).
17. JUDGE - Margaret, Bridgie, Joseph Hefferon, Mary Murray, (shopkeeper).
18. WALSH - Francis and Kate, Patrick, William, Mary, Francis, Ellen, James, Annie Melody, Pat O'Roarke, (saddler & publican).
19. Pub
20. EGAN - Bernard, Honoria Walsh, Maria McHale, Patrick Loftus, Thomas Egan, Patrick Broderick, Martin Harte, Thomas Duffy, (merchant).
21. RUANE - William and Bridget, (grocer & publican).
22. SWEENEY - Martin and Mary, Mary, Annie, John, Bridget, Martin, Patrick Judge, Ellen Judge, (shopkeeper).
23. KELLY - William and Catherine, Amelia, Esther, Patrick, Mary, (grocer & spirit mcht.).
24. BEIRNE - Patrick, (baker).
25. CORCORAN - Mary, Patrick, James, Annie Lynon, Margaret Naughton, James McDonnell, (grocer & publican).
26. WALSH - Anthony, Mary, Agnes, Maggie, Katie Finnerty, Annie Kelly, Mary Sweeney, (grocer & publican).
27. COOLICAN - James, Philip Cronin, (victualler).
28. McCAWLEY - Walter and Bridget, Michael, Margaret Jennings, (grocer & publican).
29. CAFFERTY - Patrick, James Deignan, Patrick McGuire, Dominick McGuire, Michael Kearney, Ellen McMullen, Mary Commons, Roda O'Connell, Mary Culkin, Kate Finlan, (draper).
30. vacant
31. MALONE - Patrick and Mary, Annie, Lucas, Agnes McCarthy, Margaret McCarthy, Mary Munnelly, Sarah Carey, (wholesale bacon trader).
32. MURPHY - John, John, Hugh Donnelly, Thomas McHale, Edward Walsh, Sarah Shannon, Norah O'Brien, (draper).
33. vacant
34. CARROLL - Mary, William, Mary, Patrick, (shopkeeper).
35. HOWLEY - John, Mary, Maggie McHale, (pawnbroker).
36. BEIRNE - Jane, Michael, John, Clare, Jane, Florence, Catherine Conway, (mcht.).

BROOKE STREET

ABBEYHALFQUARTER

1. BOLAND - Catherine, James, Kate, Michael, Anne.
2. vacant
3. McMANUS - Celia, Michael, Teresa.
4. CONVY - Arthur, James, Maggie, John McManus, (shoemaker).
5. HALLORAN - John and Mary, Patrick, Maggie, Anthony McKenzie, (Black

smith).
6. store
7. MUNNELLY - Mary, James, Michael, Mary.
8. CONNOLLY - Maria.
9. SWEENEY - Jane, Patrick.

BROOKE STREET

ARDNAREE or SHANAGHY

1. O'CONNELL - Patrick and Catherine, Michael, McNULTY: Bridget, Andrew, (shop).
2. CONVY - Martin and Bridget, Sarah, Bridget.
3. RUSH - Ellen, William, Margaret.
4. MURRAY - Peterp and Elizabeth, James, Mary, Peter, Thomas, Maggie, Martin, Teresa, John.
5. SIZE - William and Bridget, Thomas, Mary, John, Annie, Martin.
6. CALLAGHAN - Mary, Catherine Dempsey, Anne Tolan.
7. LOUGHNEY - Lawrence and Margaret, Kate, Mary, Margaret, Laurence.
8. CARROLL - Catherine and Ellen, Mary Doherty.
9. STODDART - John and Ellen, Mary, Anne, Martin, John, Patrick.
10. CLARKE - Catherine, John, Willliam, Henry, Mary Caslin, (dressmaker).

BROOK STREET (Ballina)

1. SHERIDAN - Mary, (shopkeeper).
2. DEMPSEY - John and Anne, (grocer).
3. McNALLY - Thomas and Maggie, Martin, Michael.
4. NEALON - Margaret, Mary, Bridget, Michael J.
5. WARDE - John and Margaret, Maryanne, Christopher, Bridget, Margaret.
6. FUERY - Anthony, William, Maryanne.
7. FUERY - James and Maryanne, Michael, Anthony, Maryanne.
8. ORME - Thomas and Mary, Michael, Bridget, May, Florence, Anney, (bootmaker).
9. FLANNERY - John and Kate, Mary, Bridget, Sarah, Annie, Mary Quinn, (tailor).
10. McLOUGHLIN - John and Margaret, John, James, Michael, Annie, Elizabeth, Thomas, Bridget Devaney.
11. McDERMOTT - Michael and Julia, Michael O'Horo, (post office porter).
12. COLLEARY - Andrew.
13. NICHOLSON - James and Catherine, Margaret, John, James, Hannah, Mary, (tailor).
14. SWEENEY - John and Annie, Jennie, Berty, Mary, Maggie, (tailor).
15. vacant
16. FALLON - Mary, Julia, Elizabeth, Michael, Francis, George, Albert, (shopkeeper).
17. HOLMES - John and Kate, Patrick, Kate, Mary Judge, Winifred Judge, (shoemaker).
18. FOX - Pat and Bridget, Mary, (tailor).
19. CARROLL - John and Celia, Patrick, William, John, Martin, Maryanne, Celia, Alice, Kate, (shoemaker).
20. PATTEN - Mary, Elizabeth, John, Michael.
21. FALLON - Martin and Maria, FOX: Bridget, Annie, Larry, John, (fish dler.).
22. vacant
23. McLOUGHLIN - Michael and Bridget, Jane.
24. CONVEY - Patrick, Anne, Bridget Lordan.
25. REYNOLDS - James and Mary, Mary, James, Michael, Maggie, Bridget, Annie, Pat, John.
26. GALLAGHER - Catherine, Anne Duffy.
27. vacant
28. DUFFY - Ellen, Winifred Graham, (ex postmistress).
29. JUDGE - Thomas and Mary.
30. COX - Henry and Norah, Lizzie, Kate, (hardware dler.).
31. BOURKE - William, Robert, Jack, Maggie, Lizzie, Josie, Agnes, Michael, Annie, Mary Hogan, (printer).

BROUGHAN LANE

1. KILBRIDE - Margaret.
2. FERGUSON - Anthony and Maggie, Mary, Maggie, Patrick, Bridget, (postman).

BALLINARAHA

FINNERTY - Patrick and Julia, Maria, Thomas, Susan, Julia, Lizzie.
ROBINSON - Mary, Thomas, Catherine.
CLARKE - Thomas and Mary, John, Honor.
JUDGE - Patrick and Kate, John, Annie, Bridget.
TIMLIN - Anthony, Patrick, John, Bridget, Tom, CASSIDY: Bridget, Thomas.
CLARKE - James and Bessie, Michael, James, Kate, Bridget, Mary, John, Elizabeth, Anne, (teacher).
TIMLIN - Richard and Mary.
Rahins Nat. School

BEHYBAWN

COOLICAN - Ellen, Patrick Healy, Mary Barns.
McHALE - Patrick, Michael, Mary, Annie M., Mary Henry.
EGAN - Patrick and Ellen, Mary, Kate, Martin, Patrick, Lizzie, James, Martin.
CONNELL - Mathew and Anne, Frances, Mary, Margaret, Bridget, Bridget Tigue, (rail signalman).
FINNERTY - Patrick, William, Honor, Ann Murphy.
NOLAN - Thomas and Anne, Michael, Thomas, John, Edward, Mary, Ellen, Nicholas, (rail platelayer).
McHALE - Patrick.

BELLEEK

BARRETT - Margaret, QUINN: Mary, Thomas.
SAVAGE - Robert and Frances, Frances, Margaret, Charles, Lucinda, Edith, Victor.
OXLEY - Frederick and Elizabeth, Frances, Elizabeth, (gamekeeper).
CONROY - Denis, (gamekeeper).
KILDUFF - Patrick and Bridget, Patrick.
DOHERTY - Thomas and Kate, Patrick and Mary, Margaret, Thomas, Margaret, Patrick, Mary, Michael, MOORE: John, Robert, (farm steward).
MARSH - George and Julia, Annie, Lizzie, John, George, Julia, BOLAND: Anne, Bridget, (blacksmith).

BALLYHOLAN

McDERMOTT - Patrick and Catherine.
SHERIDAN - Margaret, Anne Gilroy.
LOFTUS - Patt and Mary, John, May, Patrick, Daniel, Agnes.
FERGUSON - Anthony and Bridget, Margaret, Patrick, Bartholomew, Charles, Bridget, Sarah, John.
FERGUSON - Patrick and Bridget, Anne, John, Mary, Delia, Patrick.
JORDAN - Mary.
WALKER - Thomas and Margaret, Robert, John, Emma, A.Lizzie, James, William, Ernest.
JUDGE - Michael, HARKIN: Thomas, William, Celia, Bridget Calpin.
CLARKE - Patrick and Anne, Thomas, Michael, Mary, Andrew, Dorrinda, Bridget.
RAFTER - Martin and Annie, Michael, Bridget, Richard, Martin, Mary, James, Margaret, O'HARA: Mary, Patrick.
RUDDY - Thomas and Mary, Andrew, Thomas, Patrick, Anney, Jane, Lizzie, James, Margaret.

BUNREE

DWYER - Catherine, Thomas, Minnie, Charles, Anne, Hugh, Frederick, Winifred Gillespie.
KELLY - William and Mary, Mary, James, Patrick.
LAVELLE - John and Bridget, Patrick, Margaret, Tom, Annie, William, Martin, Mary, Bridget, (fisherman).
VAUGHAN - Winifred.
MORAN - Mary, Thomas.
WARD - Kate.
RUTLEDGE - John and Bridget, Mary, Bridget, Thomas, Alice.
DOHERTY - Mary, Edward, Kate, John, Michael, Lizzie.
ARMSTRONG - Catherine, Mary.
ROLSTON - Margaret, Edward, James.
COLLINS - Patrick and Mary, John, Kate.
DUFF - Thomas, Maryanne, Bridget, Nelly, Sarah, Michael.
KANE - William, Mary, William, Kate, (fisherman).
KENNEDY - William, Lizzie.
DOLAN - Catherine.
FOLEY - Michael and Maria, James, Michael, Mary, Bridget, William, Charles, Lizzie, Thomas, (mason).
JORDAN - John and Bridget, Mary, Patrick, William, Ambrose, Martin, (miller).
KELLY - Anne.
CORABINE - Mary, John Shea.
DUNCAN - William and Mary, James, Mary, Edwin, Kathleen, Daniel, Charles, (fisherman).
KELLY - Elizabeth, Barbara.
DWYER - Catherine, Mary, Anne.
LOFTUS - James.
CORCORAN - Patrick and Kate, John, Michael, Patrick, Andrew, Martin Cawley, (carpenter).

GALLAGHER - Charles, Annie, Agnes, Mary Guerin, Bridget O'Hora, Michael Mulroony, (mcht.).

CASTLE ROAD

1. NEWEY - John and Matilda, William, (ex RIC).
2. McEVOY - Catherine, James, Eliza, Joseph, (laundress).
3. RUANE - Anthony and Maria, Mary, William, Anthony, James, Ellen, Thomas, Patrick, Joseph, (painter).
4. HAMILTON - David and Maria, Ellen, William, Cecil, Hector, Ellen McDonald, Annie Boland, Margaret O'Horo, (vet. surgeon).
5. BARKLEY - Thomas and Jane, Stephanie, Nellie, Ruth, Naomie, Belinda Ormsby, Ellen Cunningham, (bank accountant).
6. ROONEY - Annie, Cecelia, Charlie, Patrick, Eileen, Nora, Annie McNally.
7. CARNEY - Patrick and Mary, George, (bank porter).
8. FARMER - Kate, John, Charles, Patrick, Kate, Alice.
9. BRODERICK - Johanna, James, Harry, Michael, (grocer).
10. SHERIDAN - Bridget.
11. GARDINER - James, (painter).
12. BURKE - Margaret.
13. LEWIS - John and Ruth, William, Charles, (ex coast guard).
14. HENDRY - Patrick and Bessie, Mary, Sarah, (bank porter).
15. McCARRICK - Anthony and Kate, Eva, Maggie, Willie, (bank porter).
16. HUIE - Ellen, Charles, Elizabeth.
17. KILDUFF - James and Elizabeth.
18. vacant
19. HICKS - Isabella, Mary, Lizzie, Annie McLoughlin.
20. ANDERSON - John, Henrietta, Ethel, Jessie, Bessie, Richard, Annie West, Jack Glenaiming, (ex RIC sgt.).
21. BANKS - Mary, Mary, Maggie Butler, (grocery).

CHARLES STREET

1. Royal Irish Constabulary Barracks - P.R., J.M., M.McG., H.J., J.C., W.D., J.G., J.G., A.H., M.L., P.McG., A.K., P.T..

1. ROONEY - Pat and Sarah, Helena, Mary, Patrick, (hd. Constable).

1. MORTON - James and Lizzie, George, (RIC).
2. MORRISSON - Hugh and Margaret, Kate, Elizabeth Hanna, (ex RIC).
3. CAIRNE - John and Mary, Joseph, Elizabeth, Albert, William, Frank, Marie Harte, (presby. clergyman).
4. Presbyterian Church.
5. National School.

CONWAY'S LANE

1. CALLAGHAN - Thomas and Mary, Patrick.
2. NASH - Thomas and Mary, Henry, Mary, Patrick, (tailor).
3. COYNE - Bridget.
4. HOLMES - Anthony and Bridget, Kate, Bridget, Michael, Catherine, DOHERTY: Mary, Mary, Kate, Martin, Elizabeth Moore.

CHAPEL LANE
ABBEYHALFQUARTER

1. KELLY - Charles and Bridget, Martin, Patrick, Martin, Christy, James.
2. HEALLY - Mary.
3. WALSH - Mary, William.
4. MURRAY - Anthony and Catherine, Sarah.
5. CULLEN - Mary, Jane.
6. CORCORAN - Winifred, Kate, Sarah.
7. MURRAY - Mary, Ellie, Martin, Kate, Thomas.
8. KILKER - Catherine, Ellen, Bridget.
9. FITZGERALD - Michael and Catherine, Kate.
10. LYNCH - Bridget, Michael, Edward, Bridget Naughton.
11. McGLYNN - Catherine, Barrett: Thomas and Anne.

CHURCH ROAD
ABBEYHALFQUARTER

1. SMYTH - Patrick and Elizabeth, Catherine, Bridget, (RIC).
2. ATKINSON - Harry, Isabella, William, Elizabeth Black.
3. McNULTY - Anne, Bridget, Thomas, Michael.
4. MULLROONEY - Annie, Margaret, Edward, Helena, Frederick, Harriett, Annie, Teresa, Robert.
5. GUILFOYLE - Edward and Margaret, Michael, May, Annie, William, (RIC).
6. LEONARD - Philip and Anne, Mary, Annie, Patrick, Eugene, John, Philip, Joseph, Thomas, Francis, (summons server).
7. RUDDY - Bridget, Margaret, Sarah, John, Kate, (publican).
8. KENNEDY - Thomas and Katie, Thomas, Bridget, Kate, Sarah, Pat, Dan, Michael, (publican).

CHURCH ROAD
ARDNAREE or SHANAGHY

1. CLARKE - John and Anne, Mary, Anna, Patrick, Bridget, Martin, Ellen, (travelling agent).
2. ARMSTRONG - Thomas and Mary, Louie, Charlotte, Violet, Annie Kelly, (RIC).
3. WALKER - Maria, Minnie.
4. GLEN - Bertha.
5. BROOKE - James and Elizabeth, Ethel, Gertrude, Margaret Fitzgerald, Sarah Conlan, Annie Cogan, (RIC).
6. McGILLYCUDDY - Michael and Julia, Annie, Ellen, Michael, Boctius.
7. MURRAY - Pat and Mary, Teresa, Lily, (butcher).
8. GILMARTIN - Bridget, John.
9. HOLLERAN - Thomas, Kate.
10. McNULTY - Rose, John.

CLARE STREET
ABBEYHALFQUARTER

1. WALSH - Michael and Margaret, Patrick, Jane Quinn, (publican).
2. DUNCAN - Winifred, Lizzie, Winifred McDonnell.
3. KELLY - John and Bridget, Kate, James, John, Michael, Thomas, Bridget, William, Peter, Joseph, Maud, fisherman
4. BARRETT - Margaret, Ellen. C
5. CROSBY - Edward and Jane, Catherine, Denis, Mary, Bridget, Margaret, Edward, (RIC sergt.).
6. KENNEDY - Patrick, Ellen, (mason).
7. QUEENAN - Andrew and Margaret, Patrick Hegarty, Joseph Chynch.
8. McCARRICK - Jane, Annie, (dressmaker).
9. CULLIN - Thomas and Mary, Mary, Kate, James, Maria, (fisherman).
10. JORDAN - Hanna, (shop).
11. REGAN - Richard and Jane, Christy, Anne, Mary, (carpenter).
12. CONWAY - Matthew and Annie, John, Kate, Teresa, Bridget Moran, James Hynes, William Stenson.
13. BURROWS - Maria.
14. KENNEDY - James and Anne, Bridget, Martin, Maria, Patrick, Amy, John, Bridget Judge, (clerk).
15. DUFFY - Martin and Helena, (carpenter).
16. ATKINSON - Esther, Esther, Kate Bryce.

CARROWCUSHLAUN WEST

TIMLIN - Patrick.
HALLERAN - James and Mary, Bridget, Michael, John, James.
MURRAY - Martin and Kate, Pat, Michael, Mary, Bridget.
ARMSTRONG - John and Jane, William, Alex, Jane, Mabel, John, Thomas, Frederick, Eleanor, Kathleen, Catherine May, (watchmaker).
DIAMOND - Catherine.

CARROWCUSHLAUN

STUART - James and Annie, Patrick, Annie, James Lynn, Bridget Halron.
HENIGAN - Patrick, Mary, Patrick, Roger, Bridget, Anne, Michael, John.
HENNEGAN - Mary, Lizzie, Patrick, Margaret.
HAMILTON - Thomas, John, Joseph, Annie, Catherine.
MELVIN - Martin and Nabby.
MULLEN - John and Barbara, William, John, Kate, Bridget, Anthony, Agnes, Thomas Gaughanp.
MURRAY - Mary, Annie, James, McNALLEN: Mary, Mary.
HOLERAN - James and Bridget, Mary, Jane, Pat, James, Annie, Denis.
HOLLERAN - John and Mary, Patrick.
QUINN - Martin and Mary, Celia, Anthony, Stephen, Kate.
MULDERRIG - Pat and Sidney, Mary, Kate, Ellen, Maggy, Michael, Barbara, Pat, (builder).
QUINN - John and Mary, Patrick.

TIIMLIN - Thomas and Mary, Patrick, William, Ellen, Anthony.
RALPH - Mary, Michael, Margaret.
GAWLEY - William and Anne, Mary Quinlan.
DEMPSEY - Bridget, Mary, Lizzie, Anne.
MUNNELLY - John and Jane, Mary, Martin, Pat, Jane.

CLOONSLAUN

CONVEY - Maria, John, Patrick, Bridget, Catherine, Thomas Robinson, Michael O'Hora.
WALL - Mary, Josephine, Mary, Alphonsus, Francis, Gertrude, Leo, (Nat. teacher).
DOHERTY - John and Bridget, Patrick, John, Anthony, Mary, Bridget, James, Thomas, Annie, Stephen, Agnes, Joseph, Michael.
MURRAY - Mary, Michael, John.
McGOWAN - Mary, Kate, Mary, Bridget, Patrick, Martin, Anne.
TIMLIN - Dominick and Catherine, Mary, Pat, Michael, Bridget, James, William, Katie, Simon, Dominick, Ellen.
MURPHY - Catherine, John, Anthony, James, Peter.
BURKE - Patrick and Bridget, Bridget, Michael.
MURRAY - John, Anne Hession.
MUNNELLY - Patrick and Anne, Anne, Sarah, Maggie, James, Mary Timlin.
HIGGINS - Bridget, Mary, Patrick, Martin, Anne.
MELODY - Bridget, Maria, Catherine, Michael.
MURRAY - Patt, Patt, Catherine, William.
MURRAY - Martin and Winefred, Patrick, Anne, Michael, Winefred.
McGOWAN - Michael and Anne, Ellen, Patrick, Margaret.
PADDEN - Michael and Ellen, Patrick, Mary, Bridget, Ellen, Kate.
O'HARA - William and Julia, Catherine Walshe.
PHILBIN - Richard and Bridget, Honoria, Patrick.
DOWD - James and Winifred, Edward, Patrick, Anne, Mary.
TIMLIN - James and Catherine, John, Michael, Stephen, Mary, Ellen, James.
HALLORAN - Margaret, Maria, William, Bridget, Patrick, Maggie.
WALSH - Anthony, Mary, Thomas, Kate, Anne, John.
MULDERRIG - Michael and Ellen, William, Mary, Michael, Patrick, Kate.
LUNDY - James and Margaret.
MULDERRIG - Patrick and Catherine, Sarah, Patrick.
FERGUSON - John and Mary.
McGOWAN - Mary, William, Anthony, Kate, Ellen, Maggie, Agnes.
CONVEY - Bridget.
O'BRIEN - Mary.

CROCKETSTOWN

1. SHAW - Robert and Bridget, Anthony, Teresa, Annie, Robert, (clerk).
2. WALSH - Patrick and Bessie, Michael, Kate, Peter, Annie.
3. BROWN - Adam, John Markham, (shipping agent).
4. HATELY - George and Priscilla, Margaret, John, William, Margaret, Mary Hegarty, (harbour master).
5. HENIGAN - Henry.
6. HENNIGAN - Peter and Maria, Henry, Michael, Joseph, William, Edward, (dock porter).
7. LACKEN - Mary, Bridget.
8. McCLEARY - Mary, Eliza.
9. BATTLE - Catherine, LOUGHNEY - Mary, John.
10. WALSH - James and Ellen, B.Ellen, P.Stephen, J.Joseph, Thomas, John, Michael, James.
11. HUMBER - Anne, Mary McNulty.
12. CARNEY - Peter and Bridget.
13. MELVIN - Pat and Bridget.
14. MELVIN - James and Anne, Edward, Patrick, Anne, Bridget, Ellen, Sarah, John.
15. TEMPLE - Mary, Joseph, Mary, Julia, Winifred, Margaret, (grocery dler.).
16. TEMPLE - John and Mary, James, Kate, Teresa Loftus, (seaman).
17. KILCULLEN - Owen and Mary, Mary, Kate, Mary, (sailor).
18. TIGUE - Michael and Kate, Pat, John, Joseph, Mary.
19. GORDON - Bridget.
20. MELVIN - Martin and Mary, Annie, Sarah.
21. RUDDY - Patrick and Bridget, Patrick, WALTON: Mary, Maggie.
22. LACKEN - Mark and Bridget, Sarah, Bridget, Patrick, Michael, Mary, Anne Convey.
23. SEAFIELD - Maria, HUMBER: Anne, Bridget, Sarah.
24. McNULTY - Bridget, Michael, Mary Melvin.
25. DONNELLY - Patrick, Mary.
26. McNULTY - Patrick and Maryanne, Joseph, Mary, Kate, Patrick, William, John, Annie, Teresa, Owen.
27. TEMPLE - William and Mary, Mary, Ellen, Bridget, Kate, Annie.
28. BAKER - Pat and Mary, Pat, Bridget.
29. LACKEY - Bridget.
30. LOFTUS - Honor, Mary.
31. FITZGERALD - Charles, Desmond, Gerald, R.Maurice, Una,, J.E. Roy, Margaret Queenan, Mary Freeney, (banker).
32. HATELY - Elizabeth, John.

CLONTYKILLEW

MOORE - Pat and Mary, Katie, Michael, Bridget Brogan.
GILLESPIE - James and Sabina, Patrick, Bridget.
DOUGHERTY - Barbara, Pat, James, Kate.
JENNINGS - Andrew and Mary, Maria, William, Kate.
EGAN - Michael, Hannah, Michael, Belinda, Maggie, Agnes, Winifred.
MUNNELLY - Thomas and Maggie, John, Mary.

COOLCRAN

LEVINGSTON - Thomas and Marie, Ellen McGlynn, (land agent).
CAFFERKEY - Patrick and Honoria, Mary, James, Celia, Bridget, Jane Keane, teacher
TOOLE - William and Bridget, Thomas, James, Michael, Anne.

CROFTON PARK

HUNTER - Robert and Margaret, Robert, Alice, Lizzie Fury, James Lavin, Michael McAndrew.
O'HORA - Daniel and Winifred.
HOBAN - James and Bridget, Anne, Bridget, Eliza, Kate, Michael, Margaret, Nora, Winifred, Patrick, Anne McAndrew.
McANDREW - Patrick and Alice, Patrick, Mary, Eliza, Anne, Alice, John, Peter, William.
EGAN - Daniel, Mary, Bridget, Ellen, Michael, Anthony, Agnes, Anne, Jane, Patt.
EGAN - Patrick and Catherine, John, Pat, Bridget, Martin, Bridget Gallagher.
CONVEY - Honor, Michael, Patrick, James, Bridget, Honor.
CONVEY - Patrick, Mary.
CRONIN - Philip and Maggie, John, Richard, Bridget, Annie, Margaret, Mary Egan.
DURKIN - Martin and Bridget, John.

CULLEENS

BRENNAN - Pat and Mary, HIGGINS: John, Pat.
O'HORA - Mary, (caretaker).
CARR - John and Mary, Bridget, Bridget, Mary, Catherine, Winifred, John, Margaret, Patrick, Robert.
ROGAN - Patrick and Anne, Mary, Annie, Charley, John.
WALSH - Peter, Michael and Mary, Mary, Thomas, James.
McLOUGHLIN - John and Catherine, Annie, Agnes, Patrick, Michael, Winnie, John, Kate, Maggie.
WALSH - Anne, John, Tom, Pat, Maria.
WALSH - Michael and Mary, Anny.
WALSH - Thomas and Mary, Pat, Thomas, John, Mary, Edward, Michael, Lizzie, Martin, Anthony.
HIGGINS - Sarah, Mary Rogan.
HEALY - Peter and Mary, Bridget, William, Lizzie, John, Ellen, Peter, Mary, Annie, Kate, Sarah.
WALSH - John, John, Maria, Michael, Patrick, Thomas, James, Bridget, Ellen.
LANGAN - John and Kate, Patrick, Martin, Anthony, Bridget.
ROGAN - John and Mary, Pat, Peter, Bridget, Maryellen.
LOFTUS - Michael and Mary, Catherine, Maggie.
BRENNAN - John and Mary, Pat, Bridget, John Rogan.
PATTERSON - Matthew, James.
GOULDING - Michael, Bridget, (rail ganger).
CONVEY - James and Mary, Pat, Bridget, Kate, Anne, Michael, Norah, John, Ellen.
KEAVENEY - Mary, Bridget, Peter.
KEAVENEY - John and Bridget, Michael, Bridget, Kate, John.

CREGGAUN

NAUGHTON - Michael and Sydney, Martin, Bridget, Eliza, Sydney, Edward, Patrick.
JORDAN - Ellen, Patrick, Peter, Anthony,

Ballina town one early morning. Looking out on Knox Street (now Pearse St.) and up at King St. (now O'Rahilly St.) The Ulster Bank was on the left, and at the top of O'Rahilly St. was the Post Office building.

Francis.
McHALE - William, James Hannahoo.
McHALE - Margaret, James, Ellen, Sarah.
HOWLEY - Martin and Kate, Mary, Michael, Martin.
MELVIN - Barbara, Thomas, Pat, Bridget, Kate, Annie, Ellen, Agnes.
GERAGHTY - Thomas and Catherine, Mary, Honor.

CRANNAGH

CAWLEY - Michael and Maggie, Jane.
HANAHOE - Richard and Honor, Mary, Bridget.
MUNNELLY - Thomas and Anne, Thomas, Mary, Bridget.
McAWLEY - Mary, Agnes, Delia.

CLOONTURK

CLARKE - Patt.
O'HORA - Patrick and Bridget, James, Mary, Bridget, Anne.
RALPH - Bartley and Mary, John, Patrick, Bridget.
LEONARD - Francis and Mary, Owen, Anthony.
MELVIN - Anthony and Ellen, Annie, Patrick, James, Kate, Bridget.
HANNAHOO - Edward and Mary, Honour, Mary, Michael Hart.
MURPHY - Ellen.
MELVIN - John, Michael, Annie, Patt, Anthony.
MELVIN - John and Bridget, Michael, Anne, Maggie, Marie Cawley.
MELVIN - Michael and Anne, Michael, Anne, Annie.
MELVIN - Margaret, Michael, William Howley.

CLOONGLASSNEY

CLARKE - William and Margaret, James.
GILLESPIE - Margaret, Pat.
SWEENEY - Patrick and Mary, Winnefred, Maria, John, Kate, Margaret, Bridget.
BIRRANE - Michael and Bridget, John, Thomas, Kate, William, Maria, Margaret, Michael, James, Joseph.
CLARKE - Martin and Julia, Agnes.
MUNNELLY - Michael and Bridget, Mary, Thomas, Barbara, Bridget, Patt, Anne, Ellena.
CLARKE - Thomas and Mary, Patrick, Michael, Anthony, John, Martin, Anne, Maria.
BIRRANE - Winnefred, James, Michael, Thomas, Patrick Foody.
CLARKE - Michael, Mary.

DIXON'S LANE

1. KILGALLON - Bridget, Rose,(fish dler)
2. McKENNA - Catherine, Mary Coleman, Patrick Coleman, John Coleman, (fish dler.).
3. O'BEIRNE - John and Mary, Mary, John, (tailor).

DOWD'S LANE

1. MYLES - William and Margaret.
2. MARLEY - James and Mary, Mary, Fanny, Patrick, Bridget, James.

DURKAN'S LANE

1. BRENNAN - John and Bridget, Mary.
2. McMANUS - Michael and Sarah, Patrick, Catherine, Sarah, Annie Ferguson, (tailor).
3. NEALON - John and Margaret, Bridget, Margaret, Lizzie, John, Arthur, Patrick, John.
4. KELLY - John, William, Thomas, Maria, (tailor).
5. DOHERTY - James, Michael, James, Patrick, Edward, Mary, (blacksmith).
6. DUNNE - Peter and Maria, Mariekate, Jane, Henry, Fanny, (sawyer).
7. McMANUS - Margaret, John, Bridget.

DILLON'S TERRACE

1. DILLON - Elizabeth, Thomas, Andrew, Mary Kennedy.
2. BAKER - Bridget.
3. MACMILLAN - William and Juiet, Bridget Cafferty, (N.school inspector).
4. DUNCAN - Elizabeth, James, Maria Howley.
5. RUDDY - John and Anne, Hugh, Norah, Michael, James, (wine store manager).
6. WALSH - Edward and Isabel, Cyril, (Baby daughter not baptised yet but 1 month old), Bridget Hope, (bookseller and stationer).
7. EGAN - John, Gerald Murray, Norah Birrane, (wine mcht.).

FRANCIS STREET

1. Bridewell.
1. CAMPBELL - John and Emma, Emma, (bridewell keeper).
2. LAING - George and Alice, Margaret, Willie, Eric, Geo. Sutton, Patt Flynn, Jeanie Irwin, Ellen Curran, Maggie Byrne, Mary O'Boyle, (doctor).
3. COOLICAN - Anne, Michael, Vincent, Mary Ginty, Annie Minnie.
4. CROTHY - Richard and Agnes, Richard, William, Dorothy, Marjorie, Esther Cahill, Irene McBride, (resident

magistrate).
5. MACAULAY - Roger and Louisa, Roger, Winifred, Florence, Henry, Mona, Octarid, Leotine McGregor, Margaret Redington, Thomas Feaney, Martin Egan.
6. ATKINSON - Edward and Harriette, Edward, Mary Sheridan, Annie Tuffy, Anthony Foy, (petty sessions clerk).
7. MacNULTY - Patrick and Mary, Georgina, Margaret Collins, John Scott, (council clerk).
8. ORCHARD - William and Mary, Reginald, Mary, Mary Judge, Bridget Judge, (civil engineer).
9. ADAMSON - Robert and Anny, Robert, Edith, Kate Doughan, Mary Hallinane, (chemist & druggist).
10. COOLICAN - Edward and Bridget, Edward, Ethel, John, Isabella, Michael, Arthur, Margaret Kelly, Mary Donnellan, (gen. mcht.).

FRANKLIN'S LANE
1. MUNNELLY - Anne.
2. WALSH - Patrick and Bridget, Nannie, Mary, John, (baker).
3. BROWNE - Mary.
4. MARLEY - Bridget, Michael.
5. DUFFY - John, Thomas, Martin, Joseph, Maggie, (baker).

FARRANDEELION
GARDNER - Thomas and Winifred, Thomas, James, Michael, Francis.
O'HORA - Patrick, Bridget, John, Annie, Thomas, Patrick.
BOLAND - William and Margaret, Thomas, Michael, Kate, Mary, William, Dolly, Margaret, Bridget O'Hora.
BOLAND - Thomas and Catherine, Bridget, Bridget Canning.
COSGRAVE - John and Bridget, Patrick, John, Katie, Catherine, Bridget Bryce.
HANAHUE - Margaret, Bartley, Michael.
COSGRAVE - Thomas and Ellen, Michael, George, Mary, Mary McDonnell.
HOWLEY - Charles and Margaret, FLYNN: Matthew and Mary.
MURRAY - Anthony and Anne, Michael, Patrick, Mary, Thomas, Anthony Nolan.

FARRANOO
MULDERRIG - Patrick and Mary, Maria, Patrick, Michael.
O'HORA - Peter, Maggie, Bridget, Patrick, Mary, Michael, John.
FRASER - Edward, Bella, Pat McNulty.

GORTEEN
CLARKE - James and Mary, Mary, Luke, Bridget, Annie, Margaret, Katie, Michael.

GALLAGHERS LANE
1. CALLAGHAN - Mary.
2. COX - Bridget, SMYTH: Bridget, Lizzy, Patrick, (fish dler.).
3. QUIGLEY - John and Bessie, (fisherman).
4. LOVE - James and Mary, George, Daniel Grahen, Francis Roach, (shoemaker).
5. McNAMARA - James and Anne, John, Ellie, (victualler).
6. CORCORAN - John, Mary McKenna, George McKenna, Martin Quigley, William Quigley, (tailor).

GARDEN STREET
1. HANLON - James and Mary, John, Mary, Katie, Malachi, (bootmaker).
2. CONLON - Patrick and Margaret, John, Mary, Patrick, Maggie, Katie, David, (shoemaker).
3. CORCORAN - James and Mary.
4. MELVIN - Bridget, James.
5. MORGAN - Martin.
6. HEFFRON - John and Mary, (painter).
7. O'HORA - Winifred, (shopkeeper).
8. ROONEY - Michael, Bridget, Michael, George Gordan, James Malley, (musician).
9. NEALON - Bridget, Elizabeth.
10. QUINN - Michael and Bridget.
11. MURRY - Patrick and Mary, Jane, Willie, Christie.
12. DEVERS - John and Susan, Thomas, Amelia, Anna, John, Lillian, William, Adeline, Irene, Alexander, George, Joseph, Muriel, Herbert.
13. HAMILTON - William and Sarah, Alexander.
14. TRIMBLE - John, Ruth, Francis, Sophia, Ida.
15. FARMER - John, Anne, James, Maggie, David, (grocer's asst.).
16. LENEHAN - Isaac and Elizabeth, Mary Edey, (auctioneer).
17. GRAHAM - Mills and Maggie, (N.S. teacher).
18. HOEY - Peter and Theresa, Francis, Peter, Sarah, (butler).
19. DEVERS - Anne, Rose Nealon, Edward Nealon, (laundress).
20. McHALE - Annie, Mary Higgins, (maternity nurse).
21. GREHAM - Joseph and Margaret, Patrick.
22. CAHILL - James and Elizabeth, Martin, Gertrude.
23. NASH - Patrick and Mary, John, Thomas, George, Levina, Robert.

GARDEN STREET LANE
1. STOKES - William and Mary, Francis, Mary, Sabina, Edward, Patrick, (tinsmith).
2. O'HORA - John and Mary.

GORE STREET
1. KERR - George and Annie, John, (ex RIC).
2. BROGAN - John and Mary, Bridget, Sarah.
3. HOBAN - Michael and Ellen, Mary, John, Patrick, Annie.
4. HASSEY - Robert and Winifred, Richard, Margaret, (mechanic).
5. BOSHELL - Bridget, William, Ernest, John, Margaret, Josephine, Francis, Mary Timlin.
6. CANAVAN - Martin and Maria, John, Margaret.
7. JORDAN - Henry and Annie, Mary, Owen, Patrick, Annie.
8. O'BRIEN - Mary, Joseph, Ellen, (grocer).
9. HOBAN - Michael and Anne, Mary, Martin, Maggie.
10. O'BOYLE - Catherine.
11. CLARKE - Patrick and Catherine, John, James, Patrick.
12. SWEENEY - John and Kate, Mary, Owen, Bridget, (stone mason).
13. MOYLES - Bryan and Annie, Katie, Bridget, James, Sabina.
14. CONNOR - John and Mary, John, Mary, Norah, Anthony, Patrick.
15. KELLY - John and Mary, Mary, Francis, John, Edward, Anastasia, Teresa, (shoemaker).
16. WALSH - Mary, Peter.
17. CARR - Michael and Mary, Michael, John, Mary.
18. PADDEN - James and Kate, Michael, Annie, John, (tailor).
19/20. vacant
21. CAFFREY - Michael and Elizabeth, Frederick, (railway gateman).

GLEBE (ARDNAREE)
SKIPTON - Rev. William, Eliza, Sibella, Mary Morrison, Annie Sheridan, (clerk in holy orders).

GORTATOGHER
MOYLES - James and Anne, James, Michael Redington.
HANNICK - Michael and Ellen, Mary, Thomas, John Moyles.
ORMSBY - James and Annie, Maggie, Thomas, Pat, Kate, James.
MERRICK - Pat, Pat and Mary, Ellen, John, Bridget.
CADEN - Patrick and Kate, John, Patrick, Mary.
MULDERRIG - Ellen, Patrick, Winifred, Patrick, Winifred, Michael, Bridget, Mary, William.
BARRETT - John and Bridget, Thomas, Ellen, Annie.

HARTS LANE
1. MAUGHAN - John and Maryanne, Margaret, Catherine, Patrick Callaghan, Mary McGuinness, (butcher).
2. FARRELL - Anne, Kate, (dressmaker).
3. FLYNN - William and Mary, Francis, Thomas, Christopher, George, (bootmaker).
4. CLARKE - John, (sawyer).
5. JENNINGS - Michael, John, Kate, (ex army).
6. DEVANEY - Mary, (milliner).

HILL STREET
1. SEXTON - Mary, Mary, (dealer).
2. CALLARY - Michael and Eliza, (tailor).
3. JORDAN - Maryanne, Mary, Sarah, Annie, (nurse).
4. Store
5. QUINN - John and Maria, Ellen, James, Patrick, Annie, Sarah, John, Margaret, William, Agnes, Edward, Bridget, (cooper master).
6. CALLEARY - James and Ellen, Michael, James, Phelim, Thomas, Ellen, Annie, Mary Tolan, (grocer).
7. WARNOCK - Daniel and Mary, Mary, Ellen, Kate, Emmelia, (ex RIC sergt.).
8. Store
9. CALLAGHAN - Edward, (horse dler.).
10. JENNINGS - James and Ellen, (shop).

11. BRODERICK - Henry and Bridget, Annie, John, Ellen, Henry, Michael, (baker).
12. CULKIN - Bridget, Pat, John, Delia, Michael, William, (boarding hse.).
13. STAUNTON - Michael and Maria, Annie, Thomas F., Maggie Kenny, Bridget Joyce, James Roche, (pub/grocer
14. BOLAND - William and Bridget, Maria James, (grocer).

JOHN STREET

1. DUFFY - Elizabeth, Charles, (shopkeeper).
2. O'REGAN - Michael and Margaret, (carpenter).
3. ORMSBY - Michael and Barbara, Silvia Barrett.
4. REDDINGTON - John, Mary, Margaret, (grocer & publican).
5. LEONARD - John and Sidney, May, Patrick, John McDonagh, Maria Ferguson, (carpenter).
6. GILLESPIE - Sarah, Elizabeth Curren, Thomas Curren, Anne Timlin, (shopkeeper).
7. BATTLE - Anthony and Mary, Mary, Winifred, Bridget, John, Annie, Teresa, (tailor).
8. BAINE - William and Mary, Louisa, Sidney, (ex RIC).
9. HANNON - Mary, Delia, Stephen, May, John Doble, Lily Doble.
10. COSGROVE - Elizabeth, Matthew, Michael, Bridget, Elizabeth, John, Sarah, Patrick Convey, John Casey, (publican).
11. National School
12/13. vacant
14. MORAN - John and Maria, Bride, Patrick, John, Annie, (coachbuilder).
15. CLARKE - John and Mary, Mary, Annie, John, Patrick, Michael, (coachbuilder).
16. BOURKE - Robert, Henry, Robert, Margaret, (solicitor).

JOYCE'S LANE

1. McGINTY - Ellen, John, Martin.
2. WALSH - James and Mary, Kate.

KING STREET

1. MULLEN - John and Anne, May, James, Bridget, James Sullivan, Pat Reilly, John McAndrew, Peter O'Brien, Robert Rogan, James Doyle, James Stephens, John Kierans, Charles Kevany, Mcihael Cosgrave, (gen. mcht).
2. McDONNELL - John, Michael O'Moyle, Michael Ormsby, Patrick Jordan, Michael Gavaghan, Ignatius O'Brien, Martin Flynn, John Cavanagh, Patrick Gilmartin, Sarah Rafter, Bridget Hogan, James Foley, Thomas Ormsby, John Cabrey.
3. DAVIS - John and Margaret, Patrick, William, Mary O'Malley, (mcht.).
4. MAUGHAN - Patrick and Mary, (butcher).
5. KEANE - Robert and Bessy, Margaret Spain, (bootmaker).
6. GARVEY - John and Lena, Patrick, Patricia, Peter, Michael Hallinane, (baker).
7. KELLY - Winifred, Mary, Bridget, Winifred, Maggie, Elizabeth, William Carroll, Christopher Carroll, (grocer & publican).
8. BOURNS - John, Sarah, May, Mary Loftus, (printer).
9. GAUGHAN - John, Bridget, John Regan, (cooper).
10. HEALY - Anne, May Duffy, (shopkeeper).
11. GILLESPIE - Mary, May, Celia, Teresa, John Murphy, Michael Carrabina, James Ferguson, Julia Hanahoe, Jane Brogan, (publican & grocer).
12. JONES - Mary, Bertha, Veronica Pelly, Francis Pelly, Francis Pelly, Bridget McLoughlin, Patrick Monaghan, (hotel proprietoress).
13. vacant
14. BROWNE - Francis, Michael, Patrick, Martin, Mary, John, (carpenter).
15. RONAN - Jane, Denis, James.
16. CORCORAN - Hannah, James, Tessy, Hannah, Bridget Ford.
17. JORDAN - Patrick and Sabina, Joseph, William, George, Gertrude, John, Patrick, Thomas, Francis, (sailor).
18. BOURKE - Cummin and Mary, Mary, Gertrude, Patrick, Anthony, Teresa, Charles, Christopher, Grace, Florence, (saddler).
19. WEHRLEY - Engelbert and Bridget, Mary, Michael, Engelbert, Maggie, Marion, (watchmaker).
20. SHERIDAN - Michael, Martin, Joe Feeney, Mary Sheridan, (shopkeeper).
21. O'HORA - Michael and Ellie, Mina, Violet, Annie McGuinness, James Sweeney, (shopkeeper).
22. Medical Hall
23. Drapery Estd.
24. GARVIN - James and Annie, Anne, Mary, John, Anne, Kate, Charles, James, Edward, Maria Melvin, (merchant).
25. HEASLIP - John, Richard Gibson, Kingsley Lewis, James Speer, John Hoare, (boot saleman).
26. ERSKINE - James and Emily, Norman, Cyril, Bertha, David Armstrong, James Clarke, Robert Sherlock, William Layng, John Cathearh, Maggie Campbell, Jennie Wallace, Jessie Wiseman, Bridget Carden, Mary Kevany, (draper).

KNOX STREET

1. FLYNN - Mary, James Stewart, William Brown, Patrick Geogehan, William Paul, Henry Richards, Annie Breslane, James Coyle, Bartley Coyle, Anne Lally, Anne Sampey, William McGurrin, Vincent Peel, Eveline Peel, Gertrude Peel, (hotel proprietoress).
2. FLYNN - George and Mary, William, John Harper, James McGrath, Nannie Lynam, Maggie Murphy, Joseph Murray, (hotel proprietor).
3. JOHNSON - Benjamin and Christina, Benjamin, Jeannie, Kate Ormsby, (saddler).
4. DOOHER - James, (land agent).
5. HEWSON - Margaret, Rev. Patrick, Thomas, Mary, Eliza, Ellen, George, James Boland.
6. BEATTY - George, Anthony McCarrick, Bridget O'Connor, Lizzie Delaney, (bank agent).
7. MURTAGH - Elizabeth, Julia, Susan Dalphin, Glady's Dalphin, Edmund Dignam, W. John Marshall, John Kennedy, John Heuston, William Murphy, Minnie Murphy, William Lee, John McNaghten, Margaret Finegan, Julia Murray, Bridget Murray, Philip Murray, James Reidde, James Flynn, John Duffy, Richard Doyle,(hotelkeeper)
8. BAIRD - John H. and Mary, Clarissa, Mary, Clara, Eleanor, Olive Galbraith, David Lowry, William King, Henry Leitch, Mary Grier, Bridget Grier, (postmaster).
9. SCROOPE - Henry and Kate, Florence, Blanche, Geoffrey, Arthur, Gervase, Charles, Mary McGuire, Margaret O'Sullivan, (bank manager).
10. O'REILLY - Michael and Bridget, Timothy, William, Patrick Doyle, John Walsh, Thomas McQuinn, William Connolly, (gen. mcht.).
11. GALLAGHER - William, MULLARKEY: Catherine, Anne, Margaret, Hugh, Mary Kelly, (ex leather mcht.).
12. McMUNN - John, Norah McNulty, Bridget McNulty, (bank manager).
13. ADAMSON - William, Margaret, William McMillan, Patrick Sweeney, (chemist).
14. MAGEE - William and Ellen, James Mathews, (carpenter).
15. O'DOWD - Margaret, Martin McNulty, James Connolly, James Lavell, Patrick Haire, Mary Wallace, (grocer & pub).
16. AHEARN - James and Mary, Glady's, Patricia, Kathleen, Arthur, Arthur Muffany, Thomas Gilmartin, William Hughes, Celia Hennigan, Bridget Reilly, Margaret Byrne, Pat Cooke, (gen. mcht.).
17. WILDE - Joseph and Annie, John, Robert, Charles, THomas McAllister, James Evans, (shopkeeper).
18. WILLS - Henry and Annie, Percy, Harry, Geoffrey, Joy, Patrick Roland, James Devanny, Rebecca Trimbill, Harriet Bears, Celia Kelly, (draper).
19. HARNEY - Patrick, Laurence, Martin Corcoran, Martin Moran, Patrick Walshe, Kate O'Rourke, Agnes Doyle, Maggie Barrett, (draper).
20. NALLY - Francis, James Duffy, (grocer's asst.).
21. FLANAGAN - John, Patrick Robinson, James McHale, Patrick Sweeney, Bridget McGoff, Anne McGoff, (publican & gro

cer).
22. LAING - Mariah, E.H.B., George, Edith, Lizzie McDonnell, Essie McDonald, Ruby Trurers, Edward McMann, P.J. Carolin, Frank Farrell, Robert Patterson, Tom Boyd, Mary Coleman, Mary Larkin, (draper).
23. BAIRD - John, Henry Hewson, James Doble, (post office).
24. JOYNT - Richard and Fannie, Madelenie, Irene, Marion, Helen, Kate Brogan, Annie Deammin, (newspaper proprietor).
25. BARRETT - Margaret, Annie, Marion, (confectioner).
26. ANDERSON - Robert, Sarah, Elizabeth Patterson, Agnes Hopkins, Bridget Sullivan, Margaret O'Keefe, Catherine Munnelly, Maurice Carolan, (corn agent).
27. ADAMS - Jane, Bessie Smith, Hartford Smith, James Cather, Oliver Bourke, Mary Kilgallon.
28. BOURKE - Kate, Bridget McDonnell.
29. WILSON - Robert, Mary, Sarah, Eliza, Kate Hegarty, (ex grocer).
30. McLOUGHLIN - Maria, Mary, Winifred, Sarah Morrison, Delia Taylor, David Stanley, Patrick O'Callaghan, Bridget Fox, (boarding hse.).
31. KELLY - Patrick and Jane, Norah, Mary, Augusta, (boot maker).
32. SLATER - Albert and Annie, Lavina, Edward, Maud, Maria, Louis, Annie Sweeney, (photographer).
33. NEALON - Pat and Margaret.
34. HOWLEY - Henry, Maria Gilligan, Henry Lynch, Thomas Lynch.
35. O'REILLY - R.James, Annie, (commission agent).
36. CROTTY - Maurice and Kate, Edward, Mary, Elizabeth, (RIC).
37. TIMONY - John and Julia, Francis, Michael, Christina, Julia, Mary.
38. PATTON - Sarah, Mary, Bridget, Margaret Malone.
39. KELLY - James and Maria, Belinda, Patrick, James, Mary, Annie, Elizabeth, Joseph Hallanan, (tailor).
40. EVANS - Mathew and Mary.
41. O'HARA - Edward, Mary, Agnes, (plumber & gas fitter).
42. ERSKINE - John and Margaret, Helena, Kate McAvoy, Mary Ruane, (Provincial bank manager).
43. Shipping Office
47. Reading Room.

KNOCKANELO

GILGIN - Mary, Pat, Maggy, Thomas Lavin.
LOFTUS - Jane, Thomas, Mary, Ellen, Kate.
CAVANAGH - Martin, Kate, Catherine Munnelly, Mary Cullen.
CAVANAGH - Anthony, James, Katie, Francis Loftus.
CAVANAGH - James, Patrick, James, Bridget, Ellie, Bridget Walsh.
WATTS - Henry and Balenda, William, Lizzie, George, JOYNT: Andrew, Lyons.

KNOCKLEHAUGH

MULLEN - Patrick and Anne, Annie, Maggie, Patrick Colman.
FLAHERTY - Edward and Bridget, Bridget, Patrick, (coachman).
CAFFERTY - Michael and Bridget, Hanoria, Pat Nolan.
KELLY - Michael and Mary, Anne, John Moran.
CLARKE - Thomas and Bridget, John, George, Mary, Annie, Bridget.

KNOCKEGAN AND CLOONAGH BEG

DIAMOND - James and Bridget, Ellen, Patrick, Martin, Mary, Thomas, Michael, Belinda, Margaret, Sarah, Norah.
HARRISON - Michael and Mary, Anthony, Anne O'Neill, Martin Moran.
CADEN - Patrick and Bridget, Mary, Margaret.
O'NEILL - Sabina, John, Michael, Anne.
REAPE - Thomas and Mary, Selia, Thomas, Mary, John Madden.

KILMOREMOY

GERAGHTY - Michael, Catherine Devins.
McLOUGHLIN - Patrick, HEALY: Mary, Mary, Maggie, Willie, McNALLON: Mary, Michael.

KNOCKSBARRETT

PETRIE - Peter and Caroline, Annie Jordan, (fishery lessee).
DISKIN - James, Mary, Katie, Anne, Belinda, Thomas, (ex RIC).

KNOCKALYRE OR DOWNHILL

LITTLE - Thomasina, Margaret, Edward O' Boyle, Elizabeth Keane , Mary Devany, Jane Ruane, (fishery proprietor).

KNOCKALYRE OR DOWNHILL

ARDNAREE URBAN

GARVEY - John and Harrie, Ruth, Ivan, Douglas, Lora, Kate Noaks, Patrick Clarke, Patrick Kelly, Kate Thompson, Agnes Kilfeather, Maria Munnelly, Martha Finly, (solicitor).
KILGALLON - Kate, Michael, James, Alice, Agnes.
ROACH - John and Bridget, Mary, Patt, Tom, John, James.
MULROONEY - Mary, Patrick, Michael, Adelaide.

LOWER PIPER HILL

1. DUGGAN - Thomas and Mary, Elizabeth, Sarah, Thomas, Joseph, James, Patrick, (railway guard).
2. LYNCH - Denis and Anne, Kate, Annie, Patrick, Denis, James, Maud, Mary, (carpenter).
3. McKENNA - Mary, Mary Cahill, Jane Coppinger, (boarding hse.).
4. MALLON - Edward and Mary, Edward, Mary, Annie, (railway helper).
5. RYAN - Richard and Maria, John, James, Richard, Robert, (carpenter).
6. KELLY - James, John, (shoemaker).
7. ROWAN - Michael and Mary, Rose, FLANNERY: Mary, Pat, May, Lily.
8. FLYNN - John and Mary, John.
9. O'HARA - James and Kate, John, Michael, Edward, Patrick, Kate, Maggie, (shoemaker).
10. McHALE - Patrick and Mary, John, Ellen, Mary Harris, (shoemaker).
11. McGUIGAN - Bridget, Anthony, Elizabeth.
12. Workshop.
13. KILGALLON - Mary, Anne.
14. LYNCH - Bridget, Vincent, Edward, Winifred.
15. DIAMOND - William and Bridget, Annie, Amellia, (shoemaker).
16. DIAMOND - Michael, Michael, Kate, (bootmaker).
17. CALLAGHAN - Michael and Mary, Bridget, Katie, Essie, Mary, (publican).
18. GREEN - John and Mary, Martha Topley, (methodist minister).
19. GILBERT - John and Elizabeth, Mary Loftus, (teacher).
20. MERRICK - Martin and Katie, Annie, Martin Hegarty, John Hegarty, Robert Carney, Edward Scanalan, William Smyth, Patrick Lee, Edward Cary, Patrick Cary, Patrick Healy.
21. MORAN - Margaret, Maria, Maggy, QUINLAN: Frederick, Mary, Michael, Bridget, Bridget Hopkins.
22. RUTLEDGE - Michael and Mary, William, Mary, Richard Forristal.
23. CLARKE - Michael, Michael, Mary, Patrick, Bridget, Joseph, Edward, Peter, (bootmaker).
24. BARRETT - John and Bridget, (blacksmith).
25. CONNOR - Michael, Bridget, Maggie, (shoemaker).
26. GALVIN - William and Mary, Annie Feeney, Mark Conlon, (carpenter).
27. MORAN - Pat and Bridget, Mary, Kate, Michael, John, Pat.
28. McDONNELL - Ellen, Willie Kelly, Thomas Callaghan, (lodging hse.).
29. GENTY - Mary, Michael, Margaret, Mary Mulderrick, Mary Blizzard, Edward Courtney, James Kendrick.
32. KELLY - John and Mary, Mary, Katie, George, (shoemaker).
33. HEGARTY - William and Catherine.
34. GIBBONS - Michael and Anne, (pub).
35. BRODERICK - Andrew and Sarah, Elizabeth.
36. CURREN - Mary, Ellen, Thomas, Mary, (nurse).
37. LYNCH - Margaret.
38. CONNOR - Bridget, Patrick, Mary, Bridget Keane.
39. DUFFY - Mary, John.
40. CARRABINE - Bridget, Mary, Joseph, James, Selia, Margaret McHale.
41. GINTY - James and Annie, Mary, Sarah, Edward, James, Ellen Bradley.
42. MEENEGHAN - Anthony and Maggie, Patrick, Ellen Hennelly.
43. ORMSBY - Robert and Bridget, Thomas, Mary McCarick.
44. QUIGLEY - Patrick and Anne, TOLAN: Anthony, Margaret, Michael.
45. TULLY - Martin and Honor, Mary.
46. CLIFFORD - Mary, Annie, Lillie, Alfred, Joseph Foy, (boarding hse.).
47. DONNELLY - Thomas and Bridget,

Patrick, Edward, Mary, Maggie, Stephen.
48/50. vacant
51. SWEENEY - Pat and Bridget, Thomas.

LAND LEAGUE AVENUE

1. SWEENEY - Michael, Patrick, James, (baker).
2. KILGALLON - John and Bridget, Bridget, Joseph, Agnes, Michael, Rose, William.
3. vacant
4. LOFTUS - John and Kate, Mary, William, Patrick, Kate, Bridget.
5. BARRETT - Anthony and Annie, Thomas, John, Bridget, Annie, Maggie, Michael, Anthony, (blacksmith).
6. TOGHER - Catherine, John, James, Bridget, Thomas.
7. McNALLY - Mary.
8. McGINTY - Manus and Winifred, John, James.
9. SHEA - Margaret, Patrick, James, John Barrett, Margaret Barrett.
10. HUNTER - William and Ellen, Mary, John, Maggie, James, (mason).

LLOYDS LANE

Plymouth Brethern Church

LAGHTADWANNAGH

QUINN - Michael and Catherine, Mary, Kate, Michael, Agnes, James, Bridget, Lizzie.
O'HORA - Edward and Anne, Mary, Nora, Eddie, Bridget, (carpenter).
McDONNELL - Thomas and Margaret, James, Mary, MONAGHAN: Michael and Bridget.
MONAGHAN - Michael and Catherine.
GRANAGHAN - Anthony and Mary.
SCANLAN - Patrick and Kate, Michael, Mary, Ellen, Lizzie.
HANAHOE - Edward, Anthony, Kate, John McDonnell.
O'HORA - John and Mary, John, Mary.

MILL STREET (MULLAUNS)

1. HEARNS - James and Mary, Patt, Henry, Mary, James, A.Jane, Michael, Frank, Essie.
2. BARRETT - Patrick, (baker).
3. vacant
4. O'HARA - Michael, John.
5. O'HORO - Michael, John.
6. CONVEY - James and Sarah, Mary, Annie, James, (shoemaker).
7. WALSHE - Michael and Sarah.
8. vacant
9. MURPHY - Pat and Eliza, Susan, Mary, Michael, Lizzie, James, (musician).
10. WALSHE - Pat and Margaret, Mary, Annie, Thomas, Lizzie, John, Martin, Bridget, Patrick, James, (carpenter).
11. SHEA - Joseph and Margaret, John, Michael, Mary, (tailor).
12. MANGAN - Michael and Sarah, Katie, John, James, Thomas, Patrick, Michael, (butcher).
13. LENEHAN - Mary, William, (upholster).
14. McLOUGHLIN - Michael and Sabina, Mary, Annie, Michael, John.
15. CAFFREY - John and Nora, Muriel, Nora, (plasterer).
16. CUNNINGHAM - Andrew and Maggie, Lizzie, Henry, Patrick, Michael, Alice, Molly, Kathleen, (tailor).
17. CURRY - Bridget, Edward, Martin, Patrick, Katie, John.
19. ROBINSON - Patrick and Mary, Nannie, Kate, Winifred, Patrick, Martin, Mary Meenehan, Norah Meenehan.
20. vacant
21. FORBES - Mark, Richard, Ellen.
22. ROONEY - Katie, Kathleen, Nellie, Jack, (dressmaker).
23. CONVEY - Catherine, Patrick, Maggie, Thomas, Joseph, Annie, Julia, Michael.
24. vacant
25. REILLY - John and Margaret, Joseph, Jane, Anny, Maggie, Mary, Michael, James, (sawyer).
26. DEVIRS - Terence and Mary, Bridget, Thomas, Kate, Julia, Martin, Agnes.
27. McCANN - Patt and Mary.
28. HEFFERNAN - William and Anne, Patrick, Mary, Jane, Thomas, Ellen, Francis, Michael, James.
29. DOWD - James and Sarah, James.
30. BROWN - James and Margaret, Anne, Ellen Tolan.
31. REID - Jane, Martha, Jessie, Thomas.
32. BECKETT - Isaac, Sarah, Robert Acton, Annie Acton, (miller).

MULLAUNS (Ballina urban)

1. RUTTLEDGE - Francis and Bridget, Patrick, Joseph, Edward, Mary, Annie, James, Sarah Kilcullen, Pat Dignan, John Sweeney, John King, William Rutledge, Thomas O'Donnell, Kate Connery, Kate McShane, Kate Mulroney, (shop& hotel).
2. Railway Station.
2. CASSERLY - James and Maria, William, Henry, Charles, Madeline, Robert, Eva, Florry, May, Frederick, Albert, Anna, (station master).

MULLAUNS (ARDNAREE)

KILGALLON - Patrick and Margaret, Michael, John, Pat, James, Agnes, Teresa.
WILLIS - Pat and Bridget, Katie, John, Birty, Catherine.
KILGALLON - Thomas and Maria, Margaret, John, Michael.
KILGALLON - James and Lizzie, Joseph, Fred, Julia, Mary McNulty.
KILGALLON - William, Barbara, Winifred.
KILGALLON - Patrick and Anne, James, Mary, Bridget, Michael, Anne, Barbara, Margaret, Winifred.

Mrs. BEIRNS LANE

(in LOWER PIPERHILL)

McGINTY - Martin.
WALSHE - James

McLOUGHLIN'S LANE

1. MALLEY - Winifred, Bridget, Anne.
2/3. vacant
4. KEAVENY - Margaret, John, James.
5. vacant
6. CORCORAN - Michael, Cathleen, Bridget.
7. KELLY - Jane, Annie, James.
8. GALLAGHER - William, Anne Greham, (bootmaker).
9. HOPKINS - Anne, Martin, Mary, John, Michael, Robert, Peter Marley, (solicitor's wife).
10. SKEFFINGTON - Patrick and Margaret, Michael, Winifred, Bridget, Charles Hannon, Catherine Hannon, (tin smith).
11. HOPKINS - Patrick and Bridget, Mary, Michael, Patrick.

NEW GARDEN STREET

1. LUCY - Denis and Eily, Michael, Denis, Minnie, Beatrice, Julia, (RIC sergt.).
2. MORGAN - William and Katherine, Kathleen Rawlins, (school master).
3. MORAN - Thomas and Margaret, Oona, (methodist minister).
4. BOLAND - William and Hannah, Annie, Eileen, Eva, David Baird, Mary Gardner, (auctioneer).
5. CANAVAN - James, Richard, Anne, Bridget, Margaretta, (carpenter).
6. HOLMES - William and Margaret.
7. FRIEL - Charles and Kate, Thomas, William, Susan, Maurice, Lizzie, Frederick, Sarah, (RIC sergt).
8. DOLPHIN - Catherine, Margaret Timlin.
9. COPPIN - Henry and Mary, John, Agnes, Anthony Hall, (tailor).
10. CARROLL - Thomas, KILCULLEN: Michael, Mary, Maggie, Christina, Annie.
11. MOUNTAIN - George and Catherine, (tailor).
12. REILLY - John and Mary, William, Jack, Violet, Clare, Joseph, Agnes, George, Gertrude, (waiter).
13. LEONARD - Patrick and Bridget, May, Ellen Cormack, (carpenter).
14. HOWLEY - Ellen, Maurice, Martha, Nannie, Ellen Harte, (ex grocer).
15. PATTERSON - Joseph and Mary, Mary, Agnes, (flour agent).
16. FERGUSON - Kate, Patrick, Thomas, John, Anthony, Martin, Francis, Michael, John.
17. CARROLL - John.
18. DOHERTY - Mary, Bridget Merrick.
19. LOFTUS - Mary, Andrew.
20. CULLEN - Honor, (grocery).
21. FORDE - Myles, Catherine, Mary Taylor, COSTELLOE: Martin, Thomas, Bridget, Catherine.
22. O'NEILL - Thomas, Francis, John, Bridget Ferguson.
23. MOORE - Robert and Mary, Maggie, Patrick, Bridget, Jane, (shoemaker).
24. O'HARA - Mary, James.
25. O'DONNELL - John and Bridget, Joseph, Bridget, Thomas, James, Kate, Michael, Fredy.

NURE

DODD - John, Martin, Margaret, Michael, Anne, Eugene, Andrew, Mary.

O'DOWD'S LANE

1. MYLES James and Mary, William, James, Martin, Dan Murray, Mary Murray.
2./5./8. vacant
3. HARTE - Ellen, (fish dler.).
4. GRAHAM - Mary, Patrick, Owen, Michael, Joseph, Anthony, Margaret.

6. MALLEY - Patrick and Maria, James.
7. SALMON - Michael and Bridget.
9. LINDSAY - Bridget.

OLD GARDEN STREET

1. FOX - Francis, Mary, Mary Harrison, (grocer & publican).
2. CARROLL - John and Maria, Andrew, Margaret, Delia, James, Hugh, Margaret Tolan, (grocer & publican).
3. HOLMES - Anne, Patty, Gerald, Anne Curran, Hanoria Durcan, Peter Langan, (shopkeeper).
4. WATERS - Henry and Maria, Charles, Henry, Delia O'Connor, Bridget Waters, (publican & grocer).
5. LENNOX - William and Rose, William, Alexander, Agnes, Catherine, (tailor's cutter).
6. ROUSE - William, Annie.
7. BATTLE - Patrick and Maria, Isabella, Edmund Scanlon, (baker).
8. CURRAN - Maria, James, Patrick, John, Martin, Bridget, Francis, (grocer).
9. MOORE - John and Anne, Patrick, Mary, Sarah Early.
10. O'DOWD - Delia, Maggie, Cecelia, Margaret O'Boyle, (publican).
11. BOURKE - John and Catherine, Bridget, John.
12. MULDERRIG - Mary, Bridget Golden, Marie Loftus, (lodging hse.).
13. CORDON - Henoria, Francis, Catherine Lynch.
14. PRICE - Michael and Bridget, Patrick, Martin, Michael.
15. HUGHES - Pat and Kate, (blacksmith).
16. MERRICK - John and Hanoria, John, Michael, (grocer).
17. HARRISON - Mary, Anthony Gillespie, Ellen Gillespie.
18. LAVELLE - John and Bridget, Sarah, Edward, Teresa, (compositor).
19. HENEGAN - Mary, James Maughan, (lodging hse.).
20. SWEENEY - Mary, Ellen O'Hora, (lodging hse).
21. HOWLEY - John and Mary, Martin, Thomas, Edward.
22. LALLY - Edward and Catherine, Edward, Mary, John, Kathleen, William, (ex RIC).
23. RUDDY - Patrick, Mary, O'HARA: Patrick, Thomas, Margaret, Margaret McKenna, (N.S. teacher).
24. CARROLL - Michael, Patrick, Hugh, Gertrude, Catherine Igoe, Bridget Igoe, (mcht.).
25. SULLIVAN - John and Kate, James, Bridget, Celia, Cathleen, Thomas Keaveny, Edward Denning, Patrick Golden, Celia Beirne, Margaret Beirne, (grocer & publican).
26. TIMLIN - Maria, Anthony, James, Maggie, Bridget, (grocer & publican).
27. MELVIN - Maria, Bridget, Winifred Howley, (grocer & publican).
28. BRISLIN - James and Bridget, Belinda, James, Mark, Annie, Katie, Mat, (coach builder).
29. RUTLEDGE - John and Anne, Christopher Boland, (corn & flour agent).
30. NAUGHTON - Mary, James, Minnie, Kate, William, (mcht.).
31. DUFFY - Margaret, Bridget, Edward, Honoria, Elizabeth, (shopkeeper).
32. CONNOR - Bridget, Margaret,Patrick, Thomas, Ellen Quigley, Ellen Beirne, (grocer & publican).
33. MURPHY - Sarah, Thomas, Mary, Michael, Alice Forde, Eliza Forde, (laundress).
34. CORCORAN - William and Anne, Edward, John, Maria, Anne, Agnes, (harness maker).
35. McBEAN - John and Margaret, William, Margaret McManus, James McManus, Patrick Keating, Mary Moffatt, Annie Meagher, John Kilmartin, Ellen Durkan, (Temperance Hotel Keeper).

POUND STREET

1. SHANLEY -Anne, Ellen.
2. FORDE - Richard and Mary, Mary, John, Patrick, William, Thomas, Sarah, Bridget, Richard, James, Joseph, Charles, Patrick Munelly, (coach builder).
3. GALLAGHER - Anthony and Bridget, Anthony.
4. O'REILLY - Peter, Francis, Patrick, James, (weaver).
5. CARABINE - Mary, John.

POUND LANE

ABBEYHALFQUARTER

1. TIGUE - Michael.
2. REGAN - Patrick and Mary, Thomas.

PAWN OFFICE LANE

1. WALSH - Dan, (nailer).

2/4. vacant

5. Pawn office.

PIG MARKET STREET

1. CONNOLLY - James and Catherine, James, (mason).

POLKS LANE

1. FLYNN - Michael and Maria, Thomas, (baker).
2. WALSH - Patrick and Bridget, Edward, Bridget, Thomas, Maria, (shoemaker).

PADDENS LANE

1. MYLES - Bridget.
2. DUFFY - John and Mary.
3. ENGLISH - Patrick and Mary, (shoemaker).
4. HEALY - Anthony and Mary.
5. EGAN - Anne.
6. FLANNERY - Michael and Julia.
7. McHALE - Bridget, (laundress).

QUIGNALECKA

GALLAGHER - Maria, Bridget Kelly.
JOYCE - John and Bridget, Mary.
LOUGHNEY - Matthew and Bridget, Pat, Thomas, John, Owen.
LOUGHNEY - Catherine, Bridget, Bridget, (seamstress).
McLOUGHLIN - Michael and Bridget, Martin, Michael, Anthony.
HEFFERON - Stephen and Maggie.
LACKEN - Martin and Margaret, Patrick, Mathew, Martin, Mary, Sarah.
CONWAY - Bridget, Patt.
COWELL - John and Bridget, John, Mary, Bridget, Anna.
CROWLEY - John and Bridget, Anne.
GALLAGHER - Catherine, Annie, Katie.
ROLSTON - John and Bella, Edward, Sarah, Rebecca, William, John, Matthew, Bella, Emma.

RAHANS

KNOX - Ernest and Ada, Ada, Zinna, Helena Rynd, Kate Pender, Mary Barrett, Margaret McCourt, Michael Newcome, (land agent).
HANAHOE - John and Julia, Mary, Edward.
STAKEM - Laurence and Maggie, Mary, Kathleen, Maggie, Bridget, (ex RIC).

RATHNACONEEN

O'HORA - Daniel and Anne, Mary, Norah, John, Patrick, Ellen, Michael, Daniel, William.
O'HORA - Henry and Mary, Mary, Patrick, Anthony, Bridget, Michael, Henry, Sarah, Sidney.
O'HORA - Margaret, Patrick, Bridget, Margaret, Michael, Thomas, Annie, Anthony Clarke.

RATHKIP

COLEMAN - Michael and Mary, John, Andrew, Mary, Bridget, (blacksmith).
FURY - Margaret, Thomas, John, Bridget, Francis, James, Winifred.
KILGALLON - Bridget, Thomas, John Marley.
LOFTUS - Denis and Sabina, John.
FOY - William and Bridget, Katie, Lizzie.
FURY - Patrick and Julia, Thomas, John, Francis, Mary.
CALPIN - James and Bridget, Kathy.
FURY - Michael and Bridget.
McNULTY - Thomas and Catherine, Mary, Kate, Anne, Lizzie, Thomas.
MOYLES - Patrick and Margaret, Michael, Patrick.
LOFTUS - John and Bessie, Bridget,Teresa
KENNEDY - James, Mary.
QUEENAN - John and Eliza, Margaret, Kate, John, Bridget, Anne, Patrick, Mary, Alice, James McNulty.
BROGAN - James and Mary, Michael, Ellen, Patrick.

REILLY'S LANE

1. MURRAY - Mary, Ellen, Mary Garvin, Margaret Tolan, (dressmaker).
2. REAPE - James and Bridget, Thomas, Mary, (baker).

SHAMBLE STREET

1. LOFTUS - Thomas and Bridget, Patrick, Mary, Patrick, Maud, Thomas, Josephine, Christina, (victualler).
2. McKENNA - Patrick, Thomas Murray, (butcher).

3/7. Stores.

8. LYONS - John and Bessie, John, Edward, Mary, Margaret, Bridget Coleman.
9. BROWN - Anne, Pat, Anthony, William.
10. HEFFERNAN - James and Bridget, Thomas, Mary.
11. McCANN - Anne, William, John, Francis, Margaret Keane, GALLAGHER: Patrick, Laurence, Thomas.

SHERIDANS LANE
ABBEYHALFQUARTER
1. CULLEN - Mary, Mary, Patrick.
2. DAISY - Ellen, Bridget, Mary, Anne.
3. FOX - Bridget, Michael.
4. MARLEY - Michael, Pat.
5. HEFFRON - Bridget, Maggie Naughton.
6. MYLES - James and Bridget, John, Ellen.
7. DALY - Bridget, Winifred, Wallace, Michael.
8. KELLY - Anthony.

SLIEVENAGARK
KEANE - Patrick and Anne, Patrick, Mary, James, Bridget, Michael.
SHEA - Bridget, Thomas and Mary, Bridget, Patrick, Thomas, William, James.
SHEA - Martin and Mary, Mary, Bridget, Anne, Michael, Martin, John.
CARR - Patrick and Mary, Luke, Edward, Robert, Bridget, Bernard, Peter, Mary, Thomas.
CARR - Mary, Nancy Foy.
TRAYNOR - Thomas, Ellen, Bernard, Catherine, Bridget, John.
HOBAN - Martin and Bridget, Mary, Catherine, Michael, John.
WYNNE - Anne, Peter, Honoria, John, Mary Traynor.
MORAN - John and Ellen, Pat.
HOBAN - Michael and Catherine, Patrick, Bridget, Michael, Mary, Anthony, Winifred, Thomas, James, Kate, Sebina.
HOBAN - Francis and Ellen, Mary, Michael, Catherine, Delia, Ellen, Anne, Maggie.

SOLOMON'S LANE
1. HARTE - Pat and Kate, James, Bridget, Mary, Katie, Nannie, (shoemaker).
2. STUDDARS - John and Mary.
3. COOKE - Mary, Patrick.

TULLYSLEVA
KELLY - John, Hannah.
HOWLEY - John, Mary.
REDINGTON - James and Mary, Bridget, Francis, Annie, Pat.
O'HORA - Mary, Michael, Bridget.
LOFTUS - John and Bridget.
GORDON - Bridget, MUNNELLY: Patrick and Bridget, Mary, Kate, Patrick, Maggie, Edward, Thomas.
BOURKE - Patrick and Bridget.
MUNNELLY - Mary, John, Thomas.
BATTLE - John and Bridget.
WARD - Michael and Mary, Mary, Margaret, Michael.
BATTLE - Michael and Catherine, Michael Reap.
HOPE - Michael and Anne, Michael, Mary, Patrick, John.
BARRETT - Mary, Patrick, Annie, Mary, Kate, John, Teresa, Martin McGuinness.
CUMMINS - John and Mary, Mary, Patrick.
HOLMES - John and Ellen, Thomas, John.
MOYLES - Patrick and Margaret, May, Michael, John, Bridget, Barbara, Patrick, Margaret, Andrew.
KILLIGREW - William and Lizzie, Hannah, Samuel, Catherine Hamilton, (nailor).
DOWD - Thomas and Maria, Mary, Patrick, Annie, Edward, Katie.

TULLYEGAN
MURRAY - John and Catherine, Mary, Martin, John, Annie, Patrick, James, Bridget.
MURRAY - Thomas and Catherine, John.
McLOUGHLIN - Michael and Catherine, John, Annie, Bridget, John Henighan, Bridget Melvin.
WALSH - Anthony and Bridget, Mary, Honor, Edward, Martin, Winefred.
McLOUGHLIN - Patrick and Bridget, Katie.
KENNY - Michael and Anne, John, Thomas.
HOLMES - Thomas and Winnie, Bridget, Pat, Maria, WALSH: Michael, Bridget.
PRESTON - Anne, Bridget, Mary, Thomas, Michael, Patrick, Kate.

UPPER PIPER HILL
1. MORRISSON - Morgan and Bridget, Emmie, John Dooley, John Balmer, Peter Burne, John Sweeney, Thomas Canavan, Alexander Kelly, Kate Meegan, (tea mcht).
2. CALLAGHAN - Owen and Bridget.
3. COPPINGER - Mark and Anne, Mary, Katie, Mark, (railway foreman).
4. CURRY - Patrick, Catherine, Thomas, (railway porter).
5. FORBES - John and Annie.
6. FORBES - Pat and Kate, Mark, John, Pat, William, Michael Neary, James Neary, James Carry, (railway porter).
7. LAVELLE - Peter and Ellen, Peter, Pat, Mary, Ellen, Thomas, John.
8. BRENNAN - Catherine, John Cantley, Mary Reilly, Jane Reilly.
9. KILGALLON - Thomas and Agnes, (coach builder).
10. LAVELLE - Edward and Ellen, M.John, William, Peter, Anthony, Edward, Bridget, P.James, (railway milesman).
11. MURRAY - Mary, Mary Carrollen.
12. DEMPSEY - Patrick and Mary, Katie, Michael, Mary, Patrick, Bernard, Edward, John Rigney, John Gannon, (grocer & publican).
13. DOYLE - Patrick and Bessy, Kate, (railway porter).
14. O'HORA - Anne, Mary, Edward Clarke, Honor Hannan, (laundress).
15. CAFFERTY - Michael and Maria, Bernard, Bridget, Mary, Margaret, Patrick, Michael.
16. MURRAY - Michael and Anne, Michael, Pat, Thomas, John, Charles, Bridget, Margaret.
17. LANGAN - John.
18. McGRATH - James and Mary, John, (milesman).
19. CAULEY - Michael and Ellen, Mary, Willy.
20. O'REGAN - Patrick and Bridget, Joseph, Patrick, (carpenter).
21. HOBAN - Mary, Martin, Nannie.
22. HALLORAN - Bridget, William, Mary, Pat, Sarah, Peter.
23. MURRAY - Martin and Kate, Mary, Bridget, Michael, Thomas.
24. LACKEY - Kate, John, Mary, Bridget, Annie, Thomas, Teresa.
25. McNAMARA - Charles and Anne, Alice, Maggie, Maria, Charles, (ex RIC).
26. CLARKE - Mary, William, John.
27. CONNOR - Michael and Hanora.
28. MELVIN - James and Ellen, Bridget Lynch.
29. LOFTUS - Pat and Jane, Jane, Kate, Bridget, Pat, Elizabeth, (shoemaker).
30. DUFFY - Pat and Kate.
31. BRENNAN - Julia.
32. vacant
33. SCOTT - John, William Lindsay.
34. SHAW - Frederick and Kate, Jane, Isabella, Robert, (signalman).
35. O'BRIEN - Hugh and Mary, William, Joseph, John, Hugh, Mary, Maggie, (shoemaker).
36. CAFFERTY - Paul and Mary, Bryan, Patrick, Paul, John, (bootmaker).
37. WALL - Francis, (dyer).
38. GORDON - Biddy.
39. WALKIN - Bessy.
40. FOY - Michael and Bridget, John, Bridget.
41. CAFFERTY - Kate.
42. WALSH - William, (carpenter).
43. O'FARRELL - Thomas and Mary, Bridget, Margaret, Mathew, Kate, Jane, Robert, Patrick.
44. GREENE - Patrick and Annie, Kate, Bertha, Gertrude, Scibina, Annie, Lizzie, Patrick, Anthony, Michael, Thomas, John, (sanitary officer).
45. WALSHE - Luke and Bridget, Bridget, John, Michael, Peter, Patrick, Anne Clarke.
46. RYDER - Thomas and Kate, George, Eva, David, Pat, (naimaker).

VICTORIA STREET
1. FLYNN - Michael, Patrick Culkin.
2. THOMPSON - George and Anne, Lillie, Minnie, Olive Gawley, Alfred Aldwell, Joseph McRobert, Dermot MacDermott, John Spencer, (land agent).
3. KNOX - Julia, Hannah, Joseph, (boarding hse.).
4. EGGLESTON - Lillie, Sarah Sharpe.
5. QUINN - Bernard, (clergyman C.C.).

WATER LANE
1. BRODERICK - Peter and Bridget, Mary, Bridget, Josephine, Nannie, Michael Anderson, (shoemaker).
2. CARDEN - Jane, John.
3. SHERIDAN - Thomas and Margaret, John, Annie, Margaret, Katie, James.
4. FERGUSON - Catherine, Richard, Charlotte.
5. GREGHAN - John and Kate, Weny.
6. BROWN - Bridget.
7. REDDINGTON - John and Bridget.
8. BROWNE - John and Catherine, Patrick, Mary.

WORKHOUSE LANE
ABBEYHALFQUARTER
MULLARKEY - John and Bridget, Patrick, Owen.

ALL THE TOWNLANDS THAT SURROUND BALLINA

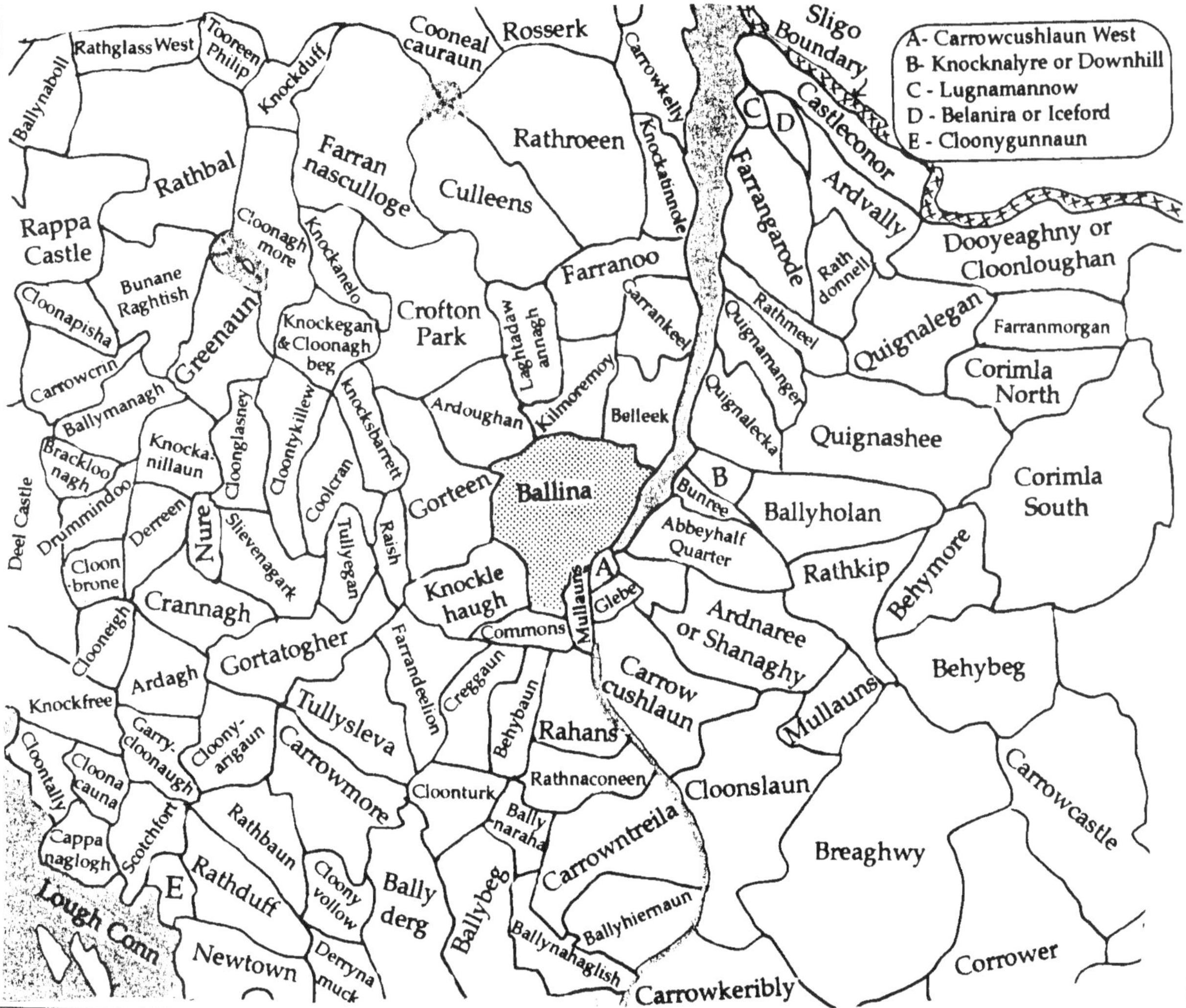

Civil PARISH	BARONY
A = Kilmoremoy,	Tirawley.
B = Kilmoremoy,	Tireragh, Co.Mayo
C = Ballysakeery,	Tirawley
D = Ardagh,	Tirawley
E = Kilbelfad,	Tirawley
F = Ballynahaglish,	Tirawley
G = Attymass,	Gallen
H = Kilgarvan,	Gallen
K = Crossmolina,	Tirawley
L = Killala,	Tirawley
N = Killasser,	Gallen
O = Toomore,	Gallen
S = Castleconnor,	Tireragh, Co. Sligo
* = Ballina	

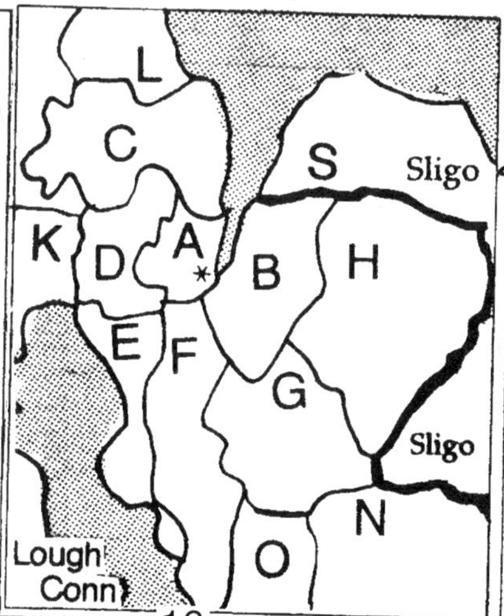

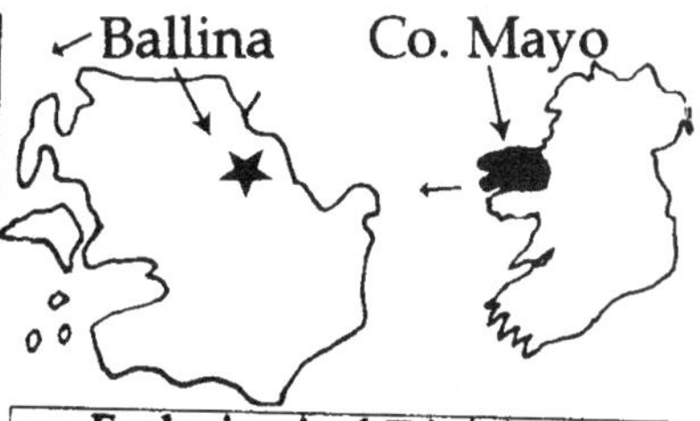

Ecclesiastical Divisions

Attymass, Kilgarvan and Killasser parish are part of Achonry Diocese. Ardagh, Kilmoremoy, Crossmolina, Ballysakeery and Killala parish are in Killala Diocese. The Church of Ireland dioceses are important for the administration of wills.

Slater's Directory of Ballina in 1894

THE nineteenth century saw the arrival of Directories of towns and cities. Ballina Town figures in Pigot's Directory of 1824, and in Slater's National Commercial Directory of Ireland 1846, '56, '70, '81 and 1894, and all are available at the National Library and the National Archives in Dublin. This extract below is from the 1894 edition. The population of Ballina Town in 1891 was 4, 662. Less informative is Ambrose Leets directorys of 1812 and 1814, and Wilsons Postchaise Companion of 1784, 1786 and 1803, which name the prominent residents of the town.

PRIVATE RESIDENTS

Armstrong Robert, Oghill hse.
Armstrong Rev. Thomas, Knox st.
Atkinson Edward E., Francis st.
Atkinson Mrs. Esther, Ardnaree.
Baxter Robert G., Arthur st.
Bourke Miss Ann, Knox st.
Bourke Mrs. Eliza, Knox st.
Bourke Mrs. Kate, Knox st.
Bourke Robert Paget, John st.
Boyd Mrs. C., Moy Fort.
Browne Rev. H.C., (curate of Ardnaree).
Cairns Rev. John, (Pres.), Charles st.
Conmy The Most Rev. John, (Catholic Bishop of Killala).
Coolican Mrs. Ann, Francis st.
Coolican Michael V., Francis st.
Crotty Richard D., Francis st.
Dillon John B., Dillon tce.
Dolphin Thomas, Francis st.
Downing Charles, Boonicoulan.
Erskine John, Knox st.
Erskine Joseph, King st.
Faussett Miss Anne, Ardnaree.
Finlay Henry, Knox st.
Gallagher Rev. Michael, (Catholic), Arthur st.
Gallagher Mrs., Millview cot., Ardnaree.
Garvey John, Riversdale hse.
Gillycuddy Michael, Ardnaree cottage.
Gordon Thomas, Knox st.
Hewson James, Dillon terrace.
Joynt George, Arthur st.
Joynt Mrs. W., Arthur st.
Keiser John F., Ballina hse.
Kelly Rev. James, Ardnaree.
Kennedy Rev. Hy. (Wesleyan), Hill st.
Kirkwood Capt. Charles, Broadlands.
Laing George M., Knox st.
Little Charles A., Iceland hse.
Malley Miss Lauria, Francis st.
Macaulay Roger, Francis st.
McDermott Standish O'G., Clongee.
McNunn John, Knox st.
Macnulty P.W., Francis st.
Naughton Rev. Jas., (Catholic), Arthur st.
Orchard William, Arran place.
Ormsby Arthur, Glen lodge.
Ormsby William, Coolcran cottage.
Pratt Joe, Enniscoe.
Pringle Miss, Farm hill.
Scrope Henry, Knox st.
Skipton Very Rev. William, (dean of Killala), Ardnaree rectory.
West William, Dillon tce.

COMMERCIAL

Adamson & Co., chemists, King st.
Anderson E. & I., confectioners, Knox st.
Anderson James, commission agent, Arran st.
Armstrong John T., watchmaker, Knox st.
Armstrong Thomas W., watchmaker, Arran st.
Baird David, cabinet maker, King st.
Baird David, grocer, Knox st.
Ballina Herald, (Richard W. Joynt, proprietor), Knox st.
Bank of Ireland, (Henry Finlay, agent), Knox st.
Barratt John, blacksmith, Hill st.
Barratt Margaret, confectioner, Knox st.
Beckett Isaac, timber mcht., Shamble st.
Beirne Michael, grocer, Arran st.
Beirne Michael, grocer, Bridge st.
Boland Sarah, spirit dler., Bridge st.
Bourke Comin, saddler, King st.
Bourns John, printer, King st.
Brislin Arthur, coach builder, Arthur st.
Brislin James, spirit dler., Garden st.
Brown Adam, ship broker, Knox st.
Browne John, grocer, Bridge st.
Callaghan Edward, shopkeeper, Bridge st.
Callaghan Michael, spirit dler., Hill st.
Calleary James, grocer, Hill st.
Calleary Michael, tailor, Hill st.
Carroll Bros., spirit dler., Garden st.
Carroll John, grocer, Garden st.
Carroll Mary, grocer, Bridge st.
Casey Thomas J., grocer, King st.
Chambers Patrick, prov. dler., Bridge st.
Clarke John, coach builder, John st.
Coleman Michael, blacksmith, Ardnaree.
Connolly Michael, tailor, King st.
Connor George, spirit dler., Garden st.
Connor Michael, bootmaker, Hill st.
Conway Matthew, spirit dler., Ardnaree.
Coolican James, grocer & gen. mcht., Bridge st.
Coolican Michael V., solicitor, Knox st.
Corcoran James, egg dler., Garden st.
Corcoran William, saddler & harness maker, Arran st.
Cosgrave Elizabeth, grocer, John st.
Daly Charles, tinsmith, Hill st.
Davis John & Co., grocers, King st.
Dempsey Patrick, spirit dler., Hill st.
Devany Henry, grocer, Bridge st.
Dodd Andrew, grocer, Bridge st.
Dolphin Edward, baker, Bridge st.
Donnelly Edward, spirit dler., Ardnaree.
Doyle J.F., spirit dler., King st.
Duffy Bros., bakers, Garden st.
Duffy Martin, coach builder, Ardnaree.
Durkan Margaret A., grocer, Ardnaree.
Durkan P.J., Temperance hotel, Ardnaree.
Egan John & Son, mineral water ma., Arran st.
Egan & Co., grocers, Bridge st.
Erskine John, insurance agent, Knox st.
Erskine Joseph, draper, King st.
Evans Michael, butcher, Arran st.
Fever Hospital, (Roger Macaulay, surgeon).
Finlay Henry, insurance agent, Knox st.
Fitzgerald Michael, tailor, Arran st.
Flanagan Patrick, grocer, Knox st.
Fleming Michael, gunsmith, Arran st.
Flynn William, Imperial & Royal hotel, Knox st.
Ford Richard, carpenter, Killala road.
Fox Frances, grocer & car owner, Garden st.
Frazer & Slater, hair dressers, Garden st.
Gallagher Hugh, grocer & gen. mcht., Arran st.
Gallagher Hugh, leather dler., King st.
Garrett John, grocer, Bridge st.
Garvey John, solicitor, Knox st.
Gas Works (Thomas John Reid, manager), Shamble st.
Gaughin John & Sons, coopers, King st.
Gibbons Michael, spirit dler., Hill st.
Gill Robert & Co., drapers, Knox st.
Gillespie Mary, grocer, King st.
Gilmartin Patrick, grocer, Ardnaree.
Gordon James, bootmaker, Arran st.
Gordon Thomas, solicitor, Knox st.
Hackett J., hairdresser, Garden st.
Hanick Anne, spirit dler., Ardnaree.
Hastings Michael, spirit dler., Ardnaree.
Healy Redmond, spirit dler., Bridge st.
Hearns Frank, shopkeeper, Bridge st.
Hearons James, shopkeeper, Bridge st.
Hewson Patrick, shopkeeper, Bridge st.
Holmes Ann, grocer, Garden st.
Howley Charles, grocer, Bridge st.
Howley John, grocer, Bridge st.
Hume Rebecca, fruiterer, Arran st.
Jennings James, shopkeeper, King st.
Johnson Benjamin, saddler & harness maker, Knox st.
Joynt Richard W., printer & commissioner, Knox st.
Joynt George, civil engineer, Arthur st.
Judge John, spirit dler., Bridge st.
Kane Robert, shoe ma., King st.
Kelly Barbara, grocer, Ardnaree.
Kelly Peter, spirit dler., King st.
Kelly William, grocer, Bridge st.
Kennedy Thos., spirit dler., Ardnaree.
Knox A.H. & Sons, land agents, Gore st.
Laing George, grocer, Ardnaree.
Laing George M., surgeon, Knox st.
Leighton R., shopkeeper, Ardnaree.
Leonard John, carpenter, John st.
Little Charles A., solicitor, Knox st.
Loftus Thomas, butcher, Shamble st.
Lynch Patrick, boot & shoe maker, King st.
Macaulay Roger, surgeon, Francis st.
McCawley Walter, grocer & commission agent, Bridge st.
M'Conn James, ironmonger, Arran st.
McDermott Elizabeth, draper & milliner, Arran st.
McDonnell John, grocer, Bridge st.
McDonnell Owen, spirit dler., Ardnaree.
McGuiness Luke, butcher, Bridge st.
M'Kenna Patrick, butcher, Shamble st.
McMullen Nathaniel, spirit dler., Ardnaree.
McMunn John, insurance agent, Knox st.
McNulty Richard, ironmonger & spirit dler., Knox st.
McNulty Robert, grocer, Knox st.
McTaggart Richard, grocer, Ardnaree.
Malone Patrick J., draper & china dler.,

Malone Patrick J., timber & slate mcht., Garden st.
Malone Patrick J., game dler., Hill st.
Marsh Patrick, blacksmith, Killala road.
Maude Anthony F., land agent, Workhouse row.
Maughan John, butcher, Shamble st.
Maughan Patrick, butcher, King st.
Meehan Winifred, bootmaker, King st.
Melvin Maria, spirit dler., Garden st.
Moran John, blacksmith, Knox st.
Moran Patrick, spirit dler., Hill st.
Muffany Arthur, newsagent & toy dler., Knox st.
Muldarig Mary, shopkeeper, Arran st.
Mullen John & Co., spirit dler., King st.
Murray John, spirit dler., Arran st.
Murtagh Elizabeth, Moy hotel, Knox st.
National Bank (Henry Scrope, manager), Knox st.
Naughton Mary, spirit dler., Garden st.
O'Boyle Michael, grocer, Ardnaree.
O'Connell Jas. & Co., grocers, Ardnaree.
O'Connor Charles, grocer, Garden st.
O'Dowd Bernard, grocer, Knox st.
O'Dowd D., spirit dler., Garden st.
O'Hara Arthur C., land agent, Workhouse row.
O'Hara Edward, bootmaker, Bridge st.
O'Horo Michael, grocer, King st.
O'Reilly Michael, grocer, ironmonger, Knox st.
Patterson John, boot & shoemaker, Bridge st.
Poland William H., watchmaker, Hill st.
Pollexsen***** W. & G.T. & Co., corn, coal mcht., Ardnaree.
Port George, watchmaker, Garden st.
Presbyterian Orphanage (Mrs. Williamson, matron), Charles st.
Provincial Bank of Ireland, (John Erskine, manager), Knox st.
Quinnen Patrick, butcher, Shamble st.
River Moy Salmon Fishery, (Little & Co. proprietors).
Ruane William, grocer, Bridge st.
Ruddy John, spirit dler., Ardnaree.
Ruttledge Francis, grocer, King st.
Ruttledge John, shopkeeper, Garden st.
Ryder Thomas, nail maker, Hill st.
St. Muredach Seminary, (Rev. James Kelly, principal), Ardnaree.
Scrope Henry, insurance agent, Knox st.
Singer Manuf. Co., (W. Speiss, manager), sewing machine makers, Knox st.
Strong James & Co., drapers, boot dlers., Arran st.
Sullivan John, spirit dler., Garden st.
Sweeney Martin, Corn mcht., Arthur st.
Timlin C., grocer, Garden st.
Timlin Maria, spirit dler., Garden st.
Trimble Francis R., draper, Knox st.
Ulster Bank (John McMunn, manager), Knox st.
Wade Timothy, coach builder, Knox st.
Walsh Anthony, grocer, Bridge st.
Walsh Edward, stationer & tobacconist, Knox st.
Walsh Francis, saddler, Bridge st.
Walsh Michael, spirit dler., Ardnaree.
Waters Henry J., grocer, Bridge st.
Western People, (Thomas R. Welsh, proprietor), Arran st.
Wills H.C., draper, King st.
Wilson J.C., corn miller, Ardnaree.
Wilson John C., salmon fishery, Woodbine cottage.
Wilson Robert, grocer & seed mcht., Knox st.
Youell FB., grocers&boot makers, Arran st

THE YEAR OF THE FRENCH: 1798

France declared war on the United Kingdom of Britain in 1793 and it lasted up until 1815. In 1791 Wolfe Tone had founded the Society of United Irishmen, whose aims were the abolition of distinctions made on the grounds of religion, the reform of Parliament, and the curtailment of British influence in the government of the country. In 1795 the society became a secret military organisation with the object of revolt against the British being its primary objective. Letters were sent to France and plans were developing. Expectations of a French invasion were mounting. Social unrest was increasing in Ireland, and confiscation of property was rife, which lead to more secret societies like the Whiteboys and other Defender organisations that wanted to seek revenge from what was happening in this country. Ideas of rebellion were spread around the small public houses of Ballina. The Government in London was well aware of the social unrest and the dangers it created. The possibility of a French Invasion was foreseen.The English Government introduced strict laws regarding the surrender of arms and the membership of the United Irish Society, and these new laws were brutally administerd.

The promise of a landing in May 1798 was agreed by the French and Irish, but spies and informers kept the Government informed. Many leaders were arrested and punished.

The Rising did break out but in small pockets of Wicklow, Carlow, Meath and Dublin. Then Wexford began to revolt against the red coats and was where the most serious fighting of the revolt was happening. Wolfe Tone was in Le Havre and did not get word of the rising until 3 weeks later. Arklow, as well as Ulster began to revolt at the start of June. Both areas were defeated. British re-inforcements restored order again. The rebellion was fought without the French. Ireland as a whole did not rise against the British. There was wide areas where there was no activity. All of Connaught and the majority of Munster was quiet. By late summer, more British soldiers were brought in.

Around August 22nd, 1798, the French carried out what was considered as the last invasion of Ireland, and landed at Killala. Wolfe Tone was hoping Napoleon would keep focused on defeating the British in Ireland, but Napoleon was starting to turn his eye towards Egypt. In Napoleons eyes, the invasion of this Island was only kept on the boil as a smokescreen to camouflage his plans in the East. He knew that Britain had command of the Seas, and therefore he realised that without being master of the seas, all plans against Britain would not materialise. But on Aug.1st, Napoleons army was defeated at the battle of the Nile by Nelson, and Napoleon re-focused his campaign for Ireland.

THE YEAR OF THE FRENCH: 1798

(continued from previous page). Eventually three French expeditions were sent to Ireland in the late Summer of 1798. The first force was over 1,000 soldiers under General Humbert sailed from La Rochelle on the Bay of Biscay. The second force had 3,000 men under Gen. Hardy, and left Brest with orders to land in Ulster and meet up with the Irish insurgents. The third force had 8,000 men under Gen. Kilmaine.

Due to severe winds, only the first force landed in Ireland. The second fleet with Wolfe Tone on board were defeated at sea near Lough Swilly on October 11th. The third force lead by Gen. Kilmaine never embarked. This was not an invasion, but merely a raid, that was lead by Gen. Humbert. The force was made up of 82 officers and 1015 soldiers, with a few troopers and gunners that had served in Italy and on the Rhine.

The British Yeomanry had little training in military matters and were recognised more as a police force to keep an eye on the locals. The British knew that it would take 4-5 days to assemble an army of up to 6,000 men, and it would take longer in Connaught. So Humbert was safe for those few days, but he was cautious because the second force did not arrive on the scene. Humbert brushed the Killala Yeomanry aside and occupied the area. Humbert then moved south to Ballina, dispersing a 500 strong troop of British Yeomanry from the area. He armed over 800 Irish men and prepared for battle. Word of the French landing spread throughout the land. A large British army left Wexford for Connaught and they reached Athlone by the 27th of August. Also a British batallion from the Galway area marched towards Castlebar. Although his objective was to march to Castlebar, Humbert marched south towards a British regiment based at Foxford. He cunningly doubled back around by Crossmolina and came down on Castlebar from the north. He outwitted and defeated the British at Castlebar and asked the local people to stand behind him and fight for the independence of ancient Hibernia. Then on the 3rd September, the British advanced towards Castlebar. The French sneaked out at night and were followed swiftly Shots were exchanged on th 5th of September at Tubbercurry, and the French made their way towards Sligo. A British batallion under Col. Vereker was based in Sligo and decided to make contact with the French army in Collooney. Shots were fired, but the French were much too cunning and they threatened to surround the British, and this compelled the British to abandon their guns and retreated back towards Ballyshannon. Had Humbert followed, he would have taken Sligo and gone into Donegal, as there was no British troops in this area. Instead of this, Humbert headed for Dromahair and Manorhamilton, where he was starting to feel the pressure. He had to abandon several of his guns, where some sank into the bogs and he lost some in the river at Dromahair. When he was near Manorhamilton, he changed directions again and marched to Drumkeeran. The British were close to Collooney and another batallion moved to Carrick on Shannon.

On the 6th of September, Humbert crossed the Shannon at Ballintra. He crossed the bridge here and moved to Drumshanbo where his rearguard shook off the British advance. He must have been in a hurry as he did not destroy the bridge. On the 7th September, the French proceeded by Fenagh to Cloone where they rested for several hours. They were truly exhausted after marching for 120 miles.

Several British regiments were hot on their heels. Another English regiment decided to set up camp in Ballinalee, in north Longford to intercept the French army, as they were convinced that the French were planning to reach Granard, where they had learned that a large number of Irish insurgents had awaited to join the French.

The British followed swiftly behind and eventually caught up with the French at Kiltycreevagh Hill, which was near Ballinamuck in north Longford. The French stood and fought for over 2 hours before several more English regiments arrived, and this finally convinced Humbert to surrender. This was the end of the French sufferings, but the start of more suffering for the Irish. Many were killed on the battlefield and in subsequent pursuit. Humbert had originally planned to reach Dublin before the British and to start a new rebellion there. The timing was terrible and with no further French landings, there was no hope of success. If Humbert had arrived in May of that year instead of August, the results would have being a lot different. The local people in Killala were severely punished afterwards.

1911 Census for Ballina

THE 1911 CENSUS is the second earliest full census returns available for the entire country and can be inspected at the National Archives in Dublin. Mayo's County Library at Castlebar has the 1901 and 1911 census returns for the county on microfilm. The official return for each household lists the occupants, their relationship to householder, name, age, occupation, religion, ability (or otherwise) to speak English/Irish. It also gives details of the house, but absentees are not listed. Ages of adults are suspect in the 1911 census due to the introduction of the pension scheme in 1908. The extracts below include townland or street, house number (in towns) and the names of all occupants, including lodgers and even servants in some cases. A photocopy of the original return for any household may be arranged from the National Archives, Bishop St., Dublin 8.

The majority of all people in the parishes of Ardagh, Kilmoremoy & Ballynahaglish (Backs) worked on the land as farmers. Any job other than farming is listed

ARDBUCKLE ROW

1. GARVIN - James and Annie, Catherine, James, Edward, Francis, Felix, Michael, Frances, Andrew, Roseline, (ex publican)
2. GALLAGHER - Mary, Eileen, John Harte.
2. CONWAY - James and Maria, John, Alphonsus, Marie, Leo, Ernest, Christina, Aloysius, Augustine, (ex RIC sergt.).
3. CONNOLLY - Michael and Mary, James, Michael, Annie, (tailor).
4. KELLY - John, Francis, Anastasia, Theresa, (bootmaker).
5. ELLIOTT - George and Harriette, John, Elizabeth, Mary Johnston, (shop).
6. MORAN - Maria, John, Robert, Kate, Josephine.
7. MORAN - John and Catherine, Nora, Catherine, (plasterer).
8. ARMOUR - Alexander and Mary, Robina, Matthew, John, (plasterer).
9. MORAN - Joseph and Bridget, Meadbh, Maurice, (solicitor's clerk).

ARRAN PLACE

1. PETRIE - Susanna, Frederick.
1. KING - Charles and Julia, Bridget Harrison, (dental surgery).
2. TUOHY - Malachi, Bridget Brogan, James Nolan, James Egan, (organist).

ARRAN STREET

1. TIMLIN - Bridget, Patrick, Kate, Cecil, Clement, Kathleen, Patrick, Timothy, Michael, Moya, Martin, Sarah.
2. McDONAGH - Mary, Mary, Annie, Agnes, Delia Ruttledge, Annie Boland, Belinda Gibson, Maria Flaherty, Michael Bourke, Mary Dixon, (trader).
3. O'BRIEN - Peter, James Kilcullen, (grocer).
4. FRAZER - William and Ellen, Henry, William, Frederick, Henry, Mary Loftus, (hairdresser).
5. STEPHENS - Daniel, Thomas Boland, Martin Connor, Patrick Callahan, Joseph Muffney, (hardware mnger.).
6. GALLAGHER - Patrick, Patrick O'Boyle, Thomas Fahey, James Devine, Percy Gallagher, John Cawley, James Naughton, John Browne, (hardware mngr.).
7. MURRAY - John, Mary, Teresa, Louisa, John, Alfred, Hubert, Constantine, (timber yard mngr.).
8. GRIMES - John and Sarah, Bell, Lucy.
9. BEIRNE - Gertrude, Louisa, Annie, James Gallagher, (post office clerk).
10. HUME - Rebecca, Samuel, Susan, Elizabeth Patterson, Glady's Mills, Bartholomew Coen, Eugene Beglen, Francis Perry, Arthur Cruickshank, William Graham, Sarah McAlister, Sarah Bracken, (boarding hse.).
11. DAVIS - John and Margaret, Patrick, Andrew, Elizabeth, John, Mary, Margaret, Enda, William Hanley, Edward McGuinness, Bessie Fury, Mary Loughney, (mcht.).
12. TEMPANY - Myles, Thomas Ryan, John McDonnell, James Carolan, Mary Reilly, Annie Durkan, (grocers asst.).
13. FLEMING - Kate, George, James Lydon, John Devirs.
14. STRONG - James and Margaret, Alice, Mary, Charles, Richard, George, Thomas Igoe, Robert Gawley, James Kirk, Frederick Bell, Charles Strong, Ella Barr, Frances Barr, Maria Rowe, (woollen draper).
14. WOODHOUSE - Annie, Lizzie Strong, Kathleen Harte, Mary McNulty, Agnes McDonnell, (dressmaker).
15. Flour Corn store.
16. Jeweller's shop.
17. Stationers & barbers shop.
18. FITZGERALD - Eva, Aileen, Gerald, James O'Neill, James Keogh.
19. Seed Store.
20. FARMER - John, Annie, Peter Kennedy, (grocer).
21. WALSH - Thomas and Frances, Rita Hewson, Mary Harlow, (journalist & newspaper proprietor).
22. McHALE - Thomas and Maggie, Ena, John, Hannah Rutledge, Kate Cawley, Patrick McHale, Thomas Coen, Michael Brislane, M. Burke, Bridget McHale, Mary Coultry, Willie Mills, B. Diamond, (draper).
23. GORDON - James, Sarah Shaw, Victor Shaw, William Reid, (boot maker).
24. MULDERRIG - John and Annie, Annie Rutledge, Kate Rutledge, Ernest Marks.
25. McLAIN - Thomas and Margaret, Mary, John, Annie, Thomas, (draper).
26. CORCORAN - Anne, BEATTIE: Joseph, Joseph, James, John Murphy, Bridgid O'Malley.
27. COURELL - Thomas and Bridget, Francis, Annie, Lillie, Joseph, James, Michael, Gerald, (printer).
27. MURPHY - John and Margaret, Patrick, (carpenter).
28. Ballina Technical School
29. Mineral Works Manuf.
30. Timber, iron, slate & coal store.

ARTHUR STREET

1. JOHNSTONE - Walter E. and Helen, Robert, Lynette, Walter, Mary Harte, Ellen Kennedy, Rose Sweeney, (soldier).
2. WALKER - Maria, Annie, Eliza Muleady
3. FAIR - Wesley and Mary, (comm. traveller).
4. HEWSON - Henry and May, Frances Devany, Winifred Howley, (post office).
5. KELLY - Mary, Thomas, Alice, Mark, Joseph.
6. PHILLIPS - William and Annie, Patrick, Aileen, Joseph, Kate Connor, Michael Carr, Thomas Thornton, (insurance inspector).
7. JOYNT - Matilda, Amy.
8. MULLEN - Bridget, William Swaine, Gerald Flood, Mary McGragh, Eugene Burn, (boarding hse.).
9. Town Hall
10. SMYTH - Margaret, Edith Hegarty, Frances Dunne, (shopkeeper).
11. GALLAGHER - Elizabeth, William, Daniel, Kate, McNALLY: Mary, Michael, Mary, Elizabeth.
12. MELVIN - Patrick and Catherine, Mary, Patrick, Joseph.
13. HOLMES - William and Margaret, Mary, John Corduff, John Gilligan.
14. McNALLY - Catherine, John, Patrick, Daniel.
15. CORDEN - Hanoria, Francis, Catherine Lunny, (grocer).
16. SWEENEY - Martin, Clare, Bartley, Michael, Bridget Kelly, (corn mcht.).

ABBEYHALFQUARTER

GILMARTIN - Patrick and Mary, Patrick, Mary, Pat Judge, John Durkan, Catherine Doherty, (contractor).
HAGAN - Catherine, John, CORCORAN: James and Isabella, Henry, James, Bertie, Bernard, Martin, Joseph, Isabella, Edward.
O'BOYLE - Patrick and Nancy, Sarah McGowan.

ABBEYHALFQUARTER
ARDNAREE URBAN

KEEFE - Mary, Margaret Hannan.
FLYNN - Michael and Maria, Thomas, Michael, May, (baker).
DOLAN - Bernard and Anne, James, Anne, (ex RIC).
MALONEY - William and Bridget, Mary, Bridget.
McLOUGHLIN - Patrick and Maryellen.
McLOUGHLIN - James and Margaret, Mary, Michael.
McLOUGHLIN - Michael, John, William, Patrick, Michael, BOURKE: William, Bridget.
QUINN - Maggie, Maria.
HOWLEY - Patrick and Wineford, Michael, Michael, William.

Bridge Street in 1901. Bridge Street was renamed Tolan Street after Michael Tolan who was a 25 year old local tailor at the time, was executed by the Black and Tans in 1921. Tolan St. joins Tone St. on the way up the Street.

CASEY - Patrick and Anne, Thomas, Maria, Michael, Annie, (tin smith).
MELODY - Michael and Bridget, John, Mary, James, Michael, Patrick Banks.
McDERMOTT - Kate.
CONLON - Margaret, Patrick, James, (dressmaker).
DAVITT - Margaret, James, Teresa, Anthony, John, Patrick Hannigan.
FLEMING - Michael and Mary, Mary, Michael, Maggie, Catherine Conlon.
MAYOCK - Catherine, Hanoria, Teresa.
HOWLEY - Michael and Margaret, Mary, Emily, Kate.
ROCHE - John, Patrick, Maggie, Tom, John, James, Bridget.
HEALY - Anthony and Annie, Michael, Joseph, May, Annie, Norah, Lillie, Lizzie, (mason).
CAWLEY - Thomas and Ellen, (postman).
KEANE - Patrick and Mary, John, Bridget, Mary, Patrick, Maggie, James, Mary, Alice, Mary, Mary Loftus.
McLOUGHLIN - Thomas, Teresa, Margaret, Edward, (ex RIC).
FUREY - Thomas and Mary, Patrick, Bridget, Margaret, Mary.
JUDGE - William and Anne, Andrew.
SEAFIELD - Maria.
FORDE - Henry and Maria, John, Henry, Denis, Patrick, Michael, Thomas, John Hope.
HEFFRON - Bridget, Kate.
CREAN - Ellen, Edward.
IRWIN - Samuel and Arabella, David, Florence, Peter Cole, John Harrison, (shop asst).
McNULTY - Patrick and Bridget, Michael, Mary.
DWYER - Thomas and Annie, William, John, Thomas, Edward.
JUDGE - John and Maggie, Patrick.
WALSH - Mary, William Burns.
CAWLEY - Ellen, Mary, William, Michael, John, Robert, Alice.
HOWLEY - James and Anne.
CULKIN - Patrick and Margaret, Bridget, John, (fisherman).
KERR - George and Annie, John, (ex RIC).
JUDGE - Margaret, John, Michael, James, William.
O'BOYLE - Patrick and Catherine, Martin, John, Mary.

ABBEY STREET

ARDNAREE

1. REGAN - Margaret, John, Michael, Bridget.
2. MELODY - Michael and Maggie, Mary, Patrick, Bridget, (coachman).
3. vacant
4. RUDDY - Patrick and Catherine, Mary, John, Patrick, Martin, (miller).
5. MURPHY - Patrick and Anne, Martin, John, (ex grocer).
6. MULLEN - John, Bridget, Michael, (publican).
7. CONMY - Annie, Thomas, Annie Cabry, Tom Bodkin, Joseph Lilly, Katie Donegan, John Cowley, Pat McGuinness, Hugh Murray, (mcht.).
8. GINTY - John and Mary, Patrick, Maryanne, James, John, Dominick, Elizabeth, Joseph, (shop).
9. MELODY - Patrick and Bridget, Ellen, Anthony, Nora, Alice, Annie Daisy, (carpenter & shop).
10. CARNEY - James and Annie, Mary, Thomas, Catherine, (tailor).
11. RUSH - Mary, Agnes, Maud, Christina, John, Anne Kelly, Robert Ryan.
12. ARMSTRONG - Thomas and Lizzie, Thomas, Joseph, George, Frances, Charlotte, Charles, (watchmaker).
13. vacant
14. QUINN - Anne, William, Daisy Belisario, William Campbell, Daniel Brien, Henry Hamilton, (boarding hse.).
15. WADE - William and Ellen, DURCAN: Kate, Bridget, John Tansey, John Doyle, (coachbuilder).
16. McGUINNESS - Patrick, Mary, WALSHE: Sarah, Kathleen, Joseph.
17/18. Forge
19. LOFTUS - Annie, Katie McNulty, Bridget Ferguson, Joseph Throdden, (publican).
20. McNULTY - Mary, Lillie, Catherine Murphy, (shop).
21. LAING - Sarah, Anne, Sarah, Bridget Doherty, Ellen Padden, (shop).
21. McDONNELL - Mary, (nurse).
22. McNULTY - Ellen, Ellen, Martin, McHUGH: Bridget, Michael, Bridget Howley, Bridget Hughes, (shop).
23. CALLAGHAN - Thomas and Mary, Mary, Daniel, (shop).
24. McMULLEN - Mary, Lucinda, Jennette O'Dowd, (publican).
25. SHIER - Hugh and Amelia, Lilian, Daniel Collins, Bridget Earley, (RIC inspector).
26. FERGUSON - George and Margaret, David, Maggie, Janie, Albert, (postmaster).
27, ARMSTRONG - Thomas and Mary, Charlotte, Violet, Cecil, George, Thomas, Isabel, John, (RIC).
27. RIC Barracks TR.A, M.P., RM.A, (constables).
27. Bridewell
28. TIMLIN - James and Bridget, Mary

Duffy, Michael Igoe, Katie O'Neill, (publican).
29. O'BOYLE - Michael and Kate, Mary, Ellen Padden, Norah Meenaghan, Ellen Walsh, Annie Mee, Hugh O'Boyle, (coal mcht.).
30. CALLAGHAN - Edward and Annie, Maggie, Michael, Thomas Ormsby, (horse dler.).
31. shop
32. TAGGART - Robert and Annie, DOYLE: Annie, John, Paul Judge, Bridget Loftus, FRAIN: Dominick, Thomas.
33. Old Seminary
34. CONWAY - Maria.
35. McCOURT - Margaret, Ellie, Lillie, Alice.
36. KEANE - William, Kate, LENNOX: Alexander and Elizabeth, Catherine, William, (fisherman).
37. vacant
38. JORDAN - Annie, Mary, Patrick, Annie, Harry, Michael.
39. KENNEDY - James and Catherine, Bridget, Thomas, Katie, Timothy, Edward, Martin, (mason).
40. CLARKE - Michael and Maryanne, Mary, Michael, Thomas, Anne, Patrick, John O'Hora.
41. MURRAY - Bridget, Kate, JACKSON: Rose, William, Michael.
42. HOWLEY - Michael and Anne, Michael, James, William, Martin, Annie, Patrick, Alice, (shoemaker).
43. HANNICK - Anne, John, Mary, (publican).
44. GANNON - John and Mary, Patrick, Annie, W.Alice, William, (ex RIC).
45. R.C. Chapel

ARDOUGHAN

HUNTER - Michael and Bridget, James, Bridget, Mary.
GALLAGHER - James, Patrick, Catherine, Anne, Thomas, BRODERICK: Thomas, Bertha, Frank Nealon.
LAVIN - Anne, GARDINER: Thomas and Sarah.
MELVIN - Patrick and Kate, Anne, Michael, Mary, Edward, Norah.
QUINN - Thomas and Anne, Patrick, Agnes, Lissie, Michael, Annie Hanahoe.
O'HORO - Thomas, Mary.
LAVIN - John and Margaret, Sabina.
O'HORO - John and Bridget, Patrick, (carpenter).
KENNEDY - John and Bridget, Patrick, Michael, Stephen, James.
GINTY - John and Bridget, Michael, Mary, John, Agnes, Mary, Bridget.
ROBINSON - John and Mary, Michael and Belinda, Katie, John, Thomas, Michael, Mary, Peter.

1906 - 1979 Students of St. Muirdeachas College, Ballina

The student role has the year in question with each pupil and their address. It also has a Surname index, with forename and year of enrolement. At the Nat. Library (Ir.259m2)

HANAHOE - Edward and Mary, Micahel, Nora, Anne, Mary, Anthony, Thomas, Margaret.

ARDNAREE or SHANAGHY (Rural)

DEMPSEY - John and Bridget, Lackey, James, John, John O'Malley, (tailor).
WALL - Mary, Richard.
KILGALLON - John and Katie, Agnes, Ellen, Mary, Julia, John, Joseph.
LYNCH - Patrick, Alisha, Margaret Ryley.
HARTE - Bridget, James and Mary.
CORCORAN - John and Mary, Patrick, James.
LYNCH - Bridget, Michael, Edward.
MEERS - Annie, John, Patrick, Michael, Bridget.
DOHERTY - Michael and Jane, Joseph, Helly, Bridget.
KING - Catherine, Richard, Sarah, Henry, Baskerville Wills.
JONES - Henry.

ARDNAREE or SHANAGHY (Urban)

NIXON - Maria, Mary, Bridget, Josephine, Patrick, Patrick Forbes.
SWEENEY - John and Maggie, (RIC).
FLEMING - Michael and Bridget, Michael, John, Annie, Pat, Edward.
STOCK - Elizabeth, Valentine, Florence.
SCANLAN - James and Ellen, William, Alice McLoughlin, Edward Sweeney.
MULROONEY - Catherine, McGOWAN: Anthony and Mary.
ARMSTRONG - Edward and Bridget, Winefred, Thomas, George, Edward, Elizabeth Kelly, (carpenter).
O'HALLORAN - Barbara, Sarah Ruane, Hannah Kelly, (shop).
MOLONEY - Elizabeth, James, Christopher.
RUDDY - James and Bridget, BRODERICK: Patrick and Catherine.
FLEMING - Patrick and Kate, McDERMOTT: William and Mary, Jane, Annie, Patrick, William.
ROBINSON - Patrick and Mary, John, Mary, Patrick, Thomas, (carpenter).
GILMARTIN - Charles and Anne, Charles, Bridgid, Martin, Mark, Barbara Culkin, (shop).
LOFTUS - Daniel and Sarah, Mary, Bridget, Kathleen, Winifred.
SWEENEY - Ellen, May.
NASH - Thomas and Anney, Mary, Patrick, Maggie, Norah, Maria, Bridget, Anney Keating, (tailor).
MANGAN - Peter, Bridget.
GILMARTIN - Thomas and Maryellen, Mary, Bridget Mullarkey, (mason).
KELLY - Maria, DURKAN: Ellen, Patrick.
SWEENEY - Thomas and Annie, John, Maggie, James, Thomas, Patrick, Malachy.
CARROLL - James and Margaret, Bridget, Mary, Margaret, (egg packer).
HOWLEY - Winifred, Peter, Patrick, Martin.
MOLONEY - Catherine, John.
CONVEY - Margaret, Agnes Loftus.
JORDAN - Anne, (shop).
CULLETON - Maryanne, Hanoria, Patrick, Joseph.
JORDAN -Patrick and Mary, John, Patrick, Martin, Anthony, Michael, William, Thomas, Ellen.
CASEY - John and Ellen, Patrick, John, Agnes, Michael, (tinsmith).
CARROLL - Thomas and Bridget, Mary, Bridget, (shoemaker).
FOSTER - Catherine, Annie, Mary.
FERGUSON - Michael and Ellen, Mary, Michael Walsh, (tailor).
CASEY - Patrick and Catherine, Michael, Patrick, (tinsmith).
FLEMING - Bridget, Katie, Patrick, John, KING: Catherine, John, (fish dler.).
KEVANY - Thomas and Margaret, Mary, (horse trainer).
JORDAN - Thomas and Bridget, John, James, Katie, Thomas, Edward.
LALLY - James and Mary, Patrick, Maryellen, Maggie, Bridget, Edward, Michael, Martin, James, (clothes mcht.).
JUDGE - Bridget, Martin, Ellen, (grocer).
NIXON - Thomas, (shoemaker).
JACKSON - Anne, Patrick, Michael, James, William, Annie, Bridget, Maggie, Michael Dolan.
BRIEN - Michael and Mary, Johanna, (barber).
CLARKE - Kate, John, William, Henry, CASLIN: Mary, Elizabeth.
O'BRIEN - William and Margaret, Hugh, Una, Winifred Kelly, William Carroll, (compositor).
LYNCH - Thomas and Kate, John, Katie, Bridget, Maggie, Annie.
DURKAN - Edward and Catherine.
MOLLOY - John and Ellen, Mary, Patrick, John Murphy, (contractor).
GORMAN - Catherine, Owen, Mathew.
CULLEN - Mary, Mary.
LAVELLE - Thomas and Mary, John, Anthony, Charles, Mary, Kate, Bridget, Ellen.
RAFTER - John, Patrick, John, Thomas.
MORRISON - John and Anne, John, Michael, Mary.
CASEY - John and Bridget, Annie, (tinsmith).
WILSON - John and Margaret, Catherine Bryce, (salmon fishery lessee & corn miller).
LEWIS - William and Elizabeth, Eileen, May, Harold, (printer).
LEWIS - Samuel and Mary, Arthur, Emily, John, Mabel, Stephen, Eva, Dorothy, (sexton).

ARDNAREE or SHANAGHY (Urban)

STUDDART - John and Ellen, Martin, John, Pat, Edward, Kate, Christina, (fish dler.).
SHAW - Anthony and Mary, Robert.
LOUGHNEY - Laurence and Maggie, Laurence, James Flynn.
CALLAGHAN - Mary, Margaret Connell, Mary Durkan.
SIZE - William, Mary, Mary Reilly.
MURRAY - Elizabeth, James, Peter, Thomas, Martin, Teresa, John.

RUSH - Ellen, Margaret.
CONVEY - Martin and Bridget, Sarah, Bridget, Martin, Catherine.
MURRAY - Pat and Adelaide, Teresa, Lillie, (butcher).
NAUGHTON - Martin and Mary, Mary, Veronica, Margaret, (blacksmith).
COBRY - John, John, Michael.
REILLY - Anne, John.
HALLORAN - Michael, Patrick.
McNULTY - Rose, John.

BROOK STREET

ARDNAREE

1. Store
2. HALLORAN - Mary, Patrick, Margaret, (dressmaker).
3. CLARKE - Mary, Annie, John, Patrick, Michael, John Heffernan, Maggie Loftus.
4. CONVY - Arthur, Maggie, McMANUS: John, Michael, Rita, Celia.
5. DURKAN - John and Bridget, Joseph, Anthony, John, Mary Gallagher.
6. vacant 7. forge

BALL ALLEY LANE

1. MARLEY - Martin and Bridget, Michael, Delia.
2. DOHERTY - Thomas and Anne, John, Winnifred, (plumber).
3. TULLY - Mary, Maggie, Patrick, Maggie.
4. WALSH - John and Bridget, (baker).
5. LOFTUS - Thomas, Michael, Patrick, Peter, (victualler).
6. GREHAN - Michael and Katie, Bridget.

BALLINA WARD

(PART OF URBAN)

1. McMAHON - John and Elizabeth, Isaac, John, Michael, Mary, Margaret, Kevin, John Jordan, Bridget Farrell, Mary McLoughrie, (N.S. teacher).
2. Convent of Mercy.
2. McCARRICK - Sr. Mary Attracta, Mary Teresa Lyons, Mary Alacoque Boyle, Mary De Sales Peyton, Mary Assisi Kelly, Mary Stanislaus O'Connell, Mary Agnes O'Donnell, Mary Berchman O'Connell, Mary de Pazzi Corden, Mary Ben. Stapleton, Mary Patrick Hennigan, Mary Joseph Garrick, Mary Bon. D'Arcy, Mary Michael McNamee, Mary Gertrude Noonan, Mary Ryan, Mary Baptist O'Brien, Mary Veronica O'Donnell, Mary Colum Neville, Mary Dympna Robinson, Mary Lyra Greely, Mary Zita Higgins, Mary Anthony O'Boyle, Mary Martha Holmes, Mary Philomena McGuire, Mary Malachy Ryan, Mary Anne McGoohan, Mary Gerard Menton, Mary Paul Brett, Mary Muredock Finnerty, (nuns - Ballina Convent).
2. DOOHAN - Alice, Mary Jordan, Kate Monaghan, Margaret Golden.
3. CORCORAN - Martin and Mary, Lizzie, William, (coachman).
4. FINNERTY - Michael and Kate, Michael, John, James.
5. DONNELLY - Patrick and Maria, Patrick.
6. WALSH - Peter.
7. GALLAGHER - Patrick, (carpenter).
8. HANLY - Margaret, Arabella, Margaret, Andrew.
9. GALLAHER - Johnnie, John O'Hora.
10. ROACHE - Edward, Anne, Bridget, Mary.
11. RUANE - Patrick and Mary, Anthony, John, Martin, (road contractor).
12. QUINN - Peter.
13. O'HORA - John and Delia, (workhouse master).
13. REAPE - William, (workhouse porter).
13. CONVY - Anne, (nurse).
13. Mental Asylum - 17 enlisted (initials only).
13. Workhouse - 104 enlisted (initials only).
13. CAHILL - Ellen, Mary, (hospital nurse).
13. MONNELLY - Margaret, James, Mary Walshe, (matron of workhouse).
13. NEVIN - Mary.

BOHERNASUP

1. KILGANNON - Anthony and Anne, James, William Kilboy.
2. O'DONNELL - John and Bridget, Michael, Frederick.
3. O'DOWD - James and Jane.
4. CARDEN - Bridget, Mary Hogan, William Bourke.
5. CASEY - James and Bridget, James, William, Patrick, Elizabeth, Susan, John, Michael.
6. GILLIGAN - Francis and Margaret.
7. McNAMARA - Michael and Anne, Alice, Norah, Patrick, Elizabeth, (bacon curer).
8. McNAMARA - Darby and Catherine, (bacon curer).
9. McDONNELL - Mary, Nora.
10. REILLY - Patrick and Maria, Patrick, William, Thomas, (fish monger).
11. McNALLY - Peter and Anne, Mary, John, James, Anne, Charles Anderson, (shoemaker).
12. JUDGE - Michael and Ellen, Mary.
13. SWEENEY - Patrick, Jane, Patrick Ruane, Annie Ruane, (baker).
14. CONNOLLY - Maria.
15. LALLY - Anthony and Mary.
16. BARRETT - Patrick and Anne.
17. GINTY - Honora, Thomas, John.
18. MITCHELL - John and Mary, Edward, Annie, Martin, Patrick, Mary Mayberry.
19. COX - William, John, (fish dler.).
20. WALSH - Patrick and Anne, Patrick.
21. COX - Catherine, Patrick, Mary Conlon, Anthony Walshe.
22. BOYTON - Mary, Thomas Walsh.
23. HELLY - Mary, William, Mary McNally, (laundress).
24. MURPHY - Bridget, Thomas, (fish dler.).
25. GALLAGHER - Bridget, Henry.
26. COX - John and Bridget, Mary, John, Margaret, Martin, Bridget, Patrick, Mary Costello, (fish monger).
27. McLOUGHLIN - Patrick and Bridget, Patrick, Margaret Tighe.
28. WADE - Thomas, Martin, Timothy, Margaret, William, Thomas, (coach builder).
29. DURKAN - Michael and Winifred, Lizzie, Thomas Mayberry, (fruit dler.).
30. McDERMOTT - Patrick and Catherine, (clerk in corn store).

BRIDGE STREET

1. LOFTUS - Patrick and Lizzie, Stephen Snea, Hugh Calry, (mcht.).
2. victuallers shop
3. MURPHY - James and Frances, Kathleen, Edward, James, Joseph, Thomas Ruddy, Michael Hughes, Peter Sweeney, James Langan, John Horan, Thomas Loftus, Thomas McDonnell, Joseph Murphy, Ellen Kearney, May Sweeney, Bridget McDonnell, Winifred Battle, Lizzie Carroll, (mcht).
4. Boot shop
5. BOYD - John and Eleanor, Thomas, Patrick, Alexander, Eleanor, Agnes-Christina, Adrienne-Nathalie, Eleanor Brusk, Michael Brusk, Catherine Mountany.
6. COOLICAN - Francis, Thomas Gilmartin, Martin Flynn, Jeremiah Cowley, Patrick Browne, Alick Kelly, Michael O'Neill, Thomas Brennan, James Donegan, Mary Quinn, Lizzie Maloney, Edward Coolican, (mcht.).
7. CORCORAN - Martin, John Murphy, William Walsh, James Quinn, Pat Kilcullen, Bridget McGuigan, Katie Connolly, Helena Clarke, Nellie McDonnell, (draper's asst.).
8. HEFFERNAN - William and Annie, Jannie, Ellen, Michael, (victualler).
9. CHAMBERS - Patrick and Mary, Ellen, Mary Gallagher, (mcht.).
10. O'HORA - Patrick, Edward, Patrick Devany, Patrick Murray, John Rushe, (grocer & spirit mcht.)
11. DODD - Andrew and Margaret, Vincent, Ellen, William Hughes, Bryan Timlin, Hana Gaughran, Michael O'Hara, (tea & wine mcht.).
12. ENGLISH - Patrick and Celia, Bridget, Celia, Mary, Edward, James, Cathleen Durcan, Patrick Durcan, Margaret Farrell, (mcht.).
13. BROWNE - John and Bridget, James, Jude, Lilley Chambers, Mary Evan.
14. shop
15. MELVIN - Martin and Nannie, Pat, Mary, Jane, (grocer).
16. HEFFERNAN - Patrick and Bridget, (publican).
17. WALSH - Francis and Kate, Patrick, William, Mary, Francis, Florrie, Jmaes, Maggie Murphy, (harness maker).

CENSUS RETURNS 1901/11

THE RETURNS for the census of 1901 and 1911 were made available for public inspection in 1961. In most countries census returns are not released until they are 100 years old, but it was decided that the returns for 1901 and 1911 should be released early because the census for 1821 to 1891 no longer survived.

18. McDONNELL - Mary, Martin, Honoria Maughan, (shopkeeper).
19. Pub
20. RUANE - William and Bridget, (shop).
21. SWEENEY - Martin, Mary, Annie, John, Bertie, Alice, Elizabeth, Sarah, Edward, Ellen Judge, (fish monger).
22. KELLY - William and Catherine, Amelia, Esther, Patrick, Mary, (grocer & publican).
23. BEIRNE - Patrick, Patrick Walsh, John Duffy, John Walsh, Eugene Duffy, Patrick Monnelly, Michael Reilly, (master baker).
24. MOLLOY - Dominick, Mary, Annie, Lizzie, Alice, John Nolan, Mary Rafter, Stephen Timlin, (shop).
25. WALSH - Anthony, Agnes, Belinda Harrison, (shop).
26. BOLAND - John and Ellen, Eileen, Michael Jordan, Mary Nash, (mcht.).
27. MacAULEY - Bridget, Michael, Agnes O'Flynn, (publican & grocer).
28. CAFFERTY - Patrick and Rosalie, Eilly, Maureen, Patrick McGuire, Thomas Rafter, Bernard Devanny, Peter Hanly, Martin McAndrew, Francis Callagher, Mary McDonnell, Mary Bourke, Bessy McNulty, Janey Duff, (draper).
29. MALONE - Patrick and Mary, Lucas, Mary, Hugh, Eleanor, Annie O'Connor, Kate Clarke, Michael Sweeney, Catherine Burke.
30. MURPHY - John and Delia, Ellen M., (draper).
31. CORCORAN - Mary, James, (egg mcht.).
32. NEARY - Michael and Bridget, Agnes Deehan, (publican & grocer).
33. BEIRNE - Jane, Michael, Florence, William McKean, Jane McKean, Clare Timony, Patrick Gallagher, (spirit mcht.).

BROOK STREET

1. SHERIDAN - Mary.
2. CARROLL - Celia, Patrick, Kate, Martin, (prov. dler).
3. NICHOLSON - James and Catherine, John, James, Hannah, Mary, Thomas, Elizabeth, Joseph, Margaret Sweeney, (sailor).
4. NEALON - Michael and Margaret, Mary, Bridget, (shoemaker).
5. FLANNERY - John and Kate, Mary, Bridget, Sarah, Annie, John, Lizzie, Maggie, Michael, Mary Quinn, (tailor).
6. SWEENEY - John and Annie, Helena, Bertie, Mary, Margaret, John, Thomas, Anne, Alice, (tailor).
7. FUERY - James and Maryanne, Michael, Anthony, Mary, William, John, James, Thomas, Anne Walsh.
8. ORME - Thomas and Mary, Michael, Margaret, Annie, (shoemaker).
9. FIMONY - John, Michael, Christina, Julia, Mary.
10. CONLON - Patrick, Catherine, (shoemaker).
11. O'REILLY - Annie.
12. O'NEILL - Thomas and Jane, Michael, John, William, Mary, Thomas, Michael Monaghan.
13. KILKER - Anthony and Mary, Anthony, James, John, Albin, Adelina, Harriett, DONNELLY: Gertrude, Edward, Patrick.
14. FALLON - Mary, William, Michael, Albert, Aileen Wade.
15. DOHERTY - Mary, Mary, John, Martin, HOLMES: Anthony, Bridget, Mary, Michael, Barbara.
16. McLOUGHLIN - Michael and Bridget, Mary, Anne, Margaret.
17. FOX - Bridget, Mary, Bridget, Michael, Patrick, Margaret, Rose Boyton.
18. McLOUGHLIN - Anthony and Mary, Martin, Mary, Michael, Anthony, Annie, Bridget.
19. COX - Henry and Norah, Elizabeth, Kate, Mary, William, Patrick, Bridget, Patrick Kelly.
20. JOYCE - Bridget, Annie Mitchell.
21. JUDGE - Mary, Winifred.
22. CONVEY - Patrick, Mary Barrett.
23. REYNOLDS - James and Mary, Mary, James, Michael, Bridget, Pat, Annie, John, Bridget Jordan.
24. FALLON - Martin and Maria, Mary, John Fox.
25. MURRAY - Patrick and Mary, Jane, Martin, Christopher, Mary, Patrick.
26. McNALLY - Thomas and Margaret, Martin, Mary, Margaret, Michael.
27. JUDGE - Thomas and Mary.
28. JOYCE - John and Kate, Mary, Bridget, Kate, Michael, (fish monger).
29. BOURKE - Robert and Mary, Robert, John, Agnes, Michael, Annie, James.

1849 Ballina Presbyterian Church Subscription List

Contains a list of all the local Presbyterians who subscribed to the building of the Church in Ballina in 1849. Only names and amounts are listed. List available from the Presbyterian Historic Soc. of Ireland

BELLEEK
PART OF URBAN

1. WALLACE - Michael and Norah.
2. CONVY - James and Marcella, Arthur, Mary, Ethel, Joseph, (clerk).

BELLEEK

LYNCH-BLOSSE - Robert and Alice, Alice, Mary McNamara, Ellie O'Sullivan, Katie Dean, Michael Kelly, (ex army).
SAUNDERS-KNOX-GORE - Matilda, William, Maria, Georgina, Mabel, Thomas Quinn, Henry Taylor, John Butler, John Sweeney, Andrew Robinson, Eliza Pendrick, Maggie Doherty, Margaret Flynn, Hannah Potts, Kate Duggan.
SAVAGE - Robert and Frances, Frances, Charles, May, Victor.
CONROY - Denis and Bridget, Edward, John, Charles, Thomas, Patrick, Mary Egan.
OXLEY - Frederick and Elizabeth, Frances, Frederick, Walter, Lillian, (gamekeeper).
KILDUFF - Patrick and Bridget.

BALLYHOLAN

CLARKE - Thomas and Ellen, Bridget, Annie, Ellen, Patrick.
LOFTUS - Patt and Mary, John, May, Joe, Daniel, Agnes, Patrick, James, Teresa, William.
FERGUSON - Anthony and Bridget, Margaret, Bartly, Charlie, Bridget, Jack .
FERGUSON - Patrick and Bridget, Annie, John, Michael, Mary, Delia, Patrick.
JUDGE - Michael and Margaret, Patrick, John, Mary, Thomas Harkin, Jane Marley.
WALKER - Thomas and Margaret, Robert, John, Emma, Jessie, James, William, Ernest.
CLARKE - Patrick and Annie, Andrew, Dorinda, Bridget.
RAFTER - Martin and Anne, Michael, Richard, Martin, James, Mary, Margaret, Annie, Mary O'Hara.
RUDDY - Thomas and Mary, Andrew, Maggie, James.

BROUGHAN'S LANE

1. DEVERS - Terence and Mary, Thomas, Katie, Martin, Agnes, Julia, James, Patrick Browne, (shoemaker).
2. McGINTY - Winifred, John.
3. DEVERS - John and Mary, Agnes, Maggie Moran.

BURY STREET

1. MORAN - Maria, Bridget, Patrick, Annie.
2. KILLIGREW - William and Lizzie, Hannah, Samuel, (nailer).
3. JENNINGS - Richard and Florence, Gabreille, Julius Holliday, Gabriel Holliday, Kate Deevers, Sarah Moran, (flour millers agent).
4. Solicitor's office
5. EGAN - John and Winifred, John, Marie, Frederick, Mary Halpin, (mineral water manuf.).

BALLYNARAHA

CLARKE - James and Bessie, Michael, James, Kate, Bridget, John, Mary, Elizabeth, Annie, Margaret, (ex teacher).
TIMLIN - Anthony, Patrick, John, Tom, Bridget.
JUDGE - Pat and Catherine, Mary Kelly, Mary Kerrigan.
CLARKE - Thomas, John, Honoria, JUDGE: John and Mary, Honoria.
ROBINSON - Mary, FINNERTY: Thomas and Bessie, Kate, Mary, Belinda, Patrick, Michael, Norah, Bessie.
FINNERTY - Julia, Thomas, Susanna, Julia, Lizzie, Agnes.
TIMLIN - Domnick and Nora, Ellen, Bridget Brislin, Michael Cullen.

BEHYBAWN

NOLAN - Thomas and Anne, Edward, Mary, Ellen, Nicholas, Annie, Richard, (rail platelayer).
McHALE - Michael and Mary, Annie, Bridget, Kathleen, Michael, Patrick, Mary Henry.
COOLICAN - Ellen, Anthony Healy.
CONNELL - Mathew and Anne, Francis, Maggie, Bridget, Mathew, Anne, Teresa, (rail man).
McHALE - Patrick and Bridget, Patrick, Michael, Martin.

EGAN - Ellen, Martin, James.
FINNERTY - Patrick, William.

BUNREE

GALLAGHER - Charles, Annie, Mary, Maria.
CORCORAN - Pat and Mary, James, Pat, Anthony, (carpenter).
Flour mill
KELLY - Barbara.
KENNEDY - Mary.
SHEA - Margaret, John, Michael, Mary.
GILLESPIE - Patrick and Annie, Annie, Mary, (wood turner).
CALLAGHAN - Bridget, Gerald.
CUFFE - Thomas and Maria, Ellen, Mary, Patrick, Michael.
QUINN - Peter and Ellen, John, William, James, Peter.
HEALEY - Anthony and Mary.
BOLAND - James and Catherine, James, Kate, Michael, Margaret.
LACKEY - Bridget.
FLYNN - Martin and Mary, James, Bridget, Anny.
COLLINS - Mary, Kate.
MURRAY - Anthony and Catherine, Sarah.
ARMSTRONG - Catherine, Maryanne.
GORMAN - Bridget, Anne, Maria.
DOHERTY - Mary, Ned, John, Michael, Lizzie, Martin Rutledge.
FLEMING - Martin and Mary.
DWYER - Catherine, Robert, Hugh, Frederick.
FERGUSON - Francis and Ellen, Mary, Michael, Martin.
LAVELLE - John and Bridget, Thomas, William, Mary, Bridget, James, Anthony, Norah, Edward, Martin, (fisherman).
JUDGE - Patrick and Bridget, Patrick.
ROLSTON - Edward.
MORAN - John.
CALLAGHAN - Owen, Bridget.
BRISLANE - Ellen, Annie, Maggie Walshe.
JORDAN - John and Bridget, Patrick, William, Ambrose, Martin, Sarah, Mary, Thomas, (miller).

CLARE STREET
ABBEYHALFQUARTER

1. REID - Thomas and Florence, Beryl, Robert, Phyllis, Hester Malony, (gas engineer).
2. NAUGHTON - James, Mary Condron, Bridget Mulderrig, Kate Langan, Julia Murphy, Thomas Clarke, John Hoban, (R.C clergyman).
2. St. Muredach's College - teachers - Rev. James Tempany, Francis Crowne, John Moran, Samuel Fahy, (teachers).
2. Students - James Mullany, Richard Barrett, Lewis Cleary, Louis McNama, John Loftus, John Hegarty, Patrick Gallagher, Thomas Goff, Thomas Heneghan, James Heffernan, David Donoghue, Thomas Moran, John Barrett, John Conmy, John Tully, Michael Munnelly, Thomas Kerins, Peter Hopkins, Patrick Groarke, Robert Kilgannon, Charles O'Reilly, Peter Colleran, Anthony Farrell, James Gordon, Patrick Nangle, Thomas Keane, Frederick Quinlan, Edwin Kelly, Patrick Lawrence, Michael Giblin, Henry O'Gara, Louis O'Boyle, Harry McCaulay, Eugene McCann, Patrick McAndrew, Michael McGuire, (students).
3. WALSH - Patrick and Elizabeth, John, Eilleen, Michael, Kate Parks, (publican).
4. DEVERS - Ernest and Winifred, DUNCAN: Lizzie, Winifred, (printer).
5/6. vacant
7. KILGALLON - Thaddeus, Alice, Alice Albon.
8. BARRETT - Margaret, Ellen, Maria Kiggins.
9. MURRAY - Philip and Anny, Mary, Alice, Joe, Phil, John, (waiter).
10. KENNEDY - James and Anne, Bridget, Martin, Maria, Patrick, John, Vincent, Margaret, (clerk).
11. MORAN - Edward and Bridget, Kathleen, Mary, Gertrude, Walter, Attracta, Winifred, Edward, Michael, Carmen, (blacksmith).
12. QUEENAN - Andrew and Margaret, Anny Dodd, Mary McGowan.
13. McCARRICK - Janie, Annie, Winnie Battle, Katie Molloy, (dressmaker).
14. McDONNELL - Mark and Bridget, Mary, Eugene, Kathleen, Celia, Bridget, Patrick, Maggie, James, (slater&plasterer
15. CULLEN - Thomas and Mary, Mary, James, Kate, Maria, Maggie, Bridget, (blacksmith).
16. vacant
17. REGAN - Jane, Mary, Eddie, John, Kathleen, Violet, Jennie.
18. CONWAY - Matthew and Anne, Teresa, Martin McLoughlin, (publican).
19. CONWAY - John and Mary, Matthew, Annie Clarke.
20. JUDGE - Bridget, Michael, Nora, Bridget Golden, Delia Barrins, (publican
21. DUFFY - Martin and Lena, (carpenter)
22. ATKINSON - Esther, Mary Morrison.
23. CONLAN - James.

CHAPEL LANE
ABBEYHALFQUARTER

1. KELLY - Charles and Bridget, Michael, Christopher, Edward, Thomas.
2. MURRAY - Joseph and Mary, Patrick, Mary, Bridget.
3. HOLMES - John and Katherine, Katherine, (shoemaker).
4. CORCORAN - Winifred.
5. DIGNAN - James and Sarah, John, Mary, Patrick.
6. KEEFFE - John and Bridget, John, Patrick.
7. MURRAY - James, Richard.
8. BARRETT - Anthony, William, Robert.
9. LOFTUS - Mary, Martin, John.
10. MELIA - Patrick and Margaret.
11. FITZGERALD - Catherine, Bridget, DEVANEY: John and Mary, Christopher.

CHURCH ROAD
SHANAGHY or ARDNAREE

LYONS - Thomas and Bridget, Ita, Martin, John, (comm. traveller).
LEIGHTON - Richard and Maryanne, Annie, John, Lillian, Lucinda, Esther, Maryanne, Richard, Alice Naughton, (tailor).
KERINS - John and Bridget, Mary, Patrick, (RIC).
FOLEY - Michael and Maria, James, Mary, Willy, Bridget, Charles, Eliza, Kate, Celia, Thady, Michael Tiernan, (mason).
HALL - Frederick and Elizabeth, Frederick, Beryl, Eva Carter, Ellen Morrison, (bank cashier).
BOURKE - Henry and Elinor, Paget, Ivy, Henry, Delia McDonnell, Maria Reape, Bina Kearney, (solicitor).

CHURCH ROAD
ABBEYHALFQUARTER

1. KEVANY - Thomas and Ellen, Patrick, Eveleen, Mary, Thomas, Mary, (cathedral clerk).
2. HARTE - Maryanne, Mary, Michael, Teresa, Gertrude, John, Katie Cooke.
3. McDONAGH - Bartholomew and Bridget, Mary, Thomas, Bridget, Annie, (RIC).
4. MULROONEY - Annie, Delia, Teresa, Robert, Louie Armstrong.
4. DURCAN - Margaret, Margaret.
5. GUILFOYLE - Margaret, May, Willie, Martin.
6. RYAN - John J. and Winifred, John, Francis, (army sergt.).
7. RUDDY - Bridget, Margaret, John, Catherine, (publican).
8. KENNEDY - Thomas and Catherine, Patrick, Daniel, Michael, DONEGAN; Annie, John, Sarah Mulderrig, Bridget McNulty, (publican).
9. MOLONEY - Richard and Catherine, Mary, Richard, Annie, (butcher).

CARROWCUSHLAUN

STUART - James and Annie, Patrick, Annie, Patrick Farrell.
McNALLY - Roger, Patrick, Roger, Bridget, Annie, Michael, John, Mary Hennigan, (ex RIC).
HENNIGAN - Mary, Patrick, Stephen Quinn.
CONNELL - Bridget, B.Teresa.
RALPH - Mary, Michael.
DEMPSEY - Mary.
TIMLIN - Patrick and Catherine, Michael, Mary.
MUNNELLY - John and Jane, Martin, Patrick, Jane, Michael.
COLEMAN - Edward and Ellen, Mary.
HOLLERAN - James and Bridget.
MULDERRIG - Patrick and Sydney.

1832 Protestants of Foxford & Surrounding Area

This census lists the local Protestant population of Attymass, Ballynahaglish, Toomore, Killasser. The list is arranged by parish and lists the head of the family, children and other relationships. 70% of 210 names are from Foxford. Nat. Library: Ms:8295

QUINN - John and Mary, Patrick.
HOLLERAN - Patrick and Kate, Marykate, Mary.
TIMLIN - Thomas and Mary, Patrick, William, Ellen, Anthony.
QUINN - Mary, Celia, Anthony, Stephen, Mary, Kate.
MURRAY - Mary, James, Mary McNally, Bridget Gilmartin, Mary McNally.
MULLEN - John and Barbara, John, Anthony, Agnes, Patrick Forbes.

CARROWCUSHLAUN WEST

HOWLEY - James and Margaret, James, Mary, LOFTUS: Mary, John, (miller).
HALLORAN - James and Mary, Bridget, Michael, James, John.
MURRAY - Martin and Catherine, Patrick, Michael, Mary, Bridget.
TIMLIN - Patrick.
ARMSTRONG - John and Jane, William, John, Thomas, Frederick, Eleanor, Kathleen, (watchmaker).
Corn mill

CLOONGLASNEY

GILLESPIE - Margaret, Patrick.
CLARKE - Michael, James, Maria.
CLARKE - Thomas and Mary, Anthony, Martin, Annie, Maria.
BIRRANE - Winifred, James, Michael.
SWEENEY - Patrick and Mary, John, Kate, Maggie.
BIRRANE - Bridget, Thomas, William, James, Joseph.
CAFFERKEY - Patrick and Nora, Mary, James, Celia, Bridget, John, Michael, (teacher).
MUNNELY - Michael, Mary, Thomas, Bridget, Patt, Anne, Helena.
CLARKE - John and Mary, Mary B., Patrick, Ellen, Bridget, Maria Herbert.

CRANNAGH

CAWLEY - James and Teresa.
HANAHOE - Richard and Honor, Bridget, GILLESPIE: Anthony and Mary.
MUNNELLY - Thomas and Mary, Bridget, Patrick, Michael, John, Agnes.

CLOONTURK

CLARKE - Patrick.
O'HORO - Patrick and Bridget, John.
MELVIN - John and Bridget, Michael, Annie, Maggie, Ellen.
MELVIN - Anne, Anne, John.
MELVIN - Anthony and Ellen, Annie, Patrick, James, Peter, Bridget, Nelly, Martin.
HANAHOE - Edward and Mary, Nora, Mary, Maggie, Patrick, Ellen.
RALPH - Bartley and Maria, John, Patrick, Bridget.
O'HORO - James and Mary, Bridget, Annie, Michael, Bridget.
MELVIN - John, Patrick, Anthony.
LEONARD - Mary, Patrick.

CREGGAUN

NAUGHTON - Michael, Martin and Bridget, Mary, Bridget.
HANAHOE - James, William McHale.
JORDAN - Ellen, Peter, Annie Melvin.
McHALE - Margaret, Ellen, James, Sarah.
HOWLEY - Martin and Kate, Mary, Michael, Martin.
MELVIN - Barbara, Katie, Pat, Annie, Helena, Agnes.
GERAGHTY - Thomas and Kate, May, John, Maggie, Cathleen, Bridget, Helena, Honor.

CLOONSLAUN

DOHERTY - John and Bridget, Patrick, John, Anthony, Mary, Bridget, James, Thomas, Anne, Stephen, Agnes, Michael
CONVEY - John.
CONVEY - Maria, Patrick, Ellen Gaughan, Frank Forbes.
MURRAY - Mary, Michael.
McGOWAN - Michael and Mary, Bridget, Patrick, Martin, Annie.
TIMLIN - Dominick and Catherine (Judge), Mary, James, Bridget, William, Dominick, Katherine, Ellen, Simon.
MURPHY - Catherine, John, James, Mary Mahon.
BURKE - Patrick, Bridget, Michael.
MURRAY - John, Anne.
MUNNELLY - Patrick and Mary, Annie, Sarah, Margaret, James, Bridget, Martin, Ellen.
HIGGINS - Michael and Anne, Anne, Bridget, Annie, Kate Mulderrig.
MELODY - Michael, Maria, Catherine.
MURRAY - Winifred, Michael, Annie, Winifred.
MURRAY - Patrick, Edward, Catherine, William.
McGOWAN - Patrick and Mary, Ellen, Michael.
O'BRIEN - Mary, PADDAN: Edward, Patrick.
PADDAN - Kate.
O'HARA - William and Julia, Edward, Catherine Walsh.
DOWD - James and Winifred, Edward, Patrick, Annie, Mary, Margaret, James, John .
PHILBIN - Richard and Bridget, Patrick, Bridget Doherty.
TIMLIN - James and Catherine, John, Michael, Stephen, James, Mary, Bridget.
HOLLORAN - Margaret, Maria, Bridget, Margaret.
WALSH - Ellen, John, Thomas, Mary, Annie.
MULDERRIG - Michael and Ellen, Michael, Patrick, Katie, Bridget.
LUNDY - James and Margaret.
MULDERRIG - Catherine, Sarah, Pat.
FERGUSON - John and Mary,, John, Mary, Patrick, Edward, Michael, Delia.
McGOWAN - Mary, William, Anthony, Agnes.

CULLEENS

KEAVENEY - John and Bridget, Bridget, John.
CONVY - James and Mary, Pat, John, Anne, Nora, Ellen.
ROGAN - Thomas, Mary.
WALSH - Michael and Kate, James, Ellen.
LANGAN - John and Catherine, Martin, Anthony, Thomas.
ROGAN - John and Mary, Patrick, Peter, Mary.
BRENNAN - Patrick, Bridget, Julia Rogan.
LOFTUS - Michael and Mary, Anthony.
HIGGINS - Patt and Margaret, John, Margaret, Ellina, John McHale.
CARR - John and Mary, Bridget, Mary, Catherine, John, Winnie, Maggie, Pat, Michael, William.
PATTERSON - Matthew, James, George Jackson.
GOULDING - Michael and Winifred, Bridget, Patrick, Annie, James, John Eakins, (rail ganger).
HEALY - Peter and Mary, John, Mary, Anne, Katie, Sarah, Agnes.
McLOUGHLIN - John and Catherine, Maggie.
WALSH - Patrick, Maria, Agnes Corcoran.
WALSHE - Michael and Mary, Maryellen, Thomas, James, Michael, Peter.
MOLLOY - Michael and Maggie, Alice, (teacher).
WALSH - Michael and Mary, Michael, Mary, James.
WALSH - Thomas and Mary, Thomas, John, Mary, Edward, Michael, Eliza, Martin, Anthony, Sarah, Kathleen.
ROGAN - Patrick and Anne, Charles, John.

CROCKETSTOWN

1. BAKER - William.
2. TEMPLE - William and Mary, Mary, Ellen, Bridget, Kate, Anne.
3. HENEGAN - Henry and Ellen, Mary, Elizabeth, Ellen, (quay porter).
4. McNULTY - Bridget, Michael, Mary Melvin.
5. BAKER - Mary, Patrick, Bridget.
6. HYNES - Edward and Jane.
7. LACKEN - Mark and Bridget, Bridget, Patrick, Peterp, Mary.
8. MELVIN - Martin and Mary, Annie, Mary, Michael.
9. vacant
10. HUMBER - James and Annie, Sarah, Michael, Patrick, Martin, Annie, Thomas, William.
11. TIGHE - Michael, James, Pat, Joseph, (quay porter).
12. KILCULLEN - Owen and Mary, Mary, Kate, Winifred Tighe, (sailor).
13. TEMPLE - Joseph, Winifred.

THE REGISTRY OF DEEDS - www.landregistry.ie

THE Registry of Deeds is located in Henrietta Street, Dublin 1, (01)8732233, and Contains information for the Family researcher in its records and deeds, business transactions, leases, marriage settlements, rent charges and wills. It has a search room and is open to the public Monday to Friday (10 am to 4 pm). There are two indexes, one is the name of the Townland in which the property is located and the other is the grantor's name (name of the party disposing of the asset).

14. MOLLOY - Michael and Mary,Michael
15. vacant
16. MELVIN - James and Anne, Patrick, Bridget, Ellen, Sarah, Norah, Maggy, John.
17. MELVIN - Patrick and Bridget.
18. MELVIN - Edward and Teresa, Robert, (clerk).
19. HUMBER - Anne.
20. McNULTY - Patrick and Mary, Martin, Bridget, Owen.
21. WALSH - James and Ellen, John, Michael.
22. LOUGHNEY - Peter and Mary, John, Peter, Lizzie, William, Joseph, Kathleen, Katherine Battle, (quay porter).
23. McCLEARY - Mary, Eliza.
24. HENEGAN - Michael and Mary, Ml. James.
25. HENEGAN - Maria, William, Edward.
26. LACKEN - Mary, Bridget.
27. HATELY - George H. and Priscilla, Margaret, Violet, (harbour master).
28. HATELY - William and Elizabeth, Mary Hennigan, (ex sea capt.).
29. RUDDY - Pat and Margaret, Maggie, Anny, Pat, Mary, Christina, Tom, Hugh.
30. KILCULLEN - Mary, Mary, Margaret, Christina, Annie, James.
31. BROWN - Adam and Emily, Jane Quinn, (shipping agent).
32. WALSH - Patrick and Elizabeth, Michael, Peter, Annie, Bridget.
33. SHAW - Bridget, Annie, Robert, Adelaide.
34. ROONEY - Patrick and Sarah, Lena, Mary, Patrick, (ex RIC).

CLOONTYKILLEW

GILLESPIE - James and Sabina, Patrick and Bridget.
DOHERTY - James and Barbara, Patrick, James.
MUNNELLY - Thomas and Maggie, John, Mary.
EGAN - Michael and Maria, Mary, Margaret, RUANE: Agnes, Anthony.
JENNINGS - Mary, Maria, William, Kate.
MOORE - Patrick, Michael.

COMMONS

PEARSON - Robert and Kate, Ada, Jeanie, Blanche, Violet, William, James, Annie, (plumber).
CLARKE - Thomas and Bridget, George, Mary, Annie, Bridget, Michael, Patrick.

COOLCRAN

LEVINGSTON - Thomas and Marie, Bridget Gallagher, (RIC).
SHEARD - Albert and Gertrude, Mildred, Norah, (timber mcht.).
TOOHILL - William and Bridget, James, Thomas, Michael.

CROFTON PARK

DURKEN - John and Catherine, Patrick, Mary, Bridget, Anne, Martin and Bridget.
CRONIN - Philip and Margaret, John, Richard, KELLY: Patrick and Margaret.
EGAN - Michael, Agnes.
HOBAN - James and Bridget, Michael, Margaret, Norah, Winifred, Patrick.
McANDREW - Patrick and Alice, Annie, Alice, John, Peter, William.
EGAN - Patrick and Catherine, John, Patrick, Martin, Bridget, Mary Gallagher.
EGAN - Anthony, Patt, Bridget, Ellen.
REGAN - John and Honoria, James, Kate O'Horo.
CONVEY - Honoria, Michael, Patrick, Norah.
HUNTER - Robert and Margaret, Robert, Alice, Robert, John, Margaret, Kathleen, Stephen Kennedy.

CALLAGHAN'S LANE

1. McLOUGHLIN - John and Bridget, Joseph, Edward, Margaret King.
2. FOX - Michael and Anne, Bridget, (bill poster).

CASTLE ROAD

1. WALSH - Edward and Isabel, Mabel, Percy, Edna, Vera, Alison McPherson, (book seller).
2. HAMILTON - Maria, Ellen, Margaret Lynott, Bridget Lynott.
3. BEIRNE - Thomas, Bridget Doherty, (R.C. clergyman).
4. DEVERS - Terence and Mary, May, (printer).
5. CARNEY - Patrick and Mary, George, (bank porter).
6. FARMER - John, Patrick, Maggie, Katie, John Coppin, Harry Coppin, (law clerk).
7. BRODERICK - Johanna, James, Michael, William Dowd, William Gorman, (lodging hse).
8. EGAN - Daniel and Bridget, John, Mary, Daniel, Kathleen, Joseph, Catherine McEvoy.
9. RUANE - Anthony and Mary, James, Joseph, Thomas, Patrick, (painter).
10. HARRISON - Michael and Ellen, Michael, William, James, Robert, Thomas, Lizzie, Ellen, Lucy, (RIC sergt.).
11. HENDRY - Patrick and Elizabeth, Mary, Sarah, John, Celia, Patrick, Bridget, William, Annie, (bank porter).
12. McCARRICK - Anthony and Kate, Eva, William, (porter in Bank of Ireland).
13. GARDENER - John and Ellen, Kate O'Neill.
14. SATCHWELL - John and Annie.
15. CROSBY - Edward and Jane, Mary, Bridget, Margaret, Edwinn, Luke, Elizabeth, Josephine, Honoria, James, (ex RIC).
16. STANSFIELD - Alfred and Ethel, Muriel, Henrietta, Eric, Eva Casserly, (photographer).
17. ANDERSON - John, Frederick, Bessie.
18. BANKS - Mary, (sweet shop).

CHARLES STREET

1. READ - Arthur and Mary, (RIC).
2./3. Presbyterian Church & School hse.
4. The Manse
4. WILSON - Francis and Jessie, Margaret, Robert, Marion Henry.
5. CARLOS - Charles and Charlotte, Margaret, Mary, Charles, Luke, William.
5. KING - Rosanna, Michael.
5. CARROLL - Joseph and Mary, Annie, James, Mary, (RIC).
5. RIC BARRACKS - initials only - C.C., A.C., P.McG., A.M., J.C., D.K., J.R., T.R..

CONWAY'S LANE

1. CALLAGHAN - Thomas and Mary, Patrick, Thomas, Mary, John, Lucie.
2. GALLAGHER - John, John O'Hora.
3. CASSIDY - John and Maggie, Mary, John, Patrick, Elena.
4. HANLON - John, Joseph, Michael, Paul, Mary Shaw, Christina Shaw, (baker).

DILLON TERRACE

1. RUDDY - John and Anne, Nora, Michael, (mngr. of grocer).
2. NAUGHTON - Mary, Kate.
3. AHEARN - Louisa, Brigid.
4. DUNCAN - James and Frances, William, Agnes Gray, William Roche, (printer).
5. HARPER - John and Marion, Bruce, Cecelia Hopkins, (bank cashier).
6. SWEETMAN - Nicholas and Margaret, Margaret, John Matthews, Edgar Phair, Ellen McHale, (ex RIC).
7. DILLON - John and Elizabeth, Andrew, Mary Munnelly, (land agent).
8. Inland Rev. bond store.

DIXON'S LANE

1. MARLEY - James and Mary, Patrick, Bridget, James, Joseph.
2. MULDERRIG - Mary, Maggie Magowan, Patrick Magowan.

DURKAN'S LANE

1. DOHERTY - Michael and Kate, Eugene, Michael, (blacksmith).
2. DEVERS - John and Teresa, Thomas, John, Adeline, Irene, Alexander, George, Joseph, Muriel, Herbert, Monica,

Madonna, Edward, (prof. sportsman).
3. DURKAN - Alice, John Walsh, Patrick Monnelly, William Kilker, Richard Forrestal, John Walsh, John Gallagher, (lodging hse.).
4. CORCORAN - William and Anne, Joseph, John, Mary, Anne, James, (saddler).
5. CORCORAN - Hannah, Bessie Ward.
6. McMANUS - Michael and Sarah, Daisy, (tailor).
7. NEALON - John and Margaret, May, Bridget, Margaret, John, Patrick.
8. KELLY - William, Thomas, (baker).
9. BARRETT - Patrick and Mary, Michael, Mary, Patrick, James, Margaret.
10. O'REILLY - Peter, (wool weaver).

FRANCIS STREET

1. CROWNE - Martin and Marguerite, Martin, Joseph, Margarite Killawee, (physics professor).
2. RUTLEDGE - John and Anne, Kate Boland, (comm. traveller).
3. vacant
4. MacNULTY - Patrick and Mary, William Loftus, Annie Padden, (clerk of union).
5. ATKINSON - Harriette, Edward, Annie Tuffy, Mary Leonard.
6. McCAULEY - Roger and Louisa, Louisa, Mary, Roderick, George, Mary Kearney, Kate Reape, Margaret Connor, (doctor).
7. ORCHARD - William and Mary, Priscilla Baine, Louisa Baine, Bridget McGrath, (surveyor).
8. COOLICAN - Anne, Kate Allen.
9. CAIRNS - William, Kate Milmine, Ellen Rafter, (comm. agent).
10. Ballina Bridewell - nil
11. Court hse.
11. CAMPBELL - John and Emma, CHAPMAN: Louis and Amy, Louis, (bridewell keeper).
12. Francis st. National School.
13. Flour, seeds, manure stores.

FRANKLIN'S LANE

1. WALSH - Patrick and Bridget, Nannie, John, (baker).
2. FOLEY - James and Anne, James.
3. WALKIN - Elizabeth, Bridget.
4. DUFFY - John, Martin, Maggie, (baker).

FARRANDELION

FLYNN - Matthew and Mary, Thomas, Michael, Matthew, Margaret Howley.
MURRAY - Anthony and Anne, Michael, Mary, Thomas, Anthony Nolan.
COSGRAVE - Michael and Kate, Patrick, Mary, Thomas, Mary Jordan, Pat McHale.
HANAHOE - Michael, Bartley, Maria.
COSGRAVE - John and Bridget, Patrick, Mary, John, Kate, Bridget, Ellen Glackin.
O'HORO - Pat, John, Annie, Thomas, Pat.
BOLAND - William and Margaret, Thomas, Michael, Willie, Kate, Derinda, Margaret, Annie, Ellen, Pat.
BOLAND - Thomas and Kate, Bridget.
DURHAM - Michael and Mary, Pat, John, Maryellen.

Mayo Voters Register of 1856
List of locals that were allowed to vote in the election of Members of Parliament in 1856. The list gives name, address, qualification to vote, and location of property. Can be located in the Nat. Archives. The lists are organised by barony. Barony of Gallen: M2784, Barony of Tyrawley: M2782.

FARRANOO

MULDERRIG - Patrick and Mary, Patrick, Maria, Mary, John, Patrick.
O'HORO - Peter, Bridget, Patrick, Mary, Michael, John, Maggie, John.
FRASER - Edward, Joseph Roberts, Owen McDonnell, Anne Boland, (estate mngr.).

GLEBE

NASH - John and Alice, Matilda Rowe, Rose Alexander, William Patterson, (clerk in holy orders).

GORTEEN

BARRETT - John and Kate, Michael, May, Agnes, John, Patrick, Anthony, Annie, Bridget.
CLARKE - James and Mary, Luke, Annie, Maggie, Katie, Michael, James, Mathew, Alice, (caretaker).
MELVIN - Michael and Maggie, Martie, Mary, Joe, Thomas.

GALLAGHER'S LANE

1. RONAN - Denis, (shoemaker).
2. QUIGLEY - John and Bessie, Mary, Martin, Willie, (fisherman).
3. McNAMARA - James and Anne, John, Ellen, (bacon curer).

GARDEN STREET

1. MASH - Patrick and Mary, Thomas, George, (blacksmith).
2. KELLY - John, (tailor).
3. O'HORA - Kate, Willie, Ida, Bertha, Florrie, (grocer).
4. McHALE - Anne, Mary Higgins, (maternity nurse).
5. DEVERS - Anne, NEALON: Michael and Rose, Edward, Michael, Margaret.
6. HOEY - Peter and Teresa, Francis, Peter, Kate, (waiter).
7. KELLY - John and Mary, Mary, John, Kathleen, Albert, (RIC sergt.).
8. LENEHAN - Isaac, Christopher Carroll, (auctioneer & cycle agent).
9. GINTY - Mary, Margaret Ginty, Mary Lacken, Bridget Timlin, Mary Crean, Mary McAndrew, (boarding hse.).
9. MAHADY - Annie, Michael, Catherine O'Boyle.
9. LOVE - Maurice and Annie.
9. O'NEILL - Patrick, Mary, (ex RIC).
10. McMAHON - Felix and Nellie, Mary, Charles, Aileen, Kathleen, Sarah, (contractor).
11. HAMILTON - Sarah, Alexander, (lodging hse.).
11. WARD - Harry and Letitia, (forester).
11. CREIGHTON - Robert and Emma, (civil engineer).
12. HANLON - James and Mary, James, John, Mary, Kate, (bootmaker).
13. ATHY - Martin and Ellen, William Gallagher, Patrick Reilly, Mary Tymony, (musician).
14. MONAGHAN - Michael and Bridget, Thomas McDonnell.
15. vacant
16. CONVEY - Catherine, Thomas, Mary Sweeney.
17. CAREY - Sarah.
18. LOFTUS - Jane, Katie, (grocer).
19. ROONEY - Michael and Winifred, Mary, Patrick, Rosaline, Paul, Kathleen, Winifred, (blacksmith).
20. NEALON - Thomas and Margaret, GREAVY: Jane, John, Mary, Margaret, (decorator).
21. DUNNE - Mary, Henry.
22. GALLAGHER - Louis and Mary, Lizzie, Mary, (tailor).
23. RYAN - Richard and Maria, Patrick, James, Richard, (carpenter).
24. WOODS - Elizabeth, Annie Kearney, ACTION: Robert and Mary, Kate Kelly.
25. O'CONNOR - Patrick and Teresa, Mary, Andrew, Winifred, (RIC sergt.).
26. SPEER - James and Minnie, Jennie, William, Bridget Munnelly, William Cottingham, (shop asst.).

GORE STREET

1. Dispensary
1. McLOUGHLIN - Margaret, Mary Timlin, William Boshell, Thomas Boshell, (nurse).
2. LAVIN - Mary, Michael, William, Owen, Kate, James.
3. HEGARTY - William and Kate, William, Thomas.
4. MEARNS - Margaret, Michael.
5. PADDEN - James and Kate, John, Patrick, James, Martin, Henry, Mary, (tailor).
6. CONNOR John and Mary, John, Nora, Anthony, Patrick, Maggie, Martin.
7. KENNY - Margaret, Mary.
8. SWEENEY - John and Catherine, Mary, Owen, Bridget, (mason).
9. CLARKE - Pat and Kate, John, James, Patrick.
10. JENNINGS - Ellen.
11. CARR - Luke and Nora, Mary, Bridget, Michael, Anne Wynne.
12. KILGALLON - John and Bridget, Francis, Joseph, Mary, Michael, Rose, Annie.
13. McKENNA - Thomas and Bridget, Molly, Annie, Patrick.
14. CANAVAN - Martin and Maria, Margaret, Martin, Mary, Michael, Anne.
15. BOSHELL - Bridget, Ernest, Austin, Frank, Josephine.
16. MASSEY - Robert and Winifred, Rick, Margaret, (blacksmith).
17. MOYLES - Bryan, (workhouse van driver).
18. HOBAN - Michael and Ellen, Patrick, Annie, Delia, Michael, Pettie.
19. FLYNN - Edward and Annie, Albert, Annie, Charlotte, Ethel, Jackson, Edward.
20. BEACON - Andrew, Annie, (clerk to land agent).

The busy Knox St. in 1901, which was called after the main Landlord family in the town. The trees in the middle of the photo are from the Beleek castle grounds where the Knox family reside. The street was renamed Pearse St. after Padraig Pearse.

21. ADAMSON - Amy, Robert, Edith, Ayesha, James, Amy, Una, Annie Monnelly, Kate Monnelly.
22. CAIRNS - Joseph and Clara, John, Alfred, Edward, Clara, Margaret McPherson, (civil engineer).
23. HOEY - Bernard, Margaret.
24. Rent office
25/26. Manure and provision store.

GORTATOGHER

CLARKE - Margaret, James and Bridget, Mary, Michael, William.
MULDERIG - Patt and Minnie, Michael, Bridget, Mary, William.
BARRETT - John, Thomas and Anne, Ellen, John, Bridget, Dan.
CADEN - Patrick, John, Patrick.
MERRICK - Patrick and Mary, Ellen, John, Bridget, Winefred, Bridget Cosgrave.
HANNICK - Michael and Ellen, Mary, Thomas, John, Julia, Michael.
MOYLES - Anne, Mary, James.

HILL STREET

1. BOLAND - Bridget, Maria James, (shopkeeper).
2. CALLARY - James and Ellen, James, Phelim, Thomas, Ellen, Annie, Patrick, Gerald, Margaret Jennings, (shopkeeper)
3. STAUNTON - Michael and Maria, Annie, Thomas, Elenia, Michael, Christina, Robert, Mary Doherty, William Ginlar, John Ginlar, Michael Frawley, John Morrison, Thomas Morrison, Bridget Mulligan, Mary Duggan, (publican).
4. CULKIN - Bridget, Mary, Michael, William, (grocer).
5. BRODERICK - Henry and Bridget, Ellie, John, Henry, Michael, (baker).
6. COYNE - John and Kate, Annie.
7. McDONAGH - John and Jennie, May, Patrick, (carpenter).
8. MORAN - Maria, Mary Quinlan, (publican).
10. WARNOCK - Mary, Mary, Kate, Nora Caffrey, (shopkeeper).
11. QUINN - John and Mary, Patrick, John, Margaret, William, Agnes, Edward, Bridget, John Kearney, (cooper).
13. JORDAN - Julia, Sarah, Annie.
14. CALLARY - Michael and Eliza, Elizabeth, (tailor).

HARTE'S LANE

1. MAUGHAN - Catherine, Mary McGuinness, William Brennan.
2. TULLY - James.
3. FLYNN - William and Mary, Katie, Bernard, Frederick, Peter, Francis, (shoemaker).
4. SYMES - William and Mary, (bill poster).
5. ORMSBY - Thomas and Mary, William, Thomas, John, Lizzie, (shoemaker).
6. MEENAGHAN - Thomas and Rose, Anthony.
7. MOYLES - James and Mary, Willie, James, Joseph, Thomas, Martin, John, Maggie, Mary.

HEALY'S LANE

1. BAKER - Bridget.
2. REAPE - Mary.
3. DIVERS - Catherine, (horse keeper).

HEALY'S LANE

ABBEYHALFQUARTER

1. MELVIN - James and Ellen, Bridget, Martin Harte.
2. CLARKE - Thomas and Bridget, Annie, Thomas, Mary, James.

JOHN STREET

1. vacant
2. HANNAN - Mary, Stephen, May, Lily Doble.
4. MacHALE - Margaret, Mary, John, Thomas Wickham, James Waters, Bridget MacHale.
5. COSGRAVE - Matthew and Margaret, Mary, Lily, Vincent, William, Delia Murphy, Bridget Howley, Frederick Casey, (publican).
6. printing office
7. CORCORAN - James, (publican).
8. LEONARD - John and Sidney, Mary, Patrick, Annie, John, Bridget, Martin, Michael, Catherine Beglin, (carpenter).
9. CORCORAN - John and Hannah, James, Mathew, Jack, Amy.
10. BATTLE - Anthony and Mary, Mary, John, Annie, Michael, Gertrude, Thomas, (tailor).

KNOCKANELO

WATTS - Henry and Belinda, William, Lizzie.
GILGIN - Mary, Pat and Margaret, Thomas.
CAVANAGH - Martin, Kate, Mary, FEURY: Anthony and Catherine.
LOFTUS - Thomas and Mary, Patrick, Thomas Lavin.
CAVANAGH - James and Kate, Pat and Maria, James.
CAVANAGH - Michael and Bridget.

KNOCKLEHAUGH

JONES - Mary.
FLAHERTY - Bridget, Patrick.
MULLEN - Patrick and Anne, Patrick Coleman.

KNOCKSBARRETT

PETRIE - Peter, Lucy Derbyshire, Sarah Martin, (salmon fishery lessee).
DISKIN - James, Belinda, (ex RIC).

KNOCKEGAN AND CLOONAGH BEG

DIAMOND - James and Bridget, Maggie, Michael, Sarah, Norah.
HARRISON - Michael and Mary, Anthony, Martin.
CARDEN - Patrick and Bridget, Mary, Margaret, John, Martin.
O'NEILL - John and Bridget, Elizabeth, Sabina.
REAPE - Thomas and Mary, Thomas, Annie, Michael, John.

KILGALLON LANE

1. TIGUE - James, Patrick.
2. DEIGNAN - Bridget, Bridget, Patrick, Mary, Elizabeth Nash, Henry Nash.
3. McNULTY - Ellen, Bridget, Ellen Toher.
4. MURPHY - Patrick and Elizabeth, James, (musician).
5. MELIA - John and Kate.
6. SHERLOCK - James and Mary, Bridget, Patrick, Stephen, Kate Murray.
7. FARRELL - John.
8. HELLY - James, John, Mary, William, Michael, (shoemaker).
9. MULLEN - Richard.
10. FINNEGAN - James and Margaret, Bernard, Patrick, Mary.

KING STREET

1. shop
2. RUSSON - Arthur, Sarah Downey, (dentist).
3. victuallers
4. MOYLETT - Michael, Joseph Trodden, Patrick Sweeney, Patrick O'Hara, (shopkeeper).
5. CALLAN - Owen and Ellen, Pauline, Alice, David Hickey, Annie Connor, (boot mcht.).
6. MULLEN - John and Annie, Evelyn, Nancy, Mary Shanley, Bridget Battle, James Clarke, (grocer).
7. Public hse.
8. LOVE - Mary, Bridget Smith, Patrick Smith, James McHugh, (prov. dler.).
9. KEANE - Robert.
10. GARVEY - John and Lena, Patrick, Patricia, Eileen, John, Laurence, Owen Murray, Thomas O'Donnell, Henry Broderick, John Broderick, (baker).
11. HEALY - Martin and Mary, John Sweeney, (publican).
12. BOURNS - John, Sarah, Mary, (printer).
13. GAUGHAN - John, Patrick Gordon, (cooper).
14. vacant
15. Ballina post office
16. BOLAND - William and Hannah, William, Eileen, Eva, Agnes O'Connor, (auctioneer).
17. GILLESPIE - Mary, Teresa, Ellen Barrett, Michael Hegarty, Peter Cane, James Ferguson, (publican).
18. JONES - Mary, PELLY: Frank and Veronica, Michael, Mary, Cornelia, Edward Hannings, Denis Corbett, William Casserly, Michael Roddy, Joseph McMonagle, James McEvoy, John Swarton, Kate Brock, Annie Dowling, Bridget Collins, Maria Padden, (hotel proprietoress).
19. Motor garage
20. JORDAN - Patrick and Sabina, William, Gertie, John, Patrick, Thomas, Francis, Sarah, Florrie, (tailor).
21. BOURKE - Cummin and Mary, Patrick, Teresa, Charles, Grace, Thomas Gibbons, George Langan, (saddler).
22. WEHRLEY - Engelbert and Catherine, Michael, Engelbert, Anthony, (jeweller).
23. SHERIDAN - Mary, Annie, John Cafferty, Julia Callaghan, Thomas Kearney, John Concannon, Thomas McGowan, Mary Gallagher, (spirit mcht)
24. store
25. O'HORA - Michael and Ellie, Mary, Violet, Helena, (shop & pub).
26. Medical Hall
27. IRWIN - John, (draper).
28. GILBOY - Francis, (publican).
29. RUDDY - Hugh and Cecilia, James, Moya, Rita, Eva C., Mary Killduff, Kate Ferguson, Francis Caffrey, Patrick McNamara, (mcht.).
30. vacant
31. ERSKINE - James and Emily, Bertha, Gerald, Emily, Jane O'Shea, Robert Sherlock, William Symington, Elizabeth McLintock, Annie Loftus, Bridget Rolston, (draper).

1796 Flax Growers List

The list gives the name & parish of over 2,000 people in Mayo. Nat. Library: (Ir633411 i7)

KNOX STREET

1. HUIE - Ellen, Charles.
2. JENNINGS - Annie, (lodging hse.).
3. KELLY - James and Maria, Belinda, Patrick, James, Annie, Lizzie, Jane, Eileen, Ellen, (tailor).
4. NIXON - Patrick and Mary, Maude, PATTEN: Mary, Bridget, Sarah, Thomas, Maria Maguire.
5. GORDON - Michael and Mary, John, Michael, William, James, Patrick, Mary, Bridget.
6. PATTEN - Mary, Eliza, John, Michael.
7. WARD - John and Margaret, Christopher, Bridget, Margaret.
8. HOWLEY - Henry.
9. NEALON - Margaret, Patrick Jordan, WALSHE: Stephen, David, William, (lodging hse.).
10. JORDAN - Joseph and Annie, Florence, Patrick, Katie Commons, (tailor).
11. HELLy - Patrick and Jane, Agusta, Bridget, (shoemaker).
12. McLOUGHLIN - Maria, Mary, Winifred, John Lee, Patrick Gaughan, Annie Hanley.
13. Commercial Club
14. Mineral water manuf.
15. KEANE - Francis, John Gordon, (doctor).
16. BOURKE - Kate E.
17. NIXON - John and Maria, DOOHER: Mary, John, Eveleen, Margaret Stapleton, May Sinnott, Bridget Lacey, Annie Davitt, Thomas Nevin.
18. HENNIGAN - Mary, Elizabeth, Teresa, Margaret, Elizabeth Brennan, Mary Murray, Mary O'Boyle, Margaret O'Malley, (hotel leasee).
18. UNIACHE - Michael and Cecelia, Ellen Duggan, (clerk).
19. DALE - Edward, (national school inspector).
18. HUGGARD - William and Anna, (solicitor).
19. BARRATT - Margaret, Annie, Marion, Maggie.
20. Printing office
21. JOYNT - Richard and Fannie, Marion, Helen, Aida Mary, R.Desmond, Mary Brogan, Honor Brogan, (newspaper proprietor).
22. Spirit/grocers shop.
23. Drapers shop
24. LAING - St. George, Lizzie McDonald, William McGurrin, Hubert Henry, Matthew Boland, Sarah Golden, Anna Ruttle, Maud Bailey, (draper).
25. FLANAGAN - John and Mary, Mary, Sarah, Celia, Maggie Convy, John Costello, William Maloney, Anthony Rowland, Bridget Irwin, (grocer & spirit mcht.).
26. Solicitor's office.
27. GALLAGHER - Peter, Michael O'Neill, Patrick Winters, Eugene Kenny, (shop asst.).
28. EAST - James and Eleanor, Harold, Janet, Roycroff, Sidney, Agnes Black, Arthur Patterson, Andrew Murphy, Bridget Mullarkey, Kate Gordon, Ellen Devers, (draper).
29. shop
30. WILDE - Joseph and Annie, Robert, Charles, William, Constance, (boot shop mngr.).
31. AHEARN - James and Mary, Mary, Patricia, Kathleen, Arthur, Louisa, Thomas, James, Vincent, Rosaline, Arthur Muffany, Ellen Brennan, Bridget Barrett, James Holleran, (gen. mcht.).
32. McNULTY - Martin, John, William McIntyre, John McDonnell, Joseph Sweeney, Michael McNulty, William Burke, Mary Jordan, (grocer & spirit mcht.).
33. Stationers shop
34. ADAMS - Charles and Sarah, Sarah, Tom, Minnie, Charles, Norah, Winnie, Maud, (tailor).
35. HUNTER - Charles, Alan, Charlotte, Margaret, Bridget Kearney, Mary Connor, (bank manager).
36. ADAMSON - Margaret, Patrick Sweeney, Joseph Thornton, Thomas Downes, Michael Munnelly, Mary Durkan.
37. ADAMSON - William and Ellen, Eveline, Rhona, Mary Molloy, Maggie O'Boyle, (chemist).
38. McCANN - James and Teresa, James, Charles, Maria, Maria, Kathleen, Silvester, Veronica, Patrick Flynn, Frederick Gannon, John Canavan, Michael Mulhearn, Mary Judge, Janie McHale, (publican).

39. WALSH - Peter and Mary, Kate Gaughan, (doctor).
40. McHALE - Sabina, Mary Rafter.
41. LOWRY - David and Jessie, Albert, Jessie, Samuel, Henry O'Hara, Mary McHugh, (grocer).
42. MURTAGH - Elizabeth, Delia, Susan Dophin, Mary Moran, Margaret Killian, Mary Touhill, Mary Williams, Thomas Sherry, Patrick Sheil, Patrick Callaghan, (hotel proprietoress).
43. MAGINN - John and Agnes, Edward, John Kelly, Anne Joyce, (bank of Ireland agent).
44. HEWSON - Margaret, James, Ellie, Rev. Patrick Howley.
45. LEONARD - Philip and Anne, Joseph, Thomas, Francis, (ex RIC).
46. JOHNSON - Benjamin and Christina, Jeannie, Rose Kelly, (saddler).
47. DOOHER - James and Mary, James Padden, William Carroll, Kate Daly, George Caldwell, Matthew O'Rourke, Peter Henry, John Fraser, (hotel proprietor & auctioneer).
48. HAINES - Charles and Bessie, Charles, Hilda, (bank manager).

KILMOREMOY

DOHERTY - Patrick and Mary, Thomas, Margaret, Patrick, Mary, Michael, Bridget, Patchious H., Robert Moore.
GINTY - John and Catherine, Mary, Gerard, Margaret, Patrick, Frederick, Anne Barnes, (cemetery caretaker & insurance agent).
QUINN - Michael and Katherine, Michael, Agnes, James, Bridget, Lizzie.
CARR - Michael and Mary, Michael, John, May, Martin, Anthony, Thomas.
MASH - Julia, Annie, John, George, Julia, Bridget Boland.

KNOCKALYRE or DOWNHILL

ARDNAREE RURAL

GARVEY - John and Harrie, Ivan, Sheelagh, Kate Noaks, Lizzie Castles, Mary McGee, Bridget Coyne, Bridget Murphy, Sarah Lackey, George Cullen, (crown solicitor).

KNOCKALYRE OR DOWNHILL

ARDNAREE URBAN

COOLICAN - Michael and Frances, Anna, James, Irene, Michael, Maureen, Noreen, Nelly Morgan, Delia Kenny, Molly Mulligan, Bridget Kelly, Michael O'Brien, (solicitor).
MULROONEY - Mary, Patrick, Michael, Teresa Dwyer.
CLARKE - Patrick and Kate, Norah, Gerald, (coachman).
Flour mill

LAGHTADAWANNAGH

LAVELLE - Peter and Ellen, Thomas, Sarah, John, Norah.
RUTLEDGE - John and Bridget, Mary, Bridget, Thomas, Alice, Martin, Annie, John, Michael, John Willis.
MERRICK - John and Hanoria, John, Michael, Willie.
O'HORO - Edward and Maria, Norah, Edward, Bridget, Sybina, Cathleen, Evelyn, (carpenter).
KENNY - Martin and Sarah, Mary, Bridget, James, Lizzie.
SWEENEY - James and Anne, Maggie, Mary, Bridget, Annie, Katie.
O'HORO - John and Mary, John, Pauline, James, Vincent, Peter, Josephine, Berty, (coachman).
SCANLAN - Patrick and Kate, Michael, Ellena, Lizzie, Patrick.
HANAHOE - Anthony and Mary, Bridget.
McDONNELL - John and Catherine, Bridget, John, Michael.
McDONNELL - Thomas and Mary, James.
MUNNELLY - Mary, James, Maria, Michael, Ellen.
MOYLES - Anne, Winnie, James, Sabina.

LAND LEAGUE AVENUE

1. LOFTUS - John and Catherine, Mary, Patrick, Kate, Bridget, John, Ellen, Margaret.
2. LACKIE - Michael and Maria, Patrick, Kathleen, Michael.
3. FLYNN - John and Bridget, Annie, Thomas, Catherine Corcoran, Patrick Warde.
4. BARRETT - Anthony and Anne, Bertie, Maggie, Michael, Anthony, Ellen, Eileen, (blacksmith).
5. HOPKINS - John and Anne, Mary, John, Michael, Charles, Stephen, Patrick, James, Peter, (shoemaker).
6. SHEA - Margaret, Patrick, James, John Barett, Thomas Barett.
7. TRAYNOR - Kate, Kate Duffy, Thomas Duffy, Margaret Heffernan.
8. SWEENEY - Hubert and Bridget, Charles, Bridget.
9. CORCORAN - Michael, Michael.

LOWER PIPER HILL

1. HEFFERNAN - Joseph and Mary, Thomas, Bridget, Patrick, Michael Clarke, Edward Clarke.
2. O'HORA - Patrick and Ellie, Joseph, Mary Conroy, (stable groom).
3. BROWNE - William and Mary, Anthony, Evelyn, Mauria, Ethina, Annie Barett.
4. MERRICK - Martin, Kathleen, Anne, James Moore, Elizabeth McNamara, Matthew Lavin, John Keating, Joseph Kearney, Patrick Brennan, Patrick Hennigan, Anthony Heally, (Temperance Hotel).
5. SWEENEY - Patrick, John, Bridget, (horse trainer).
6. CONNOR - Michael, Patrick, Maggie, (bootmaker).
7. GALVIN - William and Mary, Patrick, Elizabeth Forde, FLYNN: Michael and Kate, Kathleen, John, Michael,(carpenter)
8. MORAN - Patrick and Bridget, Mary, Katie, Michael, John, Patrick, James, Willie, Edward, Thomas Baker.
9. KNOX - John and Annie, (stable groom).
10. RUTTLEDGE - Michael and Mary, William, Mary, Margaret, John, John McEvoy, Annie Keating.
11. HASTINGS - Robert and Mary, Robert, William, Annie, (town postman).
12. KELLy - Mary, Katie, George, RYAN: John and Mary, James, John.
13. LYNN - Thomas and Maria, Mary, Michael Carabine, (mineral water maker).
14. GIBBONS - Ellen, Sabina Murphy, Patrick Lenahan, Kate Lenahan, Mary Clarke, Mary Dugan, (lodging hse.).
15. O'HORA - Patrick and Mary, Patrick, Thomas Dempsey, (blacksmith).
16. Hay and Corn store.
17. SWEENEY - Bridget, Thomas.
18. GREHAN - Daniel and Elizabeth, Ambrose, Bridget, (carpenter).
19. CALLAGHAN - Michael, Mary, (publican).
20. DIXON - Mary, Michael, Lizzie, Mary, Lizzie.
20. SMITH - James and Margaret, (porter on railway).
21. CLIFFORD - Mary, Lilly Lynch.
22. DUFFY - Bessie, Patrick, Charles.
22. BLIZZARD - Mary.
23. TULLY - Martin and Norah, Mary.
24. CLARKE - Anne, Bridget Burke, Patrick O'Hora.
25. ORMSBY - Bridget, Thomas McCarock.
26. MEENAGHAN - Anthony and Maria, Patrick, Mary, Anthony, Norah, Margaret, Bridget, Mary Carolan, Anthony Clarke, Bridget Clarke.
27. MORAN - Mary, Mary, James Kilgallon, (grocer).
28. McGINTY - Martin and Ellen, John, Martin, Michael Walsh.
29. Methodist School
29. GILBERT - Elizabeth.
29. KEATLEY - Sarah, (teacher).
30. Methodist Church.
31. ABRAHAM - Alexander and Anny, Emily, Catherine Wrench, (methodist minister).
32. BROWNE - Michael, Patrick, Martin, Mary Brogan, Margaret Herbert, (wine & spirit cellar mnger.).
33. FERGUSON - Martin, Patrick, Bridget, Thomas, John, Anthony, Martin, Francis, Michael, Catherine, (butcher).
34. DIAMOND - William and Bridget, Amellia, William Carroll, (shoemaker).
35. NAUGHTON - Ellen, Patrick, John, Thomas.
36. KILGALLON - Anne.
37. CUNNINGHAM - Walter and Mary, Mary, Aggie, Bridget, (railway goods checker).
38. McGUIGGAN - Bridget, Paul, Anthony.
39. McHALE - Patrick and Mary, Nellie, James, (shoemaker).
40. O'HARA - James, Edward, Kate, Patrick, (shoemaker).
41. BRODERICK - Andrew and Sarah, Lillie.
42. FLANNERY - Patrick and Mary, Mary, Lillie, Patrick, Kathleen, Mary Ruane,

1825 Ballina Traders List

Contains over 70 names of the local merchants making requests to extend and deepen Moy river.
Nat. Archives: OP 974/131

(tailor).
43. CARDEN - Jane.
44. WALSHE - Luke and Winnie, Sarah, Anthony, Luke, Mary, Patrick, Kate McGrath.
45. FOODY - Catherine, Patrick, Margaret.
46. ORMSBY - James and Anne, James.
47. COLLINS Annie, Patrick, Johnny, Mary, Mary McNamara.
48. CARABINE - John and Bridget, Joseph, James, Mary, Celia, Maggie, Christina, Bridget, (shoemaker).
49. DUFFY - Michael and Margaret, Mary, John, Thomas.
50. COLLINS - Ellen, Maggie, CURRAN: Mary, Kathleen, Maggie.
51. BARRETT - John and Bridget, Ellen McDonnell, (blacksmith).

MILL STREET

1. McLOUGHLIN - Michael and Sabina, Mary, Annie, Michael.
2. LENEHAN - Mary, (seamstress).
3. MANGAN - Michael and Sarah, John, James, Thomas, Patrick, Michael, Norah, Edward, Kate Hearns, (victualler).
4. O'HORA - Michael and Anne, Ellen McShane, Mary McDonagh.
5. FORBES - John and Annie, Ellen, Richard, James, Michael, (porter for excise office).
6. LYONS - John and Elizabeth, Edward, Mary, Margaret, Patrick, Anne, Bridget, Bridget Coleman.
7. BECKETT - Isaac and Maria, Isaac, Edith, Esimay, Olive, John, Margaret Henly, Mary Rape, Joseph Barret, (timber mcht.).
8. WALSH - Sarah, Joseph Duggan.
9. GRAHAM - Patrick and Mary, Mary Kate, (tailor).
10. MONNELLY - Anne.
11. CURRAN - Ellen, Thomas, Mary.
12. O'HARA - Michael.
13. DIAMOND - Michael, Michael, Annie, Michael, Katie, (bootmaker).
14. GREENE - Patrick and Annie, Gertrude, Ml.John, Thomas, Annie, Mary M., (sanitary officer).
15. HEARNS - James and Mary, Jennie, Michael, Ellie, Mary, Francis, Richard, Mary, (fishing tackle mngr.).
16. SHAW - Henry and Henrietta, Henry, Edward, Ellen Temple, (bank clerk).
17. CURRY - Bridget, Edward, Patrick, John.
18, Ballina Saw Mills

McLOUGHIINS LANE

1. LACKEY - Patrick and Mary, Patrick, Michael, Bridget, John.
2. MOYLES - James, John, William.
3. GREHAM - Charles and Anne, Mary, Bridget, Patrick, Kate, (carpenter).
4. CLARKE - Michael and Mary, John, Ellen, Patrick.
5. MURRAY - Michael and Annie, Michael, Charles, Bridget, Annie.
6. MURPHY - Sarah.
7. McGLYNN - Patrick and Mary, Patrick, Anthony, Martin, Maggie Devany.
8. KEAVENY - Margaret, John, James.
9. O'NEILL - Frank, (shoemaker).
10. FORDE - Myles, Catherine Taylor, Mary Taylor, Mary Kelly.
11. CASEY - Maria, James, Thomas, Gertrude, KELLY: Patrick and Annie, KAVANAGH: Bryan and Bridget, Bridget, (fruit & fish dler.).
12. KELLY - Ellen.

MULLAUNS (Ardnaree)

KILGALLON - James and Elizabeth, Joe, Lillie, Bertie, Annie, Jack.
HARTE - John and Barbara, Mary, Patrick, Margaret.
KILGALLON - Thomas and Maria, Margaret, John, Michael, Dan, Kate, Patrick, Thomas, Mathew, Willy, Theady.
KILGALLON - Patrick and Anne, Katie, James, Barbara, Margaret, Winifred.
KILGALLON - Patrick and Margaret, John, Pat, James, Agnes, Teresa, Augusta.
WILLIS - Patrick and Bridget, Mary, John, Bridget, Annie, Catherine.

MULLAUNS (Ballina Urban)

1. NAUGHTON - Sydney, Edward, Samuel Ludden, Robert Mash, Patrick Lyons, (boarding hse.).
2. COPPINGER - Anne, Mary, Kate, Mark.
3. RUTLEDGE - Francis and Bridget, Joseph, Maye, Annie, Kate Loftus, Bridget Loftus, John Slogan, Michael Slogan, James Finnigan, (publican & hotel proprietor).
4. MIGGINS - James and Maryjane, Margaret, Christopher Rafferty, (station master).
5. MILLAR - John and Jane, Mary, Patrick, Agnes, (supervisor of Customs & excise).

NURE

DODD - John, Maggie, Michael, Annie, Eugene, Andrew, Mary.

NEW GARDEN STREET

1. KELLY - James, Rose, Kathleen, Barbara.
1. BARRETT - Richard and Catherine, (colporteur).
2. BELL - Henry and Delia, Stephen, Ellen, (ex telegraph engineer).
3. CAHILL - Joseph and Lavinia, Patrick, Kate Daly, Hanna Galvin, (confectioner).
4. EDWARDS - Lancelot and Fanny, (motor engineer).
5. LINDSAY - Michael and Minnie, (RIC).
6. BROWNE - Matthew and Emily, (town clerk).
7. McGEE - John and Jessie, (schoolmaster).
8. KILDUFF - Michael and Annie, Maria Melvin, (sewing machine agent).
9. McGILLYCUDDY - Michael and Julia, Annie, Boctius, Ellen, (excise officer).
10. WALLACE - Joseph and Mary, Anne Hearns, Bernard O'Dowd, Joseph Lannon, Percival McCabe, Mary Callaghan, (grocer's porter).
11. REILLY - John and Mary, William, Violet, Joseph, Agnes, George, Gertie, Kathleen, Eveleen, (waiter).
12. WALSH - John and Bridget, Margaret, Minnie, Joseph, Edward, James, (RIC sergt.).
13. CANAVAN - James, Richard, Bridget, Margaret, (carpenter).
14. CAHILL - Elizabeth, Martin, Gertrude, Mary, (laundress).
15. O'HARA - Edward, (shoemaker).
15. MURPHY - John, Mary.
16. REILLY - John and Margaret, May,

CHURCH RECORDS IN BALLINA

Catholic parish Registers are kept locally by parish priests. They are also in the National Library on micro-film. Church Parish Registers date back to as follows:-

Religion	Civil Parish	Baptisms	Marriage	Burials	Location
COI	Ballysakeery	1802	1802	1802	LC/RCB
RC	Athymass	1875	1874	------	LC/NA
RC	Ballynahaglish (Backs, Rathduff)	1848	1848	------	LC/NA
RC	Kilfian	1826	1826	1826	LC/NA
RC	Killasser	1847	1847	1847	LC/NA
RC	Kilmoremoy	1823	1823	1823	LC/NA
RC	Toomore	1833	1871	------	LC/NA

LC=Local Churches; NA- National Archives. **RCB - Representative Church Body Library, Braemor Park, Churchtown, Dublin 14, Tel; (01)4923979 Fax:(01)4924770** is the Church of Ireland's principal library. The Church of Ireland and Roman Catholic Dioceses are Achonry, Killala and Tuam. Three Catholic parishes in Mayo recorded deaths - Kilmoremoy, Killasser and Kilfian. The majority of the post 1870 marriage registers list the names of both mothers. An index for 1821 & 1822 marriage registers in each deanery of the diocese of Killala is at Nat. Lib.Pos4222.

The Office of Register General, Joyce hse., 8/11 Lombard st. Dublin 2 , has all birth/marriage/death registers from 1864. We suggest some research before your visit, Birth Certs list father&mothers maiden name (01-6711000) Times9.30-12.30 and 2.15-4.30pm

This Street was originally called Arran Street after the Earl of Arran, who owned a good portion of the town back then. The Street was later called Tone Street, after the great Wolfe Tone, who was involved in bringing the French to Ireland in 1798.

William, Mary E., Margaret, Julia Convey, (journalist).
17. CLARKE - Thomas and Bridget, John, Mary, Thomas, Patrick, (mason).
18. CAMPBELL - Hugh and Elizabeth, Catherine, (plumber).
18. SCOTT - Amy, Lucy, Emily.
19. FRIEL - Charles and Kate, William, Susan, Elizabeth, Sarah, Frederick, (ex sergt. RIC).
20. MEAGHER - Annie, Anastatia, (maternity nurse).
21. McCARTHY - James and Emma, Henry, Julia, (RIC).
22. MURPHY - John and Mary, (RIC).

OLD GARDEN STREET

1. CARROLL - Patrick, Michael, Mary, Maryanne, George Polton, John Farrell, Michael Walsh, Bridget Walshe, (spirit mcht.).
2. SULLIVAN - John and Kate, Martin, Mary, Cecilia, Kathleen, Patrick Finnegan, Patrick Convey, (shopkeeper).
3. TIMLIN - Maria, James, Maggie, Bridget, Pteer Colleran, (publican).
4. BURKE - Martin and Bridget, Maria Melvin, (teacher).
5. DEMPSEY - Michael, (shopkeeper).
6. ORMSBY - Michael and Barbara, Mary, Patrick, John, Martin, Michael, Willie, Honora Barrett.
7. SLATER - Albert and Annie, Lavinia, Arthur, Maud, Annie, May, Bridget, Eileen, Elizabeth, Rachel, Arthur, Bridget Greavy, (photographer).
8. QUIGLEY - Alice, Jack, Annie, Michael Corcoran, Katie McNulty, Mary Tighe, (shopkeeper).
9. DUFFY - Margaret, Bridget, Edward, Lizzie, Nora, (shop).
10. CONNOR - Bridget, Patrick, Margaret, Sarah Sweeney, William Walshe, (publican).
11. MASH - John and Eva, Mary, Thomas, David, John, (blacksmith).
12. BROGAN - John and Mary, Bridget, Sarah, Peter, Mary, Christina.
13. GUINAN - Patrick and Mary, Mary, Mathew, Patrick, Alice, Thomas, (ex RIC).
14. RUDDY - Patrick, Mary, Margaret O'Hara, (ex teacher).
15. LALLY - Edward and Catherine, John, Kathleen, William, (ex RIC).
16. HOWLEY - John and Mary, Martin, Winney, Edward.
17. vacant
18. BRODERICK - Patrick and Maria, Pat, Mary, Anthony, Martin Lavin, William Reilly, (baker).
19. KILLORAN - Honoria, Ellen, (seamstress).
20. GILLESPIE - Anthony, Mary Harrison, (accountant).
21. GALLAGHER - Anthony and Bridget, William O'Hora, (sexton in Cathedral).
22. MOORE - Robert and Mary, Margaret, Patrick, Bridget, Jane, (shoemaker).
23. PRICE - Michael and Belinda, Patrick, Martin, Michael.
24. LYONS - Thomas and Maggie, Patrick.
25. BOURKE - Catherine, Bridget, John, Mary Heffernan.
26. O'DOWD - Delia, Margaret, Celia, (publican).
27. MOORE - John and Annie, Patrick, Mary, Bernard Doyle.
28. CURRAN - Bridget, Patrick, Frank, (shopkeeper).
29. BATTLE - Maria, Norah, Mary Convey.
30. BRENNAN - John and Bridget, Mary, John O'Hora, James Gardener, John Duffy, Thomas Lynch, Ernest Connaghton, John Devanny, Patrick Doherty, Edward Doherty.
31. LENNOX - William, Agnes, Catherine, (tailor).
32. WATERS - Henry, Agnes Gallagher.
33. McCAWLEY - Patrick and Mary, Kathleen, James, Mary, John, Frederick, Attracta, Ellen Browne, Bridie Kelly, Patrick Divers, Bridget Healy, (shopkeeper).
34. CARROLL - John and Maria, John, Andrew, Bidelia, Hugh, (ex RIC sergt.).
35. FOX - Francis and Eliza, Mary, Mary Harrison, (shopkeeper).
36. SMYTH - James, Edward, Thomas Seers, Barbara Naughton, (carpenter).

O'DOWD'S LANE

1. STOKES - William and Mary, Francis, Ed.Patrick, Catherine, Maryanne, William, Robert, Sabina, Martin, James, (tinsmith).
2. vacant
3. CONNOR - Thomas and Bridget, Patrick, Mary, Jane, Bridget, Margaret, (shoemaker).
4. DUFFY - Patrick and Kate, Mary, Bridget, Agnes, John.
5. GREHAN - Michael and Mary, Patrick, Joseph.

1798 list of People who suffered loss in 1798 Rebellion. Nat. Library JLB94107, (650 names, addresses & occupations).

6. McGRATH - Patrick and Ellen, Annie, Martin, Patrick, Ellie, Julia.
7. BYRNE - John and Mary, Annie, (tailor).
8/9. vacant
10. LINDSAY - Bridget.

PAWN OFFICE LANE

1. FERGUSON - Anthony and Margaret, Mary, Margaret, Patrick, Anthony, John, Catherine.
2. WALSH - Daniel, (nail maker).
3. vacant
4. Undertakers shop
5. Flour store.

POLKES LANE

1. WALSHE - Bridget, Edward, Bridget, Thomas, Maria.
2. O'MALLEY - Michael, Annie, Joseph, Agnes.

POUND STREET

1. FORDE - Richard and Mary, Sarah, Bridget, Richard, James, Joseph, (carpenter).
2. store
3. carpenters shop
4/5. Blacksmith's forge
6. QUEENAN - John and Bridget, Patrick, Bridget, Winifred, (fruit dler.).
7. CARABINE - Mary, Mary Murray.
8. Recreation room.

POUND LANE

ABBEYHALFQUARTER

1. BOURKE - John and Bridget, Kate, John, Ellen, Annie.
2. GALLAGHER - Patrick and Jane, Ellen, Annie, James.
3. BARRETT - John and Anne, Mary, Martin, Thomas, Annie, Catherine McGlynn.
4. REGAN - Patrick and Mary, Thomas, John, Patrick.
5. TIGHE - Michael.

QUIGNALECKA

LACKEN - Martin and Margaret, Patrick, Mathew, Martin, Sarah, Molly, Tom Conway.
COWELL - John and Bridget, Mary, John, Annie.
TIGHE - Michael and Margaret, Catherine, Aloysius, Bridget Cowley, (quay porter).
GALLAGHER - Maria, Bridget Naughton.
DUFFY - John and Catherinep, Mary, Michael, Thomas, Elizabeth.

MAYO NAMES

The main gaelic families in Mayo were the O'Malley, O'Flaherty, McEvilly, O'Henaghan, O'Flannery. The Norman families who settled here were the Burkes, Barretts, Nangles, Costelloes, Jordans. Other septs related to these Norman families were McPhilbins, McAndrews, Prendergast, and Fitzmaurice.

ROULSTON - John and Isabella, Edward, John, Matthew, Bella, Emma, Henry Atkinson.
GALLAGHER - Kate, Patrick, Annie, Owen Flynn, Margaret Roche, Anthony McLoughlin.
LOUGHNEY - Matthew and Bridget, Pat, Tom, John, Anney.
McLOUGHLIN - Bridget, Margaret, Timothy Riordan.
LOUGHNEY - John and Catherine, Bridget, Sarah, Patrick, Mary Lynn.
MULLEN - William and Bridget.
JOYCE - Bridget.

RAHINS

BARKLIE - Thomas and Jane, Ruth, Naomie, (bank accountant).
DERHAM - Patrick and Maria.
JOYNT - George and Annie, Bridget Kearney, Jane Loftus, (civil engineer).
TRIMBLE - John and Helena, Francis, Edith, Helena, Gladis.
Rahins Nat. School

RATHNACONEEN

O'HORO - Daniel and Anne, John, Ellen, Michael, Daniel, William.
HANNAHOE - Julia, Edward.
O'HORO - Henry and Mary, Pat, Anthony, Bridget, Michael, Sarah, Thomas, Edward, Sidney, Ellie.
O'HORO - Margaret, Patrick, Annie, CLARKE: Anthony, Michael.

RATHKIP

FURY - Margaret, John, Frank, James, Winifred, Margaret Loftus.
KILGALLON - John and Mary, Patrick, John, Maggie, Philip, John Marley.
LOFTUS - Daniel and Catherine, Daniel, Patrick, Sabina, James, John, Annie, Daniel.
FOY - William and Bridget, Katie, Lizzie.
FURY - Julia, Thomas, James, John, Francis, Mary, Sarah, Mary Jordan.
QUEENAN - Eliza, Bridget, John, Annie, Alice.
McNULTY - John and Katie, Mary, Kate, Annie, Lizzie, John, Teresa, Edward.
MOYLES - Patrick and Margaret, Michael, Patrick, Mathew, Mary, Thomas, Margaret.
LOFTUS - John, Bridget, Teresa, KILGALLON: Frederick, James.
KENNEDY - James and Mary, Patrick, Mary.
BROGAN - James and Mary, Michael and Mary, John, Bridget.
COLEMAN - Michael and Mary, John, Mary, (blacksmith).
MOYLES - Thomas and Bridget.

RAISH

MOORE - William.

SHERIDAN'S LANE

ABBEYHALFQUARTER

1. DAISEY - Ellen, Bridget, Joseph.
2. MARSHALL - John and Bridget, Thomas, John, Annie, Norah, May Dang
3. CREANE - Michael and Jane, James, Mary Cullen, (blacksmith).

SHAMBLE STREET

1. HEFFERNAN - Bridget, John, Thomas, Mary Harte, (grocer).
2. McCANN - Annie, John, Margaret Keane, Lawrence Gallagher, Thomas Gallagher, Michael Heffernan.
3. BROWN - James and Maggie, Annie, Patt, Bridget, Maggie, James, John.
4. MORAN - Michael and Ellen, Martin, Mary, (gas fitter).
5. CONVEY - James and Sarah, Michael, Mary, Annie, James, Patrick, Bridget, Joseph, (shoemaker).
6. LOFTUS - Patrick, (fish dler.).
7. McCANN - Patrick and Mary, Paddy, Mary, John, William.
8. COLEMAN - John and Mary, Patrick, James, Andrew, (carpenter).
9. REILLY - John, Joseph, Annie, Maggie, Mary, Michael, James, Mary McDonagh, (sawyer).
10. FORBES - Mark and Kate, Patrick, Mary, Mark, Bridget, William.
11. ROBINSON - Patrick and Mary, Kate, Patrick, Winifred, Martin, Teresa, Mary Menehan, Norah Menehan.
12. FORBIS - Richard and Bridget, Francis, Patrick, Edward.
13. BEATTY - Joseph and Kate, Joseph, James, (carpenter).
14. HUNTER - William and Ellen, John, James, (mason).
15. GREEN - Mary, Mary, Anthony, Michael, Mary Walton.
16. LOFTUS - Thomas and Bridget, Mary, Patrick, Margaret, Thomas, Josephine, Christine, James, William, Francis, (victualler).
17. RUANE - Henry and Bridget, Bridget, Henry, William, Joseph, Eva, Mary, Kathleen.
18. BROWN - Anne, Patrick, Anthony.
19. CAFFREY - John and Norah, Muriel, Norah, Eileen, Myra, Mary, (plasterer).
20. REID - Martha, Jessie, William.
21. Ballina Gas Works

SOLOMONS LANE

1. TOUGHER - James and Kate, James, Bridget, Thomas.
2. HARTE - Kate, James, Mary, Kate, Annie.
3. MORAN - Martin and Catherine, Ellen, John, Bridget Tougher.
4. MURPHY - John and Mary, Annie, Michael, Bridget, Jimmy.

SLIEVENAGARK

HOBAN - Michael and Catherine, Patrick, Mary, Anthony, Winifred, Thomas, James, Francis, Kate, Sabina, Agnes.
MORAN - Patrick and Mary, Michael.
WYNNE - John and Maggie, Patrick, Michael.
HOBAN - Martin and Bridget, Mary, Kate, Michael, John.
TRAYNOR - Thomas, Ellen, John.
HOBAN - Francis and Ellen, Michael, Catherine, Delia, Ellen, Annie, Margaret, Winefred, Elizabeth.
CARR - Patrick and Maria, Edward, Michael, John, Anthony, Maryanne.
CARR - Pat and Mary, Bernard, Peter, Thomas, Bridget, Mary.

SHEA - Martin and Mary, Martin, John, Bridget.
SHEA - Thomas and Mary, Pat, Thomas, William, James, Anthony, Michael, Bridget, Mary, Winefred.
KEANE - Patrick and Anne, Patrick, Mary, Bridget, Michael.

ST. PATRICK'S TERRACE

1. MORRELL - Patrick and Mary, Margaret, Michael, Patrick.
2. DEVLIN - Catherine, Michael, Joseph, Patrick, Charles, Robert, Catherine, Margaret.
2. CORCORAN - Patrick and Annie.
3. SHANNON - Farrell and Eleanor, Francis, Richard, Annie, Margaret, David, (ex RIC).
4. MORRELL - William and Ellen, Joseph, Francis.
5. LAVELLE - John, Edward, Mary, Bridget Morrell, (printer).
6. HUGHES - Arthur and Susan, Sarah, Susan, Mary, Arthur, Bridget, Henry, (joiner).
7. O'HARA - James, Bridget.
8. Spade Manufacturers.
9. MONAGHAN - Mary, Michael, William, Peter, Patrick, Mary.

TULLYEGAN

MURRAY - John, Martin, Anne, John, Bridget, Patrick, James.
MURRAY - Thomas and Catherine, John, Thomas.
McLOUGHLIN - Catherine, John, Ellen, Peter, John Heneghan.
WALSH - Bridget, Edward, Katie, Martin, Winnie, Bridget, Anthony, James.
McLOUGHLIN - Bridget, Bridget, John.
KENNY - Anne, John, Thomas.
PRESTON - Anne, Mary, Tom, Michael, Patrick, Kate.
HOLMES - Thomas and Winnifred, Bridget, Patt, Maria, Michael, Martin, Annie, Michael Walsh.

TULLYSLIEVA

MYLES - Patrick and Margaret, Michael, Mary, John, Bridget, Barbara, Patrick, Margaret, Andrew.
DOWD - Thomas and Maria, Patrick, Annie, Edward, Katie, John.
REDINGTON - John, Mary, Margaret, (shop).
WARD - Mary, Mary, Michael, Maggie.
HOPE - Michael and Annie, Mary, Michael, Pat, John.

1796 List of Northern Catholics recently settled in Mayo

Compiled by landlords, Browne, Altamont, and Cuffe. (Lists 1,074, 116, and 167 names). Located at State Paper Office, Reb. papers 620 (1796Series)

PLEASE NOTE

The compiler of this reference book took every care to produce it as accurately as possible, from handwritten records. He assumes no responsibility or liability for errors or omissions.

BARRETT - Patrick, Teresa, Martin McGuinness.
BATTLE - Catherine, CUMMINS: Mary, Kate.
HOLMES - Ellen, Thomas, John, Willie, Mary, Anthony.
MUNNELLY - Mary, John, Thomas.
MUNNELLY - Bridget, Patrick, Edward, Thomas.
LOFTUS - John and Bridget, Patrick Cummins.
REDDINGTON - James and Maria, Michael,Francis, Patrick, Margaret,Annie
HOWLEY - John and Maggie.
CONVEY - Peter and Kate, Honor Kelly.
BATTLE - John and Bridget.

UPPER PIPER'S HILL

1. KNIGHT - Thomas and Mary, Martin, John.
2. RUANE - Michael and Ellen, Mary.
3. RYDER - Catherine, George, David, John.
4. KELLY - Mary, John Moran.
5. CLARKE - Anne, Martin, Eccles.
6. FARRELL - Thomas and Mary, Matthew, Janie, Robert, Patrick, Delia Kingsley, Matthew Kingsley.
7. HALLORAN - William and Annie, Paddy, (tailor).
8. COPPINGER - Jane.
9. RAFTER - William and Ellen, Frank, Mary.
10. HEALY - Anne, Mary Duffy.
11. SPELMAN - Anne, Nellie.
12. O'BRIEN - Hugh and Maryanne, Mary, Joseph, John, Hugh, Margaret, (shoemaker).
13. DOHERTY - Edward and Mary, Edward, John.
14. LYNCH - Denis and Anne, Annie, Patrick, Denis, James, Maud, Mary, (carpenter).
15. LEONARD - Anthony, Mary, Annie, Catherine.
16. GARDINER - Thomas and Winifred, James, Michael, Francis, Mary.
17. LOFTUS - Patrick, Bridget, Patrick, Elizabeth, (shoemaker).
18. CALLAGHAN - Michael and Mary, Edward, Patrick, Michael, James, Mollie, (horse dler.).
19. CONNOR - Michael and Nora.
20. DUFFY - Eugene and Annie, Mary, (baker).
21. McNAMARA - Charles and Anne, Alice, Maggie, (ex army).
22. LACKEY - Kate, John, Thomas, Teresa, Kate McBride.
23. MURRAY - Martin and Catherine, Bridget, Thomas, Patrick, (tin smith).
24. HOLLERAN - Bridget, Patrick, Peter, Sarah.
25. HOBAN - Martin.
26. HOBAN - Michael and Anne, Martin, Michael, Patrick, Mary, Annie, Maggie, Bridget.
27. JUDGE - James and Mary.
28. O'REGAN - Patrick and Bridget, M.Joseph, Patrick, (carpenter).
29. FARRELL - Anne, Maggie, (seamstress)
30. MURRAY - Michael and Anne, Charles, Bridget, Maggie, Winifred McGuinty.
31. CAFFERTY - Michael and Maria, Mary.
32. McNULTY - Annie, Bridget, Michael, Michael Kelly.
33. DOYLE - Katie, Thomas Carney, Andy Lynam, (lodging hse.).
34. DEMPSEY - Patrick and Mary, Katie, Michael, Mary, Patrick, Edward, (publican).
35. LAVELLE - Edward and Ellen, Martin, Michael, Anthony, Bridget, Edward, Patrick, Sarah, Francis, Gerald, David, (milesman).
36. KILGALLON - Mary, Mary Lacken, Leontine McGregor, (grocer).
37. BRENNAN - Kate, John Cawley, Mary Reilly, Jane Reilly.
38. MELVIN - Margaret, Michael.
39. FORBES - Patrick and Kate, Mark, Jack, Patrick, Willie, Tom, Mary, Margaret, Bridget, Martina, John Sheil, Tom Kenny, Bill Deane, (railway porter).
40. DOYLE - Patrick and Mary, Annie, Edward, Mary, Patrick, Michael, Bridget, John.
41. DONNELLY - Thomas and Bridget, Patrick, Edward, Mary, Margaret, Stephen, Bridget, John.
42. DUFFY - Patrick and Bridget, John, Marcella, Patrick, Bridget, Emma Morrison, (baker).
43. CONROY - William and Catherine, Mary, Thomas, Eliza, Christina, Catherine, William, Patrick Feeney, (railway engine driver).
44. LYNCH - Mary, Jane, James, Margaret.
45. JOLLY - Thomas and Catherine, (fireman on railway).

VICTORIA STREET

1. SHANNON - George, A.Rubinia, Bridget McDermott, (mnger. Moy Fishery).
2. BEIRNE - May, Maudie, Lily, Arthur Gregson, Bertram Loughead, John Reilly, Thomas McGrane, William Gilsenan, Bridget Keane, (lodging hse.).
3. KNOX - Hannah, Julia, Bernard Egan, Margaret Bowler, Annie Beverage, Katie Jennings, (boarding hse.).

WATER LANE

1. QUIGLEY - Patrick and Anne, Michael Tolan, Jack Tolan.
2. FERGUSON - Catherine, Richard, Charlotte.
3. SHERIDAN - Thomas and Margaret, John, Annie, Margaret, Katie, James, Michael, Patrick, Christopher.
4. FLYNN - Patrick and Annie, George, (bank porter).
5. BRODERICK - Bridget, Bridget, Josephine, Nannie, Katie, ANDERSON: Michael, John, Annie.
6. McHALE - Mary, Kate, Maud, Patrick, Celia Jackson.
7. BROWNE - John and Catherine, Patrick, Mary, John, Katie.
8. LOFTUS - Mary, Margaret, Norah, Margaret.

WORKHOUSE LANE

ABBEYHALFQUARTER

1. DEVANEY - Patrick and Mary, Martin, Mary, Annie, Michael.

Primary Valuation of Tenements 1856

CONSIDERED by many as the most important civil record is Sir Richard Griffith's Valuation of Tenements 1856. The Nat. Library and the Nat. Archives have complete sets and we are pleased that Ballina's Library has the full set for the Town of Ballina and its surroundings. It gives the townland or street, house number (in towns & villages), occupier, landlord, description of property and its net annual value. I included the address, house number and occupier only, but a photocopy of a full page may be obtained from Castlebar County Library. I was fortunate to come across the old Ballina map of 1850 (p. 49) to match the Valuation Returns. (Some townlands are divided into rural/urban).

ABBEYHALF QUARTER
John Hopkins
Edward Atkinson
Col. F.A. Knox Gore
John Keane
Dr. Eccles Whyte
Jarrett Beatty
Henry A. Knox
Henry Joynt
James Hamilton
Richard Culkin
Edward McGleon
Patrick McLoughlin
Mary Shaw
William Malley
James Malley
Daniel Flanagan
Anthony Hoban
Honoria Mullarky
John Durkin
Michael O'Boyle
James Neary
Anthony Creane
Peter Murray
MichaelMcLoughlin
James Moyles
John Hogan
Michael O'Meally
Flax mill

ARDBUCLE'S ROW
1. Henry Savage
2. Michael Langan
3. Owen McKenna
4. Thomas Crean
5. Mary Mulholand
6. vacant
7. Thomas Moran
8. David Sadlier
9. Margaret Jossy
10. Peter Grehan
11. Thomas Crean
12. Samuel Willot

ARDOUGHAN
John Gallagher
Michael Ginty
Stephen Crony
Edward O'Hora
Peter O'Hora
Owen Larvan
Edward O'Hora
Peter O'Hora
James Gallagher
James Hunter
Daniel Loftus
Owen Larvan
AnthonyHannaghoe
Michael Moore
Andrew Best
James Ferguson
Patrick O'Hora
Terence Quinn
Col. F.A. Knox Gore
James Callaghan
James Hunter
Grave yard

ABBEY STREET ARDNAREE
1. John Hearne
2. Anne Hearne
3. Michael Igoe
4. Thomas Boyd
4. Corn store
5. ruins
6. Bridget Mulrooney
7. Patrick Timlin
8. Thomas Shovelin
9. ruins
10. vacant
11. Rev. John Griffin
12. vacant
13. Edward Hewetson
14. Margaret Bredin
15. James Devitt
16. ruins
17. James Murphy
18. Thomas Timlin
19. John Murphy
20. John Coleman
21/22. vacant
23. Thomas Loftus
24. Anne Hall
25. Laurence Graham
26. Honoria Knox
27. Richard Bredin
28. Eccles White
29. vacant
30. Patrick Meany
31. ruins
32. Alexander Sweeny
33/37. ruins
34. Police Barracks
35. James Gore's lodgers
36. James Kennedy
38. Alexander McDonnell
39. vacant
40. John Battle
41. Catherine Devanny
42. vacant
43. Peter Melvin
44. Peter Connor
45. Catherine Lackey
46. John Malley
47. Bridget McNulty
48. Aux. Workhouse
48b. stores
49. EdwardJennings
50. Bridget Shaw
51. Michael Boland
52. JamesMcDonnell
53. Patrick McLoughlin
54. John Devitt
55. ruins
56. Patrick McDonnell
57. Margaret Smith
58. Francis Neary
59. Neal Rooney
60. Bryan Rooney
61. Dominick Toole
62. ThomasMuffeny
63. James Gillespie
64. Francis Swift
65. James Kenny
66. Michael Fleming
67. Catherine Ford
68. Bridget Shaw
69. Anthony O'Hara
70. Andrew Carney
71. Edward McCormack
72. F.A. Knox Gore
73. John Gordon
74. vacant
75. Peter Rooney
76. Thomas Fox
77. Michael Foley
78. Andrew McDermott
79. Barbara Mayles
80. vacant
81. William Lundy
82. Charles Timlin
83. Mary Walsh
84. Michael Flannelly
85. Thomas Flynn
86. Michael Kelly
87. Patrick Ruane
88. Bridget Duffy
89. Phelim Carolan
90. Mary Walsh
91. Mary Molony
92. Anthony Cullen
93. John Walsh
94. Peter Hefron
95. John Cleary
96. Mary Devanny
97. Bridget Loftus
98. John Rooney
99. Anne Gillespie
100. ruins
101. Michael Finnerty
102. Margaret Sheridan
103.Andrew Carney
104. Thomas Loftus
105. WilliamCassidy
106. Patrick Durkin
107. Marcus Conlan
108. Thomas Conlan
109. MargaretMeally
110. John Regan
111. Andrew Battle
112. Patrick Keane
113. Patrick Garvan
114. Patrick Walsh
115/116. ruins
117. Patrick Harlow
118. PatrickFlannery
119. James Howley
120. vacant
121/122. ruins
123. Martin Loftus
124. Martin Cunningham
125. ruins
126. MichaelHowley
127. Thomas Clarke
128. Cormack Brennan
129. John Murphy
130. James McHale
131. Francis Long
132. MichaelMurray
133. Anne Bartle
134. vacant
135. Anne Melvin
136. Mary Gillespie
137. Thomas Finnigan
138. vacant
139/140. Edward Jennings
141. Edward Brennan
142. John Keane
143. George Rooney
144. Edward Jennings
145. James Kennedy
146. Patrick Melvin
147. Michael Regan
148. Michael McGauran
149. Peter Porter
150. HughGallagher
150. Corn store
151/152. vacant
153. MargaretCleary
154. Winifred O'Donnell
155. Margaret Nealon
156. Patrick Athy
157. Rev. Barracks
158/159. Rev. Thos. Feeny
160. Thomas Simpson
161. vacant
162. MargaretBredin
163. ---- Jones
164. Henry Joynt
165. Evans B.Grosse
166. Margaret Culkin
167. John Durkin
168. Edward Brennan
169. Robert Shaw

ABBEY STREET ARDNAREE
1. Thomas Fox
2. Anthony Carolan
3. ruins
4. James Burns
5. Thomas Jones
6. Peter Connor
7. Thomas Jones
8. Patrick McGlynn
9. Robert Shaw
10. Peter Connor
11. John Venard
12. John Battle
13. vacant
14. Anne Devany
15. Catherine Sweeny
16. Andrew Carney
17. Edward Murphy
18. Thomas Jones
19. Margaret Jones
20. Thomas Jones
21. John Duffy
22. WilliamCostelloe
23.ThomasMcIntyre
24. Thomas Jones
25. Andrew Judge
26. Thomas Jones
27. Thomas Fox
28. John Atkinson
29. Thomas Jones
30. Patrick Coppinger
31. Thomas Jones
32. JamesArmstrong

ARDNAREE OR SHANAGHY
James Harte
John Barrett
Bartholomew Gorman
Thomas Fox
James Kilgallen
John McGowan
Michael Corcoran
Owen Mears
Thomas Kilgallen
Michael Kelly
John Kilgallen
William Reddington
Ellen Moyles
Richard Bredin
James Hamilton
John Dunne
William G. Fox
Hugh Dunlop
Henry Joynt
John Wilson
John Hopkins
William Whittaker M.D.
Anthony McNulty
David Tolen
James Higgins
Michael McGowan
John Dogherty
Anthony Reid
Michael Furey
William Ham

ARTHUR STREET
1. Thomas Hughes
2. James McNally
3. PatrickMcDonnell
4. Martin Sweeny
5. store
6. Rev.EdwardLowe
7. Rev JohnKilwarry
8. Elizabeth Daly
9. Willoughby Fox
10. Edgar Knox
11. Peter Kelly
12. James Joynt
13. Eleanor Joynt
14. E.C.H. Perry
15. Col. F.A. Knox Gore
16. Willoughby Fox
17. National School
18/19. Martin Sweeny
20. Anne Lighton
21. Ulick McNally
22. James McGuinness
23. MichaelMcNally
24. WilliamAtkinson

ARRAN PLACE
1. vacant
2. Henry W.Gibbons

ARRAN STREET
1. William Merrick
2. Charles Lynot
3. John Prescot
4. John Devany
5. Elizabeth Daly
6. Michael Fleming

The Fair Green in Ballina, which is behind the Arts Centre, at the Market Square. There still is a market place here.

7. Hugh Hannick
8. John McMains
9. John McNally
10. WilliamGaughan
11. Charles Costello
12. Mathew Corcoran
13. Samuel McCleary
14. John Maxwell
15. John Connell
16. Alicia Reidy
17. William Burns
18. George Reidy
19. Thos. & George Bewry
20. Thomas West
21. vacant
22. William West
23. Anne Gallagher
24. Nicholas Murphy
25. Robt. & George Scott
26. Peter McDonnell

BALL ALLEY LANE

1. Anne Nealon
2. George Mash
2. Forge
3. ruins
4. Mary Maughan
5. Richard Gaughan
6. Edward Gillan
7. John Manly
8. Owen McHale
9. John Roach
10. Mary Clark
11. HonoriaHenigan
12. vacant
13. Charles Lynch

BRIDGE STREET

1. John Rooney
2. John McKenna
3. John Howley
4. James Mahon
5. Francis Wall
6. Thomas Muffany
7. John Muaghan
8. Patrick Cryan
9. Nicholas Henigan
10. Stephen Loftus
11. Andrew Derrig
12. Sidney Dixon
13. Michael Hope
14. John Hopkins
15. ThomasKilcullin
16. William Levingston
17. James Mathews
18. James McHale
19. Martin Quinn
20/22. Patrick McLoughlin
23. Anthony McLoughlin
24. Michael Cowley
25. James Hearins
26. John Commons
27. James Naughton
28. Maria Kelly
29. William Killegrew
29. Forge
30. John McCann
31. William Ham
32. Henry Devany
33. Thomas Langan
34. Francis Chambers
35. John Sweeny
36. Michael Fox
37. MichaelJennings
38. Michael Coen
39. James Coolican
40. Patrick Clarke
41. John Greene
42. Henry Broderick
43. Luke McGuinness
44. Martin Coleman
45. Patrick Crean
46. Anthony Crean
47. ThomasHenigan
48. Thomas Jordan

BROUGHANE LANE

1/2. Robert Moore
3. Martin Walsh
4. John Watts
5. Edward Richards
6. Patrick Walsh
7. Samuel Moore
8. Catherine Colby
9. Michael McHale
10. Mary Gilroy
11. vacant

BALLINA

Martin Clarke
Patrick Flynn
Daniel Loftus
Patrick Dowd
William Gillespie
James Fergus
James Mulligan
James Mahon
John Hopkins
Hugh Dunlop
Bridget Doherty
George Malley
Martin Sweeny
Michael Sweeny
Edward Atkinson
Mary Rogers
Sarah Rogers
Earl of Arran
Thomas Anderson
Edward Atkinson
John Crane
Peter Kelly
John Gill
James Mulligan
Peter Langan
William Gilboy
Anthony Ruane
Patrick Fallon
Patrick McDonagh
Edward Atkinson
Major OliverP.Burke
Anthony Joynt
John Burke
Major Crommer
Martin Timlin
Edward Timlin
Charles Timlin
James Kane
Sydney W. Jackson
Michael Doogan
James Timlin
Thomas Creane
William West
Superioress of Convent
Col. F.A. Knox Gore
John Dillon
John Golden
Patrick Egan
William Joynt
Michael O'Connor
Edward Kelly
Dispensary
William Massy
WilliamMcLoughlin
Peter Kelly
Patrick Melvin
Robert Kane
John Coolacan
Site of NewConvent
Edward Howley

BROOK STREET

1. James Jordan
2. John Dunne
3. ruins
4. William Merrick
5. Thomas Carroll
6. Mary O'Hora
7. vacant
8. Thomas Lyons
9. vacant
10. Bridget Convee
11. vacant
12. Mary Rogers
13. JohnMcCormack
14. RichardGaughan
15. Patrick Hannick
16. Mary Barrett
17. Bridget Crean
18. James Colclough
19. William Carroll
20. DanielColclough
21. BridgetMullarky
22. Richard Fawcett M.D.
23. Timothy O'Hora
24. Anne Cowley
25. Matthew Evans
26. Bryan Walsh
27. John Reilly
28. Anne Dennison
29. Mary Barrett
30. Robert Allen
31. Mary Doogher
32. Margaret Hanereagh
33. Thomas Culken
34. Denis Carroll
35. Honoria Fahy
36. William Kearney

BOHERNASOP

1. Mary Joyner
2/3. vacant
4. Mark McDonnell
5. Hugh Murray
6. John Carden
7. Michael Cawley
8. Edward O'Boyle
9. JamesMcCafferky
10. Patrick Donnelly
11. John Mitchell
12. James Cosgrave
13. Michael Hogan
14. John Daly
15. Martin Quin
16. Bryan Kelly
17. Michael Carden
18. John Donnelly
19. John Manly
20. Patrick McLoughlin
21. Michael Carlon
22. vacant
23. Michael Henaghan

24. Dominick Loftus
25. Martin Rouse
26. MichaelCoolican
27/28. vacant
29. John Gill
30. John Finnegan
31/32. vacant
33. Francis Flynn
34. James Cosgrave
35. Patt Slattery
36. John Flynn
37. MichaelCanavan
38. EleanorColeman
39. Martin Flynn
40. Thomas Quin
41. Mary Jennings
42. John Gill
43. Patrick Havey
44. Mary O'Hara
45. Arthur Dunlevy
46. MatthewEnglish
47. John Dunn
48. Roger Tighe
49. Patrick Fox
50. Sabina Gilgallin
51. Eleanor Connor
52. Honoria Walsh
53. John O'Donnell
54. Bridget Gilboy
55. John Franklin
56. vacant
57. John Reap
58. vacant
59. John Moran
60. Thady Gillen
61. Patrick Cadin
62. Peter Langan
63. John Gill
64. vacant
65. Michael Forde
66. Honoria Cunningham
67. Joseph Higgins
68. Catherine Langan
69/70. vacant
71. Peter Langan
72. Thomas Nixon
73. Arthur Dunlevy
74. William Gilboy
75. John Durkin
76. ruins
77. James O'Neil
78. Patrick Flannelly
79. Hugh Cosgrave
80. Richard Hogan
81. James Gallagher
82. John Gallagher
83. John Carroll
84. Francis Flynn
85. Patrick Carroll
86. Francis Flynn
87. Patrick Dougher
88. Thomas Sweeny
89. vacant
90. Thady Carden
91. Mary Joyner
92. Patrick Egan
93. Eleanor Cowley
94. Neal Siron
95. Michael Defly
96. James Cosgrave
97. Michael Ruane
98. Michael Atkinson
99. William Gaughan

BALLYHOLAN
Evans B. Grose
Corn mill
James Ferguson
Edward Howley
James Walker
Andrew Ruddy
Patrick O'Hara
Mary Clarke
Patrick Judge
William Jordan
Bartholomew Ferguson
Patrick Jordan
James Jordan
James Ferguson
Bridget Ferguson
Col. Edward Wingfield

BUNREE
David Kelly
Patrick Halloran
Farrel Battle
John Kelly
James Dolan
Owen Kilcawley
James Boylan
Manus Mullarky
Richard Culkin
William Kennedy
Johanna Coleman
William Ryan
Robert Jones
Thomas McGee
Anne Molloy
Patrick Coleman
John Durkin
James McCormack
Anna Gallagher
Corn mill
Ellen Hennigan
Mary Howley
Cecily Halloran
Denis Kilgallen
Robert Jones
David Kelly
Robert Jones
Ellen Hennigan
David Swift
John Moghan
Mary Donegan
Robert Jones
Catherine O'Hara
Richard Coleman
James Diamond
Robert Jones
James Loftus
John Kelly
Richard Culkin
James McAndrew
James Dolan
James McAndrew
John McNulty

BALLYNA-RAHA
Michael McGowan
Thomas Timlin
William McHale
Patrick Judge
Peter Lavelle
James Finirty
------- Clarke
Patrick Robertson
John Finirty

BEHYBAUN
John Myles
----- McHale
Patrick Barrett
James Finirty
John Lynch
Myles McHale
Anthony Sweeny
John McGowan
Patrick Crean

BELLEEK
Col. F.A. Knox Gore

CROCKETSTOWN VILLAGE
Lodgers
Henry Hennigan
Patrick Hennigan
James Lacken
James Flynn
John Hennigan
James Walsh
James Carney
Martin Cowley
Anthony Shaw
Mary Flynn
Patrick Melvin
Eleanor Hennigan
Joseph Temple
John Timlin
Samuel Ray
Michael Devitt
Edward Atkinson
John Connor
Peter Conway
AlexanderGalbraith
School hse.
Marcus McNulty
James Convy
Michael Togher
Robert Baker
Edward Atkinson
Michael Connor
Anthony McLoughlin
Patrick McLoughlin
Thomas Melvin
William Gutherie
John Joyce
Maryanne Little
Matthew Conway
Thomas Conway
Martin Cowel

CHAPEL STREET ARDNAREE
1. Abbey &grave yd
2. Henry Joynt
3. R.C. Chapel
4/5. Edward Atkinson
6. Anthony Conmy
7. Mary Devanny
8. John Keane
9. Patrick O'Hara
9. Lime Kiln
10. Thomas Boyd
11. Thomas Nealon
12. Charles Dunlevy
13. Patrick Melvin
14. Patrick Moran
15. vacant
16. George Leech
17. Patrick Kennedy
18. vacant
19. John Barrett
20. Edward Gallagher
21. Thomas Culkin
22. Anne Crawford
23. James Burns
24. Phelim Rice
25. Edward Hope
26. William Rafter

CHURCH STREET ARDNAREE
1. John Judge
2. Martin Reynolds
3. Michael Walsh
4. ruins
5. Maurice Walsh
6. vacant
7. Martin McNulty
8. Bridget Carroll
9. Patrick Brogan
10. Peter Connellan
11. Thomas Melvin

CHURCH STREET ARDNAREE
1. vacant
2. Bridget Meally
3. Mary Melin
4. Mary Power
5. Thomas Mahon
6. Anthony Timlin
7. Corn stores
8. Robert Verschoyle
9. Maryanne Little & Andrew Clarke
10/11. vacant
12. William Whittaker M.D.
13. Thomas Jones

COMMONS
Hugh Dunlop
Patrick Crane
William Merrick

CLOONTY-KILLEW
Harriet Gardiner
John Hynes
William McAdam
William Carr
James Browne
Patrick Monnelly
William Collins
William Jennings
William Doherty
Farrell Battel
James Scott

COOLCRAN
James Joynt
James Scott

CREGGAUN
William Geraghty
Michael Howley
Thomas Melville
James Loftus
Lawrence McHale
Peter Lavelle
Patrick Hanahoe

CROFTON PARK
Dr. William Whitaker
Robert Hunter
Henry Crofton
John McAndrew
Patrick McAndrew
WinifredMcAndrew
Patrick Egan
Thomas Egan
Michael Conby
Frank Conby
John Egan
Daniel Egan
Patrick Conby
John Goran
Patrick Goran

CLOON-GLASNEY
John Mullany
William Murphy
Patrick Gillespie
James Ferguson
John Kane
Edward Hare
Henry Kane
Peter Hare
James Barron
Patrick Sweeny
Mary Clarke
James Mullany
Thomas Barron
Martin Clarke
Patrick Clarke

CLOONTURK
Patrick Melville
James Murray
James Melvin
Thomas Melvin
Luke McGuinness
Thomas Jones
John Hagerty
Patrick Caverty
Martin Ralph
Edward Hobin
Michael Murphy
Patrick Kelly
John Kelly
Martin Melville
Patrick Melville

CULLEENS
Charles Atkinson
John Maxwell
Anthony Rogan
Edward Rogan
Peter Walsh
James Walsh
John Rogan
Patrick Rogan
John Moran
William Brennan
James Flynn
Patrick Rogan
Richard O'Hora
Edward Langan
Patrick Langan
Patrick Loftus
William Brennan
John Moran
Patrick Loftus
Edward Clarke
John Carr
Bryan Carr
Andrew Patterson
John Patterson
Anthony Kaveny
Philip Kaveny
Patrick Brennan
Judith Kilevary
John O'Hora

Industry in Ballina

Ballina owes its origins to O'Hara, Lord Tyrawley, who built the first street here and established a cotton factory on the Bunree river. He persuaded many skilled linen workers from Ulster to locate here. In 1801 Mr. Malley started a large tobacco and snuff production factory in the town. In the 1830's, Mr. J. Brennan from Belfast opened a large slaughterhouse and bacon curing operation. Two large ale and porter breweries were set up to make malt. Thomas Ham's father and Mr. Hendry looked after the local porter supply. Rope making was manufactured from jute yarn. Men wound the rope on drum like wheels and worked for Dillon, Merrick, Coen and Gallagher, who were eventually put out of business by cheaper imports. Fishing was the most reliable trade in town, with a bountiful supply of salmon that kept many of the townsfolk busy each year

Captain Bolton

CHURCH STREET
1. Church & Grave yard
2. Richard Diamond
3. Patrick O'Hara
4. James Matthews
5. Honoria Carolan
6. Edward Ford
7. Michael Fox
8. Richard Bredin
8. Corn mill
9. Flour mill
10. vacant
11. Michael Kelly
12. Michael McDermott
13. James Matthews
14. Patrick Moran
15. vacant
16. John Hearne
17. John McDonnell
18. Anthony Mears
19. Henry Blane

CHARLES STREET
1. Police Barracks
2. Thomas McAndrew
3. Rev. Thomas Armstrong
4. Presbyterian Church,School hse
5. Capt. John Atkinson

CLOONSLAUN
Frances Reddington
Patrick Goaghan
Patrick Reddington
Michael Kilmartin
Sarah Campbell
Patrick McGowan
John Reddington
John Willis
James Hamilton
Dominick Halloran
Timothy Halloran
Thomas Philbin
Michael Philbin
Michael Weir
Martin Conmey
Thomas Conmey
Anthony Dogherty
Richard Murray
Bridget Murray
Simon Judge
Martin Murray
Pound
James Dogherty
Richard Murray
Owen Murray
John O'Brien
Honoria Melody
Michael Murray
James McHale
Thomas Walsh
Anthony Walsh
John Philbin
Patrick Murray
Anne McGowan
Patrick Paddin
John Walsh
Bridget Philbin
John O'Brien
Thomas Paddin
Michael O'Brien
James Halloran
John Munnelly
Ellen Walsh
John Walsh
Francis Reddington
Thomas Philbin
John O'Brien
Patrick Paddin
Robert Verschoyle

CARROW-CUSHLAUN
William Ham
Garrett Beatty
Patrick Jennings
Patrick Melody
Patrick McNulty
Patrick Hennigan, s
Patrick Hennigan, j
Patrick Hennigan (Long)
Patrick McNulty
Michael Connor
Edward Myles
Patrick Melvin
Samuel Bredin
William Timlin
Dominick Halloran
Timothy Halloran
Anthony Weir
John McNulty
WinifredMcDonnell
John Wilson
John Mullins
Owen Murray
Thomas Philbin
Michael Philbin
Michael Weir
Martin Comney
Thomas Comney
Anthony Weir
Anthony Dogherty
Richard Murray
Bridget Murray
Simon Judge
Honoria Melody
James Mannock

CARROW-CUSHLAUN WEST
Rev. Joseph Verschoyle
John Hearne

CASTLE ROAD
1. Rev. William Hamilton
2. John McEvoy
3. Robert Foy
4. Michael Curran
5. Rev. William Hamilton
6. Mary Joyner
7. William Malley
8/9. vacant
10. Julia Heuston
11. Thomas Dillon
12. John Crow
13. Winifred Harris
14. Patrick Crow
15. James Gardner
16. Michael Callaghan
17. Anthony Gaughan
18. John Ormsby
19. BridgetCosgrave
20. Patrick Healy
21. Barbara Clark
22. Anne Nicholson
23. WilliamWilliams
24. D&J. McDonald
25/26.MartinHeally
27. James Hillas

CONWAY'S LANE
1. Store & kiln
2. Peter McDermott
3. Mary Gallagher
4. John Moghan
5. Margaret Foynan
6. Patrick Flynn
7. Thomas Henigan
8. MichaelHeffernan
9. Thomas Jennings

COCKLE STREET
1. Anthony Lynch
2. James Wilson
3. Bridget Molloy
4. Patrick Clarke
5/7. ruins
6. Gregory Ansborough
8. Thomas O'Hara
9. ruins
10. Mary Melvyn
11. Patrick Tobin
12. Patrick Timony
13. Michael Buckley
14. ruins
15. Michael Buckley
16/17. ruins

CRANNAGH
William Gardiner
Robert McAndrew
Michael Cawley
Ellen Timlin
Patrick Sweeny
Patrick Cawley
William Sweeny

DURKIN'S LANE
1. Patrick Hopper
2. Peter Kelly
3. Peter Cawly
4. PatrickMcDonnell
5. Charles Lynnott
6. James O'Hara
7. Hugh Andres
8. Patrick Keefe
9. Robert Mash
9. Forge
10. Mathew Corcoran
11. John Gordon

DILLON'S ROW
1/3. Monica Dillon
4. John McCormack
5/6. vacant
7. E.C.J.H. Perry
8. Rev. PeterNowlan
9. John N. Russell & Sons

DIXON'S LANE
1/2. vacant
3. Mary Flanagan
4. Martin Quinan
5. James Callaghan
6. Anne Kelly

DOWD'S LANE
(off Old Garden st.)
1. Anne McAndrew
2. vacant
3. Anne Walsh
4. Mary Walsh
5. vacant

FRANCIS STREET
1. William Malley
2. Henry Joynt
3. Patrick Crean
4. John C. Urquhart
5. Isabella Short
6. Rev. John Gore
7/8. William Malley
9. Elizabeth Handy
10/11. vacant
12. William Malley
13. Sarah Malley
14. Court hse.
15. Bridewell
16MichaelO'Connor

FARRAN-DEELION
James Ferguson
Michael Hanahoe
Thomas Howley
Michael Roche
Michael Flynn
Patrick Hora
Charles Howley
Anthony Healy
Thomas Battle
-------- Carbine
John Howley
John Hanahoe
Bartholomew Hanahoe
Patrick Cosgreve
Patrick Hoare
Anthony Hoare
Michael Cosgreve
Michael Hora

FARRANNOO
Col. F.A. Knox Gore
WilliamMcLoughlin
John Reddy
Michael O'Hora
John Kenny
Alexander Walsh
Michael Kenny
James Gaughan
Bryan Foody
Michael Meny

FRANKLINS LANE
(OFF MILL ST)
1. Bryan Scanlan
2. Mary Walsh
3. John Browne
4. Michael McKenna
5. Mary Preston
6. Michael McHale
7. Thomas Duffy
8. Thomas Goldin
9. Bryan Ward

GARRANKEEL
Col. F.A. Knox Gore

GORTEEN
Martin Clarke
Louis G. Jones
John Hopkins
James Mahon
Francis Wall
Francis Carroll
Bridget Doherty
John McCann
James Curran
John Walker

GORTATOGHER
MichaelMcLoughlin
John Myles
William Hamilton
Patrick Thompson
John Meerick
Anthony Cullen
Thomas McAnalty
Daniel Gillespie
Michael Mulderig
Alexander Gillespie
Anthony Gillespie
John Orme

GLEBE
Rev. Joseph Verschoyle

GARDEN STREET
1. Anne Daly
2. John Higgins
3. John Murphy
4. Peter Rooney
5. James Connor
6. Anthony Henigan
7. Jane Sullivan
8. Capt. John Smith
9. Susanna Stock
10. Anthony Joynt
11. Michael Sweeny
12. William Joynt
13. William Lundy
14. Samuel Strodgen
15. Francis Knox
16. Henry Cummins
17. JamesMcDonnell
18. Anthony Joynt
19. John Sweeny
20. ruins
21.PatrickCallaghan
22. Michael Cullen
23. Thomas Costello
24. ruins
25. John Gilboy
26. Robert Power
27. PatrickBroderick
28. James Moughan
29. Margaret Smith
30. James O'Regan

GALLAGHER'S LANE
(off King street)
1. Peter Murray
2. Anne Kavanagh
3/4. vacant
5. Martin Coleman
6. William Hefron
7. Margaret Clarke
8. Patrick Jennings

HART'S LANE
(OFF MILL ST)
1. John Reilly
2. vacant
3. Sarah Hart

HILL STREET
1. William Malley
2. Thomas Feenarty
3. Thomas Hegarty
4. Andrew Melvin
5. Mary Shannon
6. William Ormsby
7. Patrick Jordan
8. John Green
9. Denis McKenna
10. John Heally
11. NicholasMurphy
12. Henry Morrow
13. Martin Hart
14. Michael Walsh
15. Patrick Banks
16. Thos Geraghty
17. Michael Hope
18. Thos Geraghty
19. Mathew West

JOHN STREET
1. John Burns
2. Luke Kerins
3. John Hope
4. James Redington
5. John Hope
6. James Hart
7. Martin Roach
8. James Mahon
9. James Doheny
10. Edward Cosgrave
11. Catherine Porter
12. John Sheridan
13. John McKenna
14/15. vacant
16. David Baird
17/18. Edward Cosgrave
19. vacant
20. Baptist Preaching hse.
21. S.R & T. Brown
22. Anne Atkinson

KNOCKALYRE OR DOWNHILL
Rev. Thomas Feney
Anne Gallagher
Patrick Judge
AnthonyMulrooney
John McHugh
Anthony Flynn
James McAndrew
William Symes

KNOX STREET
1/2. James Jordan
3. John Devanny
4. Thomas Nealon
5. WilliamHeffernan
5. Market stall
6. John Hannon
7. Richard Wilson
7b. Bonding store
8. Robert Wilson
9. Nicholas Murphy
10. William Richy
11. Robert G. Baxter
12. George Higgins
13. John McAndrew
14. Edward Hanley
15. John Talbot
16. Robert P. Bourke
17. Mathias V. Ferguson
18. MaryanneJoyner
19. vacant
20/21. Nicholas Flynn
22. ThomasFinnigan
23. Andrew Clancy
24. Edward McCormack
25. John Dunne
26. Patrick Gilligan
27. Michael McAndrew
28. Michael Hynes
29. Palmer Kirkwood
30. PatrickGallagher
31. Thaddeus Loftus
32. Frederick Potts
33. vacant
34. James Ward
35. Custom hse.
36. Joseph Atkinson
37. George Higgins
38. Richard Fausett
39. Charles Bianconi
40. store
41. Thomas Anderson
42. Robert P. Bourke
43. Thomas Anderson
44. John McCulloch
45. Rev. Robert Allen & the Misses Bourke
46. Marcus Devlin
47. Old ballroom
48. Michael Foley
49. Thomas Ham
50. John McCulloch
51. St. John Purcel
51. Provinc. Bank
52. Bernard Flynn
52. Charles Boyd
53. Robertson & Dunlop
54. Robert Atkinson
55. Elizabeth Hamilton
56. Monica Dillon
57. Adam Pettigrew
58. William Merrick

KILMOREMOY
Col. F.A. Knox Gore
James Higgins
James Loftus
Michael Merry
Robert Atkinson

KNOCKANELO
Anthony Loftus
Anthony Kavanagh
John Kavanagh
Mary Loftus
Thomas Loftus
John Gilligan
Thomas Kavanagh
James Clarke
Rachael Watt
Sir William Palmer

KNOCKEGAN AND CLOONAGH BEG
Patrick Caden
John Kavanagh
Francis O'Neill
Thomas Rape
Patrick Kavanagh
Margaret Kavanagh
Anthony Hughes
Earl of Arran(Bog)

KING STREET
1. William Whelan
2. David Baird
3. Joseph Atkinson
4. Evans B. Grose
5. Mary Leacy
6. Ellen Devitt
7. John G. Swift
8. James Mahon
9. James B. Nolan
10. Margaret Irwin
11. vacant
12. Richard Grehan
13. James Barrett
14. DominickJordan
15. Eliza Lenaghan
16. Maria Devitt
17. Patrick McNulty
18. Daniel Heathen
19. John Clarke
20. Michael Hope
21. vacant
22. Sarah Smith
23. Patrick Jennings
24. Patrick Forde
25. Thomas Corcoran
26. Letitia Gillum
27. Anthony Burke
28/29. vacant
30. John Dillon
31. James Jennings
32. Thomas Conway
33/34. Hugh Gallagher
35. Mary Manley
36. vacant
37PatrickMcDonnell

KNOCKLEHAUGH
Thomas Jones
James Hamilton
William West
Edward Cosgrave
Anne Gallagher
Charles Howley
Michael Kelly
Stephen Loftus
Hugh Dunlop

KNOCKSBARRETT
Edward Atkinson

LLOYD'S LANE
1. vacant
1b. Robert P. Bourke
2. store
3/4. Matthias Ferguson
5. Diana Slevin

LOWER PIPER HILL
1. James Sproule
2. Methodist Chapel
3. Rev. Gibson McWillan
4. Patrick McLoughlin
5. Christopher Dunlevy
6. Bryan Hannan
7. vacant
8. Thomas Gilgallin
9. Patrick Clarke
10. George Huston
11. Michael Butler
12. Patrick Flynn
13. John Diamond
14. Patt Daly
15. John Cunningham
16. Edward Lynch
17. Mary McKenna
18. Edward Cosgrave
19. Luke Noone
20. ruins
21. Sabina Merrick
22. Elizabeth Mackey
23. Mary Lacy
24. ruins
25. Martin Hesneen
26. ruins
27. John Gibbons
28. Anthony Chambers
29. ruins
30. Honoria Barrett
31. Margaret Lane
32. Anthony Chambers
33. Patrick Hope
34. James Stuart
35. Peter Kelly
36. John Reid
37. Anne Ellis
38. James Mulligan
39. Patrick Clarke
40. Thomas Walsh
41. John Dunn
42. vacant
43. Thomas Boland
44. Michael Gaughan
45. ThomasMuffony
46. Edward Callaghan
47. Barbara Melvin
48. John Lawton
49. Thomas Hanaghoo
50. William McHale

LAGHTADAWANNAGH
Col. F.A. Knox Gore
Daniel O'Hora
Captain Bolton
Bryan Foody
John Kenny
Jane Gaughan
Patrick Brennan
Jane Kilevary
John O'Hora
John Lyons

LANGANS' LANE
(off Bohernasop)
1. Daniel Dowd
2. Robert Long
3. Eleanor Goldin
4. Michael Fox
5. Robert Brighton
6. vacant
7. Mary Kearney
8. vacant
9. Mary Harrisson

McLOUGHLIN'S LANE
(off Lwr. Piper Hill)
1. vacant
2. Patrick McKenna
3. Bryan Callaghan
4. John Gallagher
5. vacant
6. JamesMcLoughlin
7. Patrick Hope
8. William Hildebrand
9.ThomasNewcomb
10. PatrickMcKenna
11. George Kelly
12. Thomas Scott

McCANN'S LANE
(off Lower Piper Hill)
1. Patrick McLoughlin
2. ruins
3. John Tully
4. Patrick Kennedy
5. EdwardCallaghan

MULLAUNS
Thomas Kilgallen
Matthew Kilgallen
John Kilgallen
Patrick Kilgallen
John Willis
Patrick Goghan
John Reddington
Patrick McGowan
James Hamilton

MULLAUNS
Thomas Kilgallon
Matthew Flynn
Michael Rafter
Thomas Dillon
Patrick O'Donnell
Bernard Cafferkey

MILL STREET
1. Col. F.A. Knox Gore
2/3. vacant
4. Michael Rochford
5. ruins
6. James Cafferky
7. Bridget Brogan

MILL STREET
1/2. vacant
3. William Brislane
4. Anthony Hart
5. ruins
6. William Hefron
7. Martin Culkin
8. John McCann
9. ruins
10. Bryan Carr
11. John Franklin
12. Richard Forbes
13. Martin Murphy
14. John Howly
15. Michael Fox
16. James McHale
17. WilliamAtkinson
18. ruins
19. Francis Chambers
20. Thomas Garvin
21. John Buchanan
22. James Lynch
23. Patrick Browne
24. John Browne
25. Anthony Brogan
26. Mary Banks
27. ThomasHastings
28. Bridget McClusky
29. John Heston
30/31. James Helly
32. John McNulty
33. Patrick Hearns
34. Patrick McLoughlin
35. ruins
36. WilliamAtkinson
36. Corn mill
37. Thomas Ruddy
38. ruins
39. Thomas Loftus
40. ruins
41. Peter Walsh
42. Edward Clarke
43. vacant
44. Richard Ryan
45. Patrick Sweeny
46. Anthony Brown
47. Matthew McKenna
48. Richard Brown

NURE
James Joynt

NEW GARDEN STREET
1. Robert Moore
2. Patrick Gallagher
3. Manus O'Donnell
4/5. ruins
6. Michael Hughes
7. Patrick Joyce
8. Daniel McGovin
9. Patrick Philbin
10. John Gilbride
11. Annesley Knox
12. John Malley
13. John Brennan
14. Anne McKenna
15. Anthony Kelly
16. ruins
17. Michael O'Regan
18. Robert Jones
19. John Knox
20. Robert Moore
21. William Carr
22. vacant
23. Martin Murray
24. James Walsh
25. William Gilbert
26. John Mannix
27. John Sharkey
28. Peter Howley
29. Patrick Joyce
30. Andrew Loftus
31. James Murray
32/33. John Bourke
34. ruins
35. James Ferguson
36. ruins
37. James Murray
38. PatrickHarrisson
39/40. vacant
41. Patrick Dowd
42. Patrick Holmes
43. John Carden
44. Col. F.A. Knox Gore

OLD GARDEN STREET
1. store
2. Eleanor Joynt
2. Toll & Customs of fairs & markets
3. Campbell Fair
4. Sarah Roach
5. Robert Gill
6. James Walker
7. John Perry
8. John Neary
9. William Boyd
10. John Sweeny

11. Henry Lochran
12. Sidney Jackson
13. Peter McNally
14. Michael Walsh
15. William Foody
16. Michael Walsh
17. Joseph Robinson
18. John Kelly
19. James Timlin
20. James Preston
21. Thomas Hughes
22. Sidney Jackson
23. Patrick Egan
24. ruins
25. George Orme
26. Ellen Cassidy
27. James Patterson
28. James McNally
29. WilliamGillespie
30. Eliza Hanna
31. William Onions
32. Peter Gallagher
33. Edward Timlin
34. Martin Timlin
35. Thaddeus Loftus
36. Edward Bourke
37. Thomas Ruddy
38. Michael O'Dowd
39. Anne Nealon
40. Anne Mash
41. John Curran
42. Francis Kean
43. Michael Egan
44. Robertson and Dunlop
45. Michael Sweeny
46. Martin McHugh
47. James Currin
48. Joseph Hamly
49. Catherine Newcombe
50. John McDermott
51. Michael Doogan
52. Thomas Mangan
53. John Moyles

PAWN OFFICE LANE
(off Knox st)
1. Hugh Gallagher
2. vacant
3. Patrick Broderick
4. Patrick Jordan
5. George Higgins
6. Nicholas Murphy
7. Robert Wilson
8. Edward Hanley

POUND STREET
1. John Quinn
2. James O'Donnell
3. William McCormack
4. Anthony Joynt
5. Thomas Crean
6. Michael Cullen
7. John O'Hara
8. Catherine Dowd

POKES LANE
Off Old Garden St.
1. John Doherty
2. ruins
3. James Hart
4. Martin Clark
5. John Walsh
6. Michael Rouse
7. John O'Hora
8. ruins
9. James Loftus
10. Michael Nealon
11. John McGuigin

PADDIN'S LANE
(off Uppr Piperhill)
1/6. vacant
7. Patrick McLoughlin

QUIGNALECKA
John Rutledge
Bridget Walsh
Mary Convay
Capt.WilliamWright
John Atley
Matthew Conway
Thomas Conway
Martin Cowel
Michael Gallagher
Matthew Rolston
Thomas Naughton
Rt. Rev. Thos. Feney

RAISH
James Walker

REILLY'S LANE
1. Sarah Stanton
2. Tobias Conlan
3. ruins
4. Thomas Rutledge
5. Catherine Loftus and Mary Carolin

RAHINS ROAD
1. Bridget Butler
2. William Atkinson
3. ruins
4. William Pape
5. Col. Tobias Kirkwood
6. William Foody
7. Michael O'Hara
8. ruins
9. Patrick Hesneen
10. Patrick Foody
11. Thomas Monahan
12. Catherine Moran
13. James Kean

RATHKIP
James Brogan, sen
James Brogan, jun
Marcus Connellan
George Kennedy
Anthony Naughtin
Patrick Foy
John Willis
John Loftus
Michael Furey
James Murphy
Patrick Furey
Thomas McNulty
Mary Burke
Andrew Shaw
William McNulty
Sr. W. Roger Palmer
James Harte
John Barrett
Bartholomew Gorman
Thomas Fox
James Kilgallen
John McGowan
Thomas Kilgallen
Owen Mears

RAHANS
George Orme
James Butler
Catherine Butler
John Myles
James Finirty
Bridget Finirty
Ellen Joyce
Luke McGuiness
William Meyrick
Hugh Dunlop

RATHNA-CONEEN
George Orme
School hse.
Daniel Haydon
Catherine Butler
James Butler
James Finirty
Michael Hora
Patrick Hora sen.
Patrick Hora jun.

SHAMBLES STREET
1. Martin Murphy
2. John Brady
3. Michael Hefron
4. Martin Sweeny
5. ruins
6. Richard Flynn
7. Michael Hefron
8. ruins
9. James Sharkey
10. Luke McGuinness
10. shambles
11. Thomas Hefron
12. William Foody

SLIEVENA-GARK
Patrick Donoughan
Michael Hobin
Anthony Hobin
Philip Mulderick
Edward Carr
Luke Carr
Martin Shea
Thomas Shea
Patrick Kane
Patrick Kane jun.

SOLOMON'S LANE
(off Mill St.)
1. Michael Quinan
2. James Kennedy
3. Michael Cowley
4. William Kelegrew

TULLYEGAN
Thomas Murray
Martin Walsh, jun.
John Walsh
John McLoughlin
John McLoughlin, j
John Murray
Hugh McLoughlin
Bryan Henegan
Martin Walsh, sen
Michael Walsh
MichaelMcLoughlin
Patrick Walsh

TULLYSLEVA
Thomas Battle
Edward Ward
Michael Battle
Michael Hope
John Walsh
Bryan Mullany
John Mullany
Patrick Ruane
Winifred Holmes
Anthony Commons
Michael Mullany
Patrick Burke
John Goran
Edmund Dugan
Mary Gore
Anthony Hora
Anthony McNulty
Patrick Kelly
Anne Kelly
John Loftus
John Myles
Owen Burke
Patrick Dowd
Peter Cosgrave

TIDEWAY OF RIVER MOY
Maryanne Little and Andrew Clarke
(salmon fishery rights)

UPPER PIPER HILL
1. John Rooney
2. Mary Foody
3. John Branigan
4. Bridget Neilis
5. John Walsh
6. Michael Hegarty
7. John Gillespie
8. Patrick Quin
9. Patrick Hanaghoo
10. WilliamAtkinson
11. John Battle
12. Elizabeth Rowe
13. James Sweeny
14. Eleanor Moffitt
15.MichaelMulligan
16. Thomas Murray
17. John Geraghty
18. BernardCafferky
19. John Buchanan
20. BernardCafferky
21. vacant
22. Thomas Brown
23. Thomas Benane
24. Patrick Madden
25. Margaret Kilcar
26.PatrickO'Donnell &BernardCafferky
27. Patrick Madden
28.PatrickO'Donnell
29. John Dixon
30.PatrickO'Donnell
31. William McHale
32. Hannah McHale
33. Bridget Doyle
34. Anne Foody
35. Michael Cawley
36.PatrickO'Donnell
37. Peter McNalty
38.PatrickO'Donnell
39. MichaelCoolican
40. vacant
41. ThomasCafferky
42. Francis Wall
43. Mary Merrick
44. Thomas Jordan
45/46. vacant
47. Michael Lynch
48. Mary Duggan
49. Michael Brennan
50. Jane Kelly
51. Daniel Grehan
52. Caterine Boland
53. Patrick Feenaghty
54. John Langan
55. Patrick Hopkins
56. ruins
57. James Clarke
58. Michael Nary
59. ruins
60. John Heston
61. ruins
62. Michael Rafter
63. Michael Geraghty
64. Patrick Grimes
65. John Buchanan
66. Edward Franklin
67. Neal Duggan
68. Catherine Callaghan
69. James Duffy

VICTORIA PLACE
1. vacant
2. Charles Downey
3. John Little
4. James Higgins

WATER LANE
1. John Loftus
2. Patrick Herins
3. Michael Hope
4. Bryan Cafferky
5. James Healy
6. Peter Kelly
7. Owen Conway
8. ruins
9. Bridget Gallagher
10. William Anderson
11. John Clark
12. ruins

TITHE APPLOTMENTS AND THE NATIONAL LIBRARY

These Tithe books give the Townland name, landholders name, land area and tithes payable. Some give the landlords name. The Tithes can provide clues especially when a holding passed from father to son in the years 1828 up to the 1851 Griffiths books. They are located in the Nat. Library & Archives as well as Mayo's Co. Library. THE NATIONAL LIBRARY has a large collection of printed books, newspapers, maps, photographs and manuscripts. Well worth a visit. Catholic Parish Registers are the most frequently requested resource. Tel:(01)6030200

Ballina Electors Register of 1936/37

THE inclusion of the 1936/37 Electors List will prove interesting to locals who remember the characters from that generation. All of the old local characters we knew and heard about, are listed, before many joined the vanishing Irish on the emigration trail. All people with the same surname in each townland and street are listed together. To be listed, one had to be 18. In 1841, the population of Ballina was 5,313. In 1853 the population fell to 4,560 as a result of the famine years. By 1911, the population remained static at 4,662 and has slowly recovered since then. By 1936, it reached 5,674 and by 1998, it increased to 6,063. p.s. - where there are two townlands of the same name, this is where the townland is split into rural/urban or divided between two parishes.

ABBEY STREET

Armstrong Thomas, Edward, Elizabeth, Patrick, Lucinda, Thomas, May, Charles.
Barrett John, Thomas.
Burke James, Lizzie.
Callaghan Annie.
Carney James, Edward, Kathleen, James, James P.
Carroll Bridget, Thomas, James, Margaret, Annie, Thomas.
Casey John, Patrick, Kate.
Caslin John, Anne.
Cawley Thomas.
Clarke Mary Bridget, James, Maria, Michael, Maryanne, Mary, Patrick.
Convey Thomas.
Convy Margaret.
Courtney Mary.
Cosgrave John, Bridget.
Costello J.G.
Crean Michael, Jane.
Cunningham Mary.
Devany Thomas, Sarah.
Diamond Bridget, Michael.
Dodd Delia.
Donohoe Stephen, Ellen.
Duffy Margaret, Martin, Bridget, Sean.
Durcan Ellen, Martin, Margaret, Catherine.
Durkin Patrick.
Dwyer Thomas, Annie, Thomas, Albert.
Farris Charles, Kate.
Ferguson Bertie, Michael, Ellen, Thomas.
Finlan Margaret, Michael.
Finnerty William, Delia.
Fitzpatrick Patrick.
Flemming Patrick, Maggie.
Flynn Michael, John, Agnes, Michael, Kate, Thomas, Patrick.
Foley Lilly, Celia, William, Kathleen, Ted.
Foster Catherine.
Furlong Paul.
Gallagher Patrick, Jane, Hugh, James.
Gannon Patrick, Nancy.
Gibbons Patrick, Nora.
Gilboy Michael, Lena.
Gillan Daniel, Mary Ellen.
Gilmartin Lucy, Charles, Kathleen, Mark, Denis.
Gilvarry Winifred.
Ginty John, Mary.
Gordon Bernard.
Halloran Patrick, Sarah.
Hannick John, Margaret.
Harte John, Bridget.
Healy Lizzie, Annie, May, Michael.
Heffernan Mary, Thomas, Margaret.
Henry Paul, Agnes.
Holmes Patrick, Margaret.
Howley Martin, Paddy, William, Winifred, Patrick, Peter, Martin.
Irwin Kate.
Jackson Annie, James, Bridget, Michael, Elizabeth
Jennings John, Bridget.
Jordan James, Agnes, Mary, Eddie, Agnes.
Judge Patrick, John, Annie, Mary, John, Margaret, James, Martin, Ellen.
Kane Patrick.
Keane Bridget, Frank, Patrick, Mary, John.
Kearney William, Annie.
Kennedy Patrick, Mary, Edward, Thomas, Annie, Katie, Michael.
Kilcullen Patrick, Mary, Anthony.
Kilgallon John, Mary, Thomas.
Lally Edward, Kate, Martin, Alice.
Lavelle William, Annie.
Loftus Agnes, Margaret, Michael, Teresa, Dan,Sarah
Lynch Kate.
Lynn Thomas, Kate.
Maloney Elizabeth, John, John.
Mangan John, Mary Jane.
Marley James, Elizabeth.
Maughan Nora.
Melody Anthony, Patrick, Bridget, Margaret, Michael
Melough William.
Molloy Eileen, Paddy, John, Ellen.
Moran Michael, Belinda.
Mullen Nellie.
Murray Maryanne, Patrick, Thomas.
Murphy Thomas, Lizzie, Madeline, Martin, John.
McCaffrey Eileen, Eugene, Eugene, Peter, Mary, William, Mary, Herbert.
McDermott Nellie, Bridget, Patrick, William, Mary, Annie.
McLoughlin May, Patrick, Maryellen, John, William, Patrick, Margaret.
McMullen Susanna, Mary.
McShane Patrick, Annie.
Melody Kitty.
Monks Paddy.
Naughton Annie, Thomas, John, May, Martin, John, Bridget, Mary, Michael
O'Boyle Michael, Kate, May
O'Callaghan John, May.
O'Halloran Barbara.
Rafter Mary, Patrick, Maria, Pat, Nancy, James, Thomas, Mary, James, Patrick, Winifred.
Rattray John, Victoria.
Roache John, John, Alfred.
Robinson Bridget, Joe.
Ruane Anthony, Annie.
Ruddy James, Thomas, Mary Clare, Patrick, John, Martin, Paddy, Kate, James, Bridget, Michael.
Shaw Lena, William.
Sullivan Edward, Annie.
Sweeney Thomas, Annie, Thomas.
Stock Val.
Tierney John, Mary.
Timlin James, Bridget.
Wall Joseph.
Walsh Thomas, Bridget, Joseph, Agnes.

ABBEY STREET (HALF QUARTER)

Corley Francis, Kathleen.
McDermott J.J., Oonagh.
O'Boyle Martin.

ABBEYHALF QUARTER

Donnell Bertie.
Gallagher Helena, Hugh.
Judge Michael.
O'Donnell Patrick.
McLoughlin James.

ARBUCKLE ROAD

Connolly James.
Deane Kate.
Doherty Patrick, Lilly.
Flannery Patrick.
Foley Francis R.
Garvin Annie, Andrew, Rosie.
Hanlon James, Kate.
Heffernan Michael, Katie.
Hickey May.
Hickie William, Ellen.
Joyce Peter.
Kelly Annie.
McHale Bertha.
McNulty Michael, Maryann
Moran George, Peter, Sara.
Mullen Bridget.
Murphy John.
O'Connell Sean.
Padden John, Sarah.
Plover John.
Sweeney Nan, Michael.
Teehan Richard.
Walshe Mary.
Webb Samuel.

ARRAN PLACE

Clarke Patrick, Kate, Gerald, Norah.
O'Shea Bridie.
Regan Sheila.
Trimble Charles, Edith.

AVONDALE

Ahearn Mary, Doreen, Leo, James, Gladys, Patricia.

ARDNAREE or SHANAGHY

Corcoran James.
Doherty Joseph, Honoria, Bridget.
Foley James, Sarah.
Harte James, Mary.
Judge Patrick, Bridget, Patrick.
Kilgallon Thomas, John, Annie, Mary.
Mears Edward, Anne.
Moyles Bridget.
Naughton Patrick.

ARDOUGHAN

Broderick Thomas.
Gallagher May, Edward, Nora, Annie, Catherine, Thomas, John, Elizabeth.
Ginty John, Bridget, John, Sarah, Brigid.
Hunter Margaret, Michael, Bridget, Bridget.
Kennedy Michael.
Lavin Patrick, Mary, John, Margaret, William, Patrick.
Melvin Michael, Patrick, Kathleen, Annie, Patrick.
Neary John, Agnes.
Robinson Peter, Angela, Belendia.

BROOK STREET

Cummins Patrick.

BROOK STREET

Boland Michael, Margaret.
Clarke Anthony.
Convey Kathleen, Thomas, Bridget, Martin, Martin, Bridget, Mary.
Criehton Thomas,MaryKate
Halloran Sarah, Mary, Pat, Patrick, Sarah, Bridget.
Jordan Anthony, Mary.
Lynch Annie.
Molloy Anthony, Sabina.
Murray Richard, Mary, John, Teresa, Peter, Martin
Naughton Martin, Mary.
Rush James.
Sweeney Lily, John.
Walkin John, Maria, Patrick

BEHYBAWN

Connell Matthew, Annie, Eva.
Egan Martin.
Finnerty William, Mary, Kathleen.
Hanley Annie.
Healy Kate.
Hughes Patrick, Bridget, Michael, Thomas, Thomas, Winifred, Anne.
McHale Patrick, Michael, Michael, Martin.
Ruttledge Julia.

BISHOPS PALACE

Gallagher Bridget.
Naughton Most Rev. James, Katie, Minnie.

BALLYNARAHA

Blewitt Thomas, Delia.
Clarke Lizzie, James, Bessey, Michael, Madge, John, Bridget, May, Rita.
Finnerty Julia, Thomas, May, Thomas, Bessey.
Judge Catherine.
Murray James.
Rape Annie, Thomas.
Scott John.
Robinson Thomas.

BUNREE

Boland Kate, John, James.
Bourke Thomas, John, Agnes, Lilly.
Carney John, Annie.
Collins John, Annie, Eileen, Catherine, Bridget.
Corcoran Andy.
Devany James.
Dever Ernest, Sabina.
Devine James, Margaret.
Duffy Bridget, John, Kate.
Ferguson Frank, William.
Flynn Martin, Mary.
Furey Frank, Catherine.
Heneghan William, Bridget.
Hyland Joe, Annie.
Hynes Edward, Edward, John, Jane, Patrick.
Irwin Catherine, Barbara, Anthony.
Keegan Michael, Catherine.
Lavelle John, Bridget, James, Norah, Norah.
Loughney Delia.
Lynn Michael, Katie.
Mears John, Mary.
McGrath Martin, Emily.
Munnelly James, Kate.
Murphy John, Mary-Kate, James, James G.

Newcombe Thomas, Annie.
O'Boyle Frank, Nora.
Padden Maria.
Rafter Margaret, Richard, Michael.
Reilly Patrick, Mary.
Ruane Anthony, Mary.
Ruttledge John, Sabina.
Sweeney Katie.
Tobin John, Margaret.

BUNREE ROAD Ardnaree

Bourke John, Annie, John.
Casey John, Bea, Bridget.
Clarke Anne, Michael.
Coen Michael, Lizzie, Thomas.
Corcoran Joseph, Katie, Margaret.
Devaney Michael, Mary.
Duignan John.
Ginty Thomas, Annie.
Holmes Bridget, Michael, Lilly.
Howley Michael, Annie, Paddy, Alice.
Kelly Thomas, Bridget, Barbara, Patrick.
Loftus Mary.
Marshall Thomas, Bridget, John.
Murray Thomas, Mary-Kate, Ellie.
Moran Michael.
O'Hora John, Bridget.
Togher Thomas, Annie.
Connor Lousa-Sydney.

BARRETT STREET

Beckett Isaac, Alice, Isaac.
Bluett John, Elizabeth.
Brennan William, Margaret.
Browne Bridget.
Caffrey Kitty, John, Norah.
Clarke Mary, Annie, Patrick, Michael.
Coleman Percy, John, Mary, Patrick, James, Bertie.
Convey James, Sarah.
Davis Margaret.
Diamond John, Patrick, Michael, Anne.
Devers Thomas, Susan.
Downey Belinda, Michael.
Farrell Patrick, Margaret.
Flannery Rita, Patrick,Mary
Flynn Mary, Peter.
Forbes, Josie, Kate, Matt, Paddy, Bridget, Kathleen, Mary.
Grehan Daniel, Elizabeth.
Grennan Joseph, Martha.
Hearns James, Frank, Patrick, Thomas, Sarah, Kathleen.
Holmes William.
Hunter James.
Kelly John, Bridget, William, Margaret.
Leonard Katie.
Loftus Patrick.
Mangan Michael, Thomas, Patrick.
Marley Patrick, Annie.
Martin Joseph.
Melvin Bridget, Patrick.
Meenehan Anthony, Rose.
Moran Edward, Annie, John, John, Elizabeth, Edward, Annie, Ellen,John
Moyles Christie, Joseph.
Murphy Mary.
McCann Sean, Patrick,Mary ,William, Francis, Alice.
McLoughlin Michael.
Ormsby Lizzie.
O'Hora Joseph, Patrick, Annie, Patrick, Mary.
Popplewell Ernest, William, Mary, Rita.
Raftery Patrick, Catherine.
Regan James, Ellen.
Reid Beryl, Martha, Jessie.
Robinson Teresa.
Ruane William, Bridget, Joseph.
Robinson Mary, Martin.
Sweeney Agnes.
Symes Mary.
Walshe Robert, Alice.

BALLYHOLAN

Clarke Thomas, Michael, Ellen.
Connor Brodie, Margaret.
Ferguson John, Annie, Charles, Mary, Bridget, Anthony, Bessie.
Jordan Michael.
Judge Michael, Tom, John, Ambrose, James, Mary, Michael, Michael,Margaret
Loftus Patrick, Mary, Daniel, William.
McCaffrey James, James, Kate.
Rafter Martin, Anne.
Ruddy Andrew, James.
Walker John, Lizzie.

BALL ALLEY LANE

Beirne Martin, Bridget.
Doherty Martin, Sarah.
Kelly Thomas.
Lackey Michael.
Loftus Michael, Patrick.
Morrell Michael, Mary.
Murray Mary.
Townley James, Bridget.

BALLINA HOUSE

Cullen Mary.
Hourihane Dr. Jp, Lia.
Rafter Mary.

BELEEK

Convey Marcella, Joseph.

BURY STREET

Mulligan Patrick.

BOHERNASUP

Barrett Patrick, Margaret.
Casey Elizabeth, Thomas, Patrick, John, James, James jun., Mary.
Clarke Patrick, Catherine, John.
Cox Bridget, Martin, John.
Garrett John, Ellen.
Henry Anne.
McHale John, Ellen.
McLoughlin Bridget,Patrick
McNulty Patrick, Patrick jun., Lizzie.
Marshall Thomas, Bridget.
Mitchell Annie, Edward, Mary.
O'Boyle John, Mary.
Reilly Mary, Joseph.
Ruane Patrick, Annie, John.
Wade Thomas.

BELEEK

Boland Bridget.
Colman Edward, Mary.
Doherty Patrick, Maggie, Kate.
Holleran Jane.
Jacob Christopher, Teresa.
Marsh Alice, George, Julia, John.
Sanders Knox-Gore.

CIRCULAR ROAD

Barrett Bridget, John.
Cox Bridget, Pat.
Curran Ellen, Thomas,Mary
Doherty Bridget.
Fallon Maria, Martin.
Flynn May, Michael, Michael-Joe, Thomas.
Fox Alice, Patrick.
Furey Bridget, James, John, Katie, Maryanne, Thomas.
Gaughan Annie, Henry, John, Patrick.
Hallinane Joseph, Joseph jun., Paul.
Judge Julia, Michael.
Kelly Lizzie, Patrick.
Knight Mary, Thomas, William.
Marley Bridget.
Monaghan Michael.
Murray John, Mary.
McLoughlin Anthony, Anthony jun, Anne, Ellen, Martin.
McNally Anne, Claire, James, Mary.
Nealon Margaret.
Nicholson Bridget, Thomas.
O'Neill Jane, Thomas, William.
Queenan Annie, Patrick.
Reynolds Kate, Maria.
Ryan Annie, Thomas.
Shaw Chrissie.
Studdart Annie, Edward.
Walsh Kate, Michael,Patrick

CORCORAN TERRACE

Barrett Jack, Mary, William.
Battle Michael, Bridget.
Beckett Jack, Eileen.
Beirne Sarah.
Boyle Nellie.
Brennan Patrick.
Burke Michael.
Byrne Thomas, Mary, Michael, Edward.
Byron Andrew, May, Micael, Margaret.
Campbell Francis, Blanche.
Cassidy John, Margaret, Robert.
Coggins James, Maryellen.
Coleman Joseph.
Conmy Annie, Thomas.
Connelly Thomas.
Connolly Nellie.
Corcoran Michael, Margaret
Cowley Jeremiah, Kate.
Delaney Delia, Thomas.
Devlin Samuel.
Deehan Bridget, Thomas.
Doherty James, Mary, Mollie, Nancy.
Donnelly Jack, Margaret, Stephen, Thomas.
Duffy Edward, Michael.
Doyle Thomas, Evaline.
Durr Mollie.
Finnegan Bernard, Katie.
Forey Harry, Mary.
Graham James.
Gaughran JohnJoe,Margaret
Griffin Michael.
Gannon Michael, Harriett.
Gilroy Nellie.
Haran Maud, Michael.
Hennigan William, Annie.
Hogan John.
Hopkish James.
Hughes Patrick, Margaret, Michael, Kate.
Keane Kathleen.
Keegan James, Maria.
Kenna Bernard.
Knight Richard.
Lamb Rudolph, Bridget.
Leighton Richard, Maura.
Leonard Patrick, Kathleen.
Loftus Joseph, Mary.
Maguire Patrick, Elizabeth.
Mangan Celia, Patrick.
Marley Bridget, Mary.
Mee Patrick, Eileen.
Mooney Joe.
Moore Patrick, Letitia.
Morrell Bridget, Margaret, Patricksen, Patrick,William
Mulderrig Margaret, Michael.
Munnelly Edward, Thomas, Barbara.
McAndrew Patrick, Bridget, Walter, Margaret.
McDermot John, Annie.
McLoughlin Michael, Anne
McNamara Annie, Arthur.
Nevin Mary.
O'Connor Terry.
O'Malley Michael.
O'Neill Hugh.
Ormsby Thomas, Maryellen
Power Patrick, Bridget.
Quinn James, Mary.
Reilly Liam, Norah.
Rogan John, Katie.
Rogers Maria.
Ruane Alice, Joe.
Ryan Ethel, Joseph.
Scanlon William, Bridget.
Tolan T.P.
Troy James, Margaret.
Walker Elizabeth.
Waters Henry, Bridget.

CULLEENS

Brennan Patrick, Margaret.
Carr Michael, John, Mary.
Convey Mary.
Devers Mary.
Healy John, Aggie.
Higgins Patrick, Patrick, Margaret, John.
Hughes John, Mary.
Jackson Mary, Mathew.
Keaveney John, Bridget.
King James, Mary.
Langan Kathleen.
Loftus Anthony.
McLoughlin Catherine.
Mulloy Margaret, Michael.
Rogan Charles, Mary, Patrick, Patrick, Thomas.
Walsh Mary, Sarah, Anthony, Catherine, Mary, Kathleen, Peter, Kathleen, Patrick, Jack, Annie, Mary, James, Michael, Mary, Thomas, James, Michael.

COMMONS

Clarke Thomas, Bridget, Bridget, Patrick, Bridget.
Langan John, Bridget.

CREGGAUN

Foy Thomas.
Geraghty Lizzie, Thomas, Kathleen, Martin, Bridget.
Hanahoe James, Honor, Mary
Howley Maisie, Martin, Michael.
Jordan Peter, Anne.
McHale Katie, James.
Melvin Barbara, Thomas.
Naughton Martin, Bridget, James.

CROFTON PARK

Convey Patrick, Minnie, Michael.
Croneen Richard, Mary.
Durkan Edward, John, Catherine.
Egan Bridget, Michael, Margaret, Mary, Martin, Bridget, Patrick, Agnes, Patrick, Anthony, Alice.
McAndrew John, Alice.
McDonnell Mary K.
O'Donnell Thomas.
O'Shea Bridie.
Regan John, John, James.
Shea James, Mary, John, Martin.

CLOONSLAUN

Burke Michael, Julia.
Clarke James.
Convey John, Patrick.
Doherty Thomas, Anne, Bridget, Michael.
Dowd Alice, James, John, Winifred, James.
Ferguson Mary, Ned, John, Delia.
Higgins Michael, Pat, Annie, Anne.
Holleran Bridget, Maggie, Maria.
Lundy James, Margaret.
McGowan Mary, Agnes, Annie, Martin, Patrick, Mary, Mary, William, Martin, Michael.
Moloney Michael.
Mulderrig Michael, Patrick, Patrick, Kate, Ellen,Bridget
Munnelly James, Margaret.
Murphy John, James, Kate, Anne.
Murray Catherine, Tom, Pat, Michael, Mary.
O'Hara William, Ned.
O'Hora Mary.
Padden Ned.
Philbin Catherine.
Timlin James, Catherine, James, Catherine, Michael, William, Catherine.

CLOONGLASNEY
Birrane Michael, Annie, Joseph, John, Bertha.
Byron Patrick, Catherine.
Cafferty Bridget, Stephen, Patrick.
Clarke Anthony, Martin, Maria, Mary, Patrick.
Gillespie Patrick, Annie.
Heverin Catherine.
Monnelly Thomas, Patrick, Bridget.
Sweeney Winifred, John.

CLOONTYKILLEW
Doherty James, Margaret.
Doocey Anthony, May.
Egan Michael, Maria, Kathleen.
Gillespie Patrick, Bridget.
Jennings William, Kathleen, Maria.
Monnelly Bridget, John, Mary.
Moore Michael, Bridget.

COOLCRAN
Carey Annie.
Corr Edmond.
Doherty Patrick, Annie.
Rowe Mary.
Tohill James, William.

CLOONTURK
Hanahoe Bridget, Edward, Patrick, Mary.
Hart Michael.
Melvin Bridget, Ellen,Mary, Thomas, Joseph, Patrick, Annie, Anne, Patrick.
O'Hara Patrick.
O'Hora James.
Reape Beelinda, John.
Reilly Annie.

CRANNAGH
Cawley James, Teresa.
Barrett Bridget, Daniel.
Gillespie Anthony, Annie.
Haire Edward, Mary, Ellen.
Kane Patrick.
Keane Margaret.
Monnelly Agnes, John, Thomas, James.

CARROW CUSHLAUN
Boland Patrick, Anne.
Casey John.
Coleman Edward, Ellen.
Dempsey Bessie, Mary Jane.
Doherty Patrick,John,Norah
Gallagher John.
Hennigan Patrick, Anne, Anthony.
Higgins Edward.
Holleran James, Bridget, James.
Igoe John, Mary.
McGowan Anthony, Ellen, Tom.
McNally Mary, John, Roger.
Moloney Mary.
Mullan Pat, Sarah.
Munnelly John, Jane.
Murray James, Mary.
Philbin Michael.
Quinn John, Patrick, Winifred.
Robinson Tom, Mary, Patrick, Mary.
Timlin Patrick, Catherine, William, Dotie, Mary, Patrick, Mary.
Verschoyle A.R.

CASEMENT STREET
Baine Lousa.
Battle Anthony, Mary, Gertrude, Thomas.
Calleary Vincent.
Carrigg John.
Carney Jack.
Conway Jack, George, Catherine.
Corcoran Amy, James, Bridget, Hannah, John.
Cosgrave Vincent, Matthew, Margaret.
Cronin James.
Crossan James.
Cuff Mary.
Dobbin Gerald, Bridget.
English Eamon.
Fitzgerald Alex.
Flatley May.
Griffin Jerry.
Heffernan James, Marie.
Hoey Margaret.
Kelly Bessie.
Kilcoyne Mary.
Knox Annie, Madge, Annie.
Leonard John, Cecelia, Martin, Vincent.
Lynn Mary.
Martin James, James C.
Meerick Bridget.
Murphy John, Kate.
McKenna Bridget.
Nevin Mary.
O'Connor Mary.
Phillips Margaret.
Ruane William, Bridget.
Scanlon Michael, Ellen, Dermot, Agnes.
Stokes John.
Walsh Margaret.

DISPENSARY, GORE STREET
Reilly John, Margaret, Desmond, Rosaleen.

DIXON'S LANE
O'Donnell Margaret.

DURKAN'S LANE (Off Tone Street)
Barrett James, Norah, Mary.
Casey Mary, Patrick, Michael, Bertie.
Corcoran James, Mary.
Curran Margaret, Jack.
Devers Alexander, Agnes, Edward, John.
Develin Robert.
Doherty Michael, Sarah.
Feeney Thomas.
Hegarty Thomas, Catherine, William.
McNally Patrick, Catherine.
Nealon Margaret, Bridget, Thomas.
O'Boyle John.
Rafter William, Ellen, John F., Bridget.
Regan John.

DILLON TERRACE
Armstrong Jack, Elsie, Mary, Louisa, Violet.
Barrett Annie, Margaret, Marie, Margaret jun.
Dodd Ellie.
Johnston Edwin.
Langan Peggy, Thomas, Mary.
McDermott Maria.
Lynn Sabina.
O'Connor Rev. D.J.
Ruddy Michael, Daisy.

EMMETT STREET
Beirne Louisa.
Boland Patrick, Agnes.
Caden Mary.
Clarke J.H, Mrs. J.H.
Farmer Patrick, Nellie.
Fleming John.
Gallagher Michael, Nancy.
Glynn John, James, Mary.
Golden J., John.
Lally Bridget.
McHale Patrick, Margaret.
McNamara Annie.
Melody James.
Moran John.
Murphy Nellie, John, Delia, Edward, Mary.
Tilson Richard, Sheila.

FARRANNOO
Keaveney Thomas, Maria.
O'Hora Patrick, Nora.

FARRANDEELION
Boland Thomas, William, Maggie, Thomas, Patrick, Kate.
Browne Bridget.
Clarke Patrick, Agnes.
Connington Maria.
Cosgrave Mary, Kathleen, John, Bridget.
Cosgrove Thomas, Patrick, Patrick.
Cunningham James.
Flynn Thomas, Matthew, Michael, Mathew, Mary.
Glacken Margaret.
Hanahoe Michael.
Murray Michael, Mary.
O'Hora Patrick, John, Thomas.

GORTATOGHER
Barrett Thomas, Katie, Daniel, Annie, John, Mary, Thomas, Ellen, Bridget.
Carden John, Ellen,Winifred
Clarke Michael, James, Michael, Bridget, Mary, James.
Curran Francis, Mary.
Hannick Ellen, John, Michael.
Mulderrig Mary, William, Michael, Winifred.
Moyles James, Mary.
Quinn Mary.

GORTEEN
Barrett John, Thomas, Patrick, Anthony, Kathleen, John, Annie.
Clarke Luke, James, Michael, Mary.
Hanahoe Anthony, Maggie, Edward, Mary.
McAndrew Michael,Bridget
Melvin Joseph, Martin, Michael, Margaret, Molly, Dolly.

GALLAGHER'S LANE
Flynn James, Winnie.
Wallbridge Edward, Mary.

GLEBE (Rectory)
Harris Shelia M. Annette, Mary-Ellen, Rubert G.M., Rev. Charles J. Algernom.

GLENCARIN
Burns Doris, Thomas.
Egan John, Winifred, Frederick.

HUMBERT STREET
Beckett Matthew.
Bourke William, Mary, John, Robert, Robert, Una.
Carroll Martin, Sally.
Cox William, Norah, Norah, Patrick, William, Henry,
Flannery Lizzie, Michael, John, Kate, John.
Gilligan Michael, Bridget.
Griffin Ellen, Michael.
Heffernan John, Elizabeth.
Joyce Michael, Kate, Mary, Michael.
Murray May, Delia, Patrick.
O'Donnell Joseph.

HART'ES LANE
Devers Mary.
Kavanagh Bridget.
Studdart John, Kate.

HOWLEY STREET Ardnaree
Beirne Sarah.
Breslin Winifred.
Coghlan Dorothy, James.
Connor John.
Conway Nellie, Teresa, Mathew, John, Mary,James
Cullen Thomas.
Curry Patrick.
Dodds Hugh, Henrietta.
Duffy John, Mary.
Duncan Mary-Kate.
Durkan Bridget.
Hegarty Belinda.
Johnson Thomas, Beryl.
Kelly Alex, Alicia, John.
Kilgallon Rex, Winifred.
Moran Bridget.
Murray Thomas.
McDonnell Mark, Bridget, Kathleen.
McElwee R.J., Julia.
McLean James, Bridget.
Moran Carmel.
Nolan Hugh, Anne.
O'Neill John, Elizabeth.
Rolston John, Margaret.
Rooney Thomas, Margaret.
Rouse Kate.
Ryder George, Kate.
Stansfield Alfred, Olive, Ethel, John.
Veldon Patrick, Mary-Kate.
Wade William.
White Jack, Georgina.
Wilson John, Ethel.

HOWLEY TERRACE
Connington Bella.

HEALY TERRACE Ardnaree
Baker Patrick.
Barrett Anne, Martin, Michael, Bridget, Richard, Paddy, William.
Brogan Michael, Mary, John, Michael.
Broderick Patrick, Kate.
Casey Thomas, James, Margaret.
Cawley Thomas, Ellen, Bridget.
Cowley Belinda.
Clarke Michael, Bridget.
Conlon James, James.
Connor John, Margaret.
Corcoran James, Bella, John, Henry, Martin, Mary-Kate.
Commons Thomas, Mary.
Culkin John, Patrick, Michael.
Corcoran Bernard, Bridget, Richard, Bridget.
Dillon Joseph, Nora.
Deasey Bridget, Ellen, Stephen, Michael.
Devers James, Bridget.
Doherty Bridget, Bridget.
Fleming Paddy, Kate, Martin, Edward, Annie, Bridget, Margaret, Pat, Michael, Ellen, Margaret.
Forde Thomas, Pappy, Michael, Kitty, Annie, Denis, Bridget, Richard, Mamie.
Furey Thomas, Mary, Patrick, Sabina, Ellen.
Gaughan Thomas, Mary.
Gallagher Peter, Kate.
Hennigan Joseph, Nellie.
Howley William, Annie, Michael, Mary, Kathleen, Emma.
Jackson Rose, Michael, Bridget.
Jordan May.
Judge Margaret, Michael, Mary, John.
Johnston Bridget.
Kennedy Tim, Katie.
Lally Katie.
Langdon John, Celia,Patrick
Leonard Mary.
Loftus Michael.
Maycock Hannah, Teresa, Catherine.
Melody James, John.
Melvin Bernard, Bridget, James, Ellen.
Meenaghan Anthony, Martha.
Mullen John, Annie.
Murray Kate, Maryanne, Patrick, Kate, Sarah-Anne.
McDermott James,Margaret
Mcloughlin Michael, Annie, Paddy, James, Margaret, Mary, Michael, Margaret.
McNulty Bridget, Michael, Mary, Patrick.

Ormsby John, Mary.
O'Boyle Catherine.
Quigley Margaret.
Regan Dorothy, John, Pat.
Roache Annie, Mary.
Sherlock James, Mary.
Sweeney Patrick.
Townley James, Bridget.
Walsh Joseph, Bridget, Ellen, Michael, Anne.
White Edward, Maryellen.

JAMES CONNOLLY STREET

Anderson Ronald, Annie.
Baird J.A.
Barrett John, Anthony, Thomas.
Battle Paddy, Norah, John, Mollie.
Baxter Phillip, Katie.
Beattie Kathleen.
Beatty Joseph, Kate.
Bennett Jeanie.
Boshell Olive.
Boylan Thomas, Ellen.
Brehany Annie, Paddy.
Broderick Lily, Sarah, John, Michael.
Browne Toney, James,Maria ,Margaret, Patrick, Michael
Brown Jack.
Burns Michael, Bridget, Thomas, Marykate.
Cafferty Sarah.
Callaghan Bridget, Gerald.
Calleary James, Ellen, Elizabeth.
Carbine Bridget.
Carabine Chrissie.
Cawley Anthony, Bridget, John, Martha.
Cogger Mary.
Collins Willie, Hannah, Patrick, John, Mary, John.
Connolly Annie, Patrick.
Convey Katherine.
Coppinger Mary.
Cosgrave Patrick.
Culkin Mary, Willie.
Dempsey James.
Doyle Kate.
Duffy Patrick, Thomas, Kate, Charles.
Durcan Michael, Sabina, Mary, John, Mary.
Farrell Mary, Matthew, Robert, Patrick.
Ferguson John, Bridget, Thomas, Katie, Anthony, Francis, Michael.
Flynn Geroge, Maryanne.
Forbes Pat, Kate, Josie.
Forde Paddy, Joseph, James, Annie, Patrick.
Gallagher John, Annie, Frank.
Gannon Fred, Annie.
Gardiner Francis, Rose.
Gaughan Thomas, Mary.
Glover Harry.
Gillan Patrick.
Granaghan John, Mary.
Grehan Katie.
Grogan Martin.
Halloran Patrick, Jane, William, Mary.
Hastings Robert, Annie, Mary, Andrew.
Healy Elizabeth.
Heffernan Mary, Patrick, Molly, Frances, Collie.
Heraty Nora.
Herbert Margaret.
Holleran James, Bridget.
Hoban Anne.
Holmes William, Norah.
Hopkins Daniel, Ellen.
Hynes Kathleen, James, Bridget.
Jackson William, May, Rev. Thomas, Henrietta.
Jordan Patrick, Maggie.
Judge James, Mary.
Kelly George, Katie, Mary, Michael, Margaret, William, Agnes, John.
Kenny Henry.
Keogh Rose.
Kilgallon James.
King Patrick.
Lackey John, Patrick, Catherine, John.
Leenehan Patrick, Kate.
Loftus Mary, Maggie, Margaret.
Lynch Maud.
Lynn Thomas, Molly, John, Ellie.
Lyons Patrick, Jennie.
Marron Patrick, Mary.
McHale Frank.
Meenaghan Maria, Mary, Pat.
Merrick Mary, Helen.
Meerick John.
Melvin Michael.
Morris Joseph, Mary.
Murray Anne.
Moran Edward, William, Patrick, Bridget, Mary, James, Maria.
Muldowney Ellie K.
McFadden Neill, Kate.
McGinty Martin, Bridget, Martin, Ellen, John,Bridget
McHale Patrick, James, Bea, Bridget.
McMale John.
McNulty Mary, Michael.
O'Boyle Kate.
O'Brien Joseph, Hugh,Mary
O'Connell Michael.
O'Hara Michael, Margaret.
O'Hora Vincent, Mary.
O'Connell Michael.
O'Regan Joseph, Hannah.
Pearson Robert, William.
Quigley Annie.
Quinn Mary, Margaret, Agnes.
Rafter James, Annie.
Ralph James, Teresa.
Redington Mary.
Reddington Margaret, Margaret, Stephen.
Robinson Patrick.
Ruane Michael, Ellen.
Ruttledge John, Michael, Mary.
Ryder Margaret.
Smith Bridget.
Staunton Michael.
Sweeney Patrick, Kathleen.
Syron Manus, Kathleen.
Tuohill Charles, Helena.
Walshe Luke.
Walsh Luke, Teresa, Winifred, Michael, Aileen.
Warnock Mary.

KNOCKALYRE or DOWNHILL

McGuinness Bridget.
McNamee Tom, Brigid.
Munnelly George, Baby.
O'Brien Peter, Mary.

KNOCKALYRE or DOWNHILL -Ardnaree

Murray Patrick, Adelaide.

KNOCKNANELO

Fury Anthony, Catherine.
Gilligan Margaret, Patrick, Thomas.
Kavanagh Martin, Patrick, Michael, Nellie, Anthony, Bridget, Maria, James.
Loftus Mary, Patrick, Thomas, Mary.
Watt William.

KNOCKEGAN

Cadden Bridget.
Caden Martin.
Diamond Norah.
Harrison Patrick, Anthony, Bridget, Winifred.
O'Neill Mary, John, Bridget, Anne, Bridget.
Rape Thomas, Michael, Annie.

KEVIN BARRY STREET

Barrett Alice, Rev. Patrick,
Battle Norah.
Boggans Barbara.
Carlos Charles, Liam.
Carlis Charlotte, Mary.
Cawley Thomas, Bridget, Bridget.
Chapman Louis, Annie, Mary.
Collins May.
Dermody Eileen.
Doherty Martin.
Duffy Mary.
Feeney Rev. M.J.
Hewson Henry.
Hurst Margaret.
Jones P.J.
Kilduff Michael.
Macauley Louisa.
Maguire Thomas, Nan.
Molloy Mollie.
Moran Mary.
Mullen Annie, Eveleen.
McDonnell W.J.
Murphy Joseph.
McGivern John.
Murnaghan J.J.
Munnelly Bessie.
McHale William.
MacHale John, Una.
Newman Florence.
O'Kane Peter, Louisa.
Rice Ernest.
Ruttledge John.
Towey Margaret.

KILMOREMOY

Brady Matthew.
Carr Michael, Martin, Mary, Nellie, Thomas.
Doherty Michael, Thomas, Mary, Maggie, Patricia.
Ginty Kathleen, Gerard, Jane, Patrick.
Moore Robert.

KNOCKSBARRETT

Doocey Margaret, Michael,
Duglas Alice.
Petrie Jane.
Odlum George, Edith.

KNOCKLEHAUGH

Barrett Michael, Ellen.
Callaghan Edward, Mary.
Clarke James,Maisie,George
Conmy Michael, Margaret.
Connor Mary.
Cook Frank, Annie, John F.
Donnelly Patrick, Mary, Kitty, Sabina.
Hopkins John, Annie.
Jordan Mary, Thomas, Mary
Kelly Francis, Anna, Michael, Ellen.
Kennedy James, Pauline.
Marrins Michael, Bridget.
Monaghan Tillie, Mary.
Moyles John.
Orme Mary.
Ormsby Thomas, Bridget.
Quigley Anne.
Rowland Anthony, Mary.
Timony Michael, Ellen.
Walsh Thomas, Mary.

LORD EDWARD STREET

Ahearn May, Patrick.
Croke Kate.
Frizelle Mary.
Joyce Sarah.
McAuliffe Eileen.
O'Brien Bridget.
Orme Bernard, Florrie.
Rooney Sarah.
Treacy James, Mary, Patrick, Elizabeth.
West A.J, Charlotte.

LORD EDWARD STREET

Adamson Robert, Amie, Vivian, Violette.
Bannon Thomas, Sheila.
Bell J.J., Aileen.
Boshell Austin.
Callaghan Mary, Michael.
Carden Charles, Mary.
Commons Mary.
Commins Martin.
Connor Bridget, Nellie, John, Mary.
Cooper George.
Cullen Bernard, Mollie.
Devany Christopher, Kate, Mary, James, Lilly.
Doherty William, Mary, Eugene, Michael.
Duignan Bridget.
Duggan Patrick, Annie.
Ferguson Anthony, Bridget, Anthony (Sr.), Margaret.
Flannery Annie.
Fleming Edward.
Flemming Julia.
Flynn Baby, John, Bridget, Mary, Thomas, Christina.
Fox Bridget, Margaret.
Gaffney Myles, Lucy.
Galvin Patrick, Mary.
Gallagher Louis, Mary, William.
Grehan Ambrose, Bridget.
Gorman Owen, Bridget.
Guy G.J.
Helly Mary.
Heneghan Delia.
Holmes Michael, Nellie.
Howley Martin, Margaret.
Joyce John, Mary.
Keegan Michael, Bridget.
Loftus Martin, Julia.
Lynch Michael, Kate.
Lyons Patrick, Christina.
Kilgallon Joseph.
Maloney James, Mary.
Moran John, Maria.
Morrell Nellie, Francis, Mary, Joseph, Winifred, Thomas.
Murphy Margaret, Michael.
Murray Annie, Michael, Michael, Jane.
McDonald Michael, Bertie.
McGahan James, Bridget.
McHale Mary, Michael.
McLoughlin Mary,Margaret
O'Neill Thomas, Annie.
O'Regan Patrick, Mary.
Ralph Winifred.
Stokes Mary, Edward, William, Sabina, Martin.
Sweeney Bridget.
Studdart Martin, Catherine.
Timlin Joseph, Mary.
Wade Mary.
Walshe Peter.
Ward Alice.

LAGHTA - DAWANNAGH

Browne John.
Callaghan Mary.
Donnelly Patrick, Agnes.
Gallagher Annie.
Hanahoe Bridget, Michael, Mary.
Kenny Sarah.
Lavelle Charles, Bridget.
McDonnell James, Mary, Thomas, John.
Meerick Norah, John, William.
Melvin Patrick, Mary.
Moyles Mary, James.
O'Hora Mary, Jack, John, Patrick, Peter, Maisie, Peter, James, Maggie, Michael, Edward, Maria.
Quinn Edward, Mary, Michael, Aggie, Lizzie, James, Bridget.
Robinson Patrick, Annie.
Ruttledge Thomas, John, Bridget, Michael, Martin.
Scanlon Bridget, Michael.
Wilkinson John, Sara, Willie, Michael, Veronica.

LAND LEAGUE AVENUE

Cawley Michael, Alex, John, Kate.
Collins Margaret.
Curran Mamie.
Fox Michael, Annie.
Hopkins Stephen, Lizzie, James, Peter, John.
Kevany James.
Lackey Maria, Michael.
Newcombe Annie, Annie.

NURE

Dodd Michael, Margaret, Lizzie.

MORRISON TERRACE
Browne John, Matthew, Emma.
Bryan John, Lillie.
Conboy George, Madeline.
Curry John, Delia.
Doherty Joseph, Ellen.
Finlay James, Margaret.
Fogarty Margaret, William.
Gardiner James, Margaret, Winifred, Michael.
Grehan Patrick, Mary, Mary
Kilduff Patrick, Bridget, Annie.
Kelly Christopher, Mollie.
McGuire Sean, Nancy.
Maguire Owen, Kathleen.
Mullarkey Edward, Annie.
Murray Stanley, Mary.
McHugh Nina, John.
Naylor William, Mary.
Robston Lizzie.
Sheehan Annie, Patrick.
Timlin Mary, John, Bernard, John P.

MULLANS (Ardnaree)
Furey John, Winifred.
Harte John, Pat, Mary.
Kilgallon Francis, James, Lizzie, James, Thomas, Patrick, Mary, James, William, Michael, Patrick, Agnes, John, Thady.
Willis Patrick, Bridget, John

MULLAUNS (Ballina)
Barrett Margaret, Michael, Bertie.
Campbell John.
Healy Anthony, Mary.
Hopkins Patrick.
McDonnell Edward, Kathleen.
Ruttledge Joseph, Norah.
Timlin Edward, Mona.

McLOUGHLIN'S LANE
Grehan Jane.
Lackey Patrick, Bridget.
Morrison John, Katie.
Moyles Martin, Annie, Thomas.
McLoughlin John, Bridget.
McGlynn Mary.

MacDERMOTT STREET
Athy Ellen.
Birrane Annie, John.
Boshell William, Austin, Bridget, Ernest.
Byrne Lucy.
Casey John.
Collins Maria.
Convey Kathleen.
Corley James.
Conway James, Margaret.
Cooney Margaret.
Corcoran Martin, Bridie.
Cottrill Sylvester, Kate.
Courell David, Margaret.
Diamond Edward, Ellen.
Doherty Edward, Alice.
Dunphy Patrick.
Ferguson Frank.
Flaherty William.
Forbes Mark, Margaret.
Friel Kate, Susan.
Frizzelle Mary.
Gallagher Pat.
Gawley Nan.
Golden John, Teresa, Annie, May.
Grehan Frank.
Halpin Patrick.
Hamilton Jane, Alick.
Hanlon Mary, Kate.
Hardgraves Agnes.
Harte Maryanne, May.
Hoey Peter, Kate.
Howlett Charles, George.
Howley Terence.
Humber James, Mary.
Jolly Thomas, Catherine.
Jordan Mary.
Kenny James, Mary.
Lavan Mary.
Loftus Jane.
Lyons Belinda.
Meagher Annie.
Merrick Ellen.
Melvin Thomas.
Monaghan Margaret.
Moran John, Lizzie.
McGillycuddy Michael, Annie, Ellie.
McLoughlin Teresa, Maria, Rebecca, John, Patrick,
McMahon John F., Elizabeth, Kevin, Isaac.
Murnaghan Helena.
Murphy William.
Nealon Rose, Michael, Kathleen, Edward.
O'Connor Roger, Rory.
O'Donnell Eileen.
O'Dowd Bernard.
O'Keane Seamus.
Quinn Edward, Belinda, Maud.
Redmond Paddy, Mary.
Reilly Mary, Frank, Maud.
Rooney Winifred, Patrick, Paul, Rose.
Ryan John, Mary, James.
Shanan David.
Shannon Kate.
Sheehy Hannah, Michael, Joseph, Thomas.
Treacy George, Kathleen, May, William, Leo.
Walsh Nellie, Isabella, Mabel.
Wallace Mary.
Willis Richard, Frances.

NALLY STREET
Acton Robert, Ethel, Mary, John.
Browne Gerald, Eveleen, William, Mary, Ena, Maura
Burke Delia.
Carney George.
Carne John.
Crosbey Jane.
Crosbie James.
Crosby Norah, Josephine.
Dever Ernest, Winifred, William, Ernie.
Gardiner John, Ellen.
Glynn Christina.
Harte Elizabeth.
Healy Mary.
Heffernan Margaret.
Hendry Bridget, Patrick, Elizabeth, Sarah, Annie, Paddy.
Horan Patrick, Annie.
Kennedy Nellie, Christina, Jack.
Keegan John, Annie.
Loftus Patrick, Anne.
McCarrick Mary.
McGee John, Jessie, Ivan.
McGrath Thomas.
Mullen William, Nora.
O'Dowd Matthew.
Rolston Emma, William.
Ruane Agnes, James, Anthony.
Synnott Mary.
Wright Thomas.

O'RAHILLY STREET
Beirne Michael, Florence.
Boyd William.
Clarke Loretto, John.
Davis Michael, Ethel.
Frizzell Mary.
Gallagher Peter, Bridget, Bridget.
Garvey James, Annie, Kathleen, John, John.
Gaughan John, Elizabeth.
Geraghty Lula.
Greaney Eva.
Hopkins James.
Keaney Bridget.
Lally James, Mary.
Lindon James.
Loftus Peter, Mary.
Moylette Michael, Frances.
McGrath Timothy, May.
McManus John.
Rogan Frank.
Shevelin Ellen.
Tuffy Anthony.

O'RAHILLY STREET
Aldwell Mary.
Bourke Patrick.
Burke Mary.
Carney John P.
Clarke Bridget, Mary.
Cleary Annie.
Donnelly Annie.
Durkin Owen.
Durkan Lizzie.
Fitzgerald Alex.
Gallagher Patrick, Patrick J.
Guerini Eva.
Gaughan Elizabeth, Mary.
Jones Mary.
Jordan Patrick, Joseph, Annie, Paddy.
Kearney Mary.
Lenehan Mary.
McAndrew Norah.
McGlynn Sally.
McKane Archie, Jane.
Mannion Michael.
Mitchell Teresa.
Moran Matthew, Arthur, Mary.
Mulcair Bridie.
Mulhern Kate.
O'Hora Bridget.
O'Malley Mary.
O'Reilly Kathleen.
Reape Bridget.
Ruddy James, Annie.
Wherley Engelbert, Grace, Catherine, Michael, James.

PAWN OFFICE LANE (Off Pearse st)
Carroll William.
Derham Maria.
Reilly Nora, Thomas.

POUND STREET (Off Tone Street)
Forde James, Ellie.

PADDEN'S LANE
Devaney Martin, Maggie.
Foy John, Kate.
Gaffney Susan, John.
Grehan Anthony, Mary.
Mitchell Martin.
Morrison Michael.
Moyles William, Mary.
Murphy Eliza, James.
Murray Ellen, Charles.
McLoughlin John, Joseph.
Nash Lizzie.

PEARSE STREET
Adamson William J.
Armstrong Frederick, Margaret.
Bourke Patrick, Bridget.
Brian Larry.
Brien Michael, Rose.
Brogan Bridget.
Byron John, Elizabeth, Helena.
Calleary P.A.
Callaghan Paddy.
Campbell Hugh, Kate.
Cawley John, Annie.
Clarke Christina.
Coleman Agnes.
Coolican Martin.
Curran Hugh.
Crowley Cornelius, Mary.
Cornish Percy.
Cruise Margaret.
Deane Annie.
Dolphin Susan, Gladdies.
Donnelly M.M.
Duffy Annie.
Duncan James, Frances.
Dwyer Andrew, Catherine.
Early Kate.
Flynn James.
Forestal Kathleen.
Frizelle John.
Gilmartin Mary.
Gowley Catherine.
Grey Jeannie, Agnes.
Griffith William.
Hanly Peter, Winifred.
Harte Teresa, Michael J.(Dr.)
Healy William.
Hegarty Bridie, Mary.
Hennigan Teresa, Lizzie, Paddy, Margaret.
Hewson James, Martha, Thomas.
Hopkins Michael, Bridget.
Hunt Michael.
Hughes Thomas.
Hunter J.P, Violane-Victoria.
Jordan Michael, Sarah.
Keane Jeanie, Norah, Louisa, Francis.
Keaveney Simon.
Keegan Annie.
Kellar Kate.
Kelleher Patrick.
Kelly Jeanie, William.
Kiernan Phil.
Kilcullen John, Annie.
Kilgallon Julia.
Killeen Margaret.
Lally Mary.
Lavelle Thomas.
Lennox William, Alex, Lizzie.
Leonard James, Catherine, John, Norah.
Lowry Albert, Isabel, David, Jessie.
Lydon Bertie.
Lyons Nance.
McAndrew Martin.
McArdle James.
McConn Eugene, Minnie
MacCormack Betty.
McGarrigle Mary.
McHale James, Sadie.
McLoughlin James.
McMonagle Joseph, Bertha.
McManamon Winifred.
McNulty Christopher, Martin, Norah, Noreen.
Madden Jack.
Maguire James.
Melvin Norah.
Moffatt Michael.
Molloy Denis.
Moran Michael, Beatrice.
Murphy Patrick, John.
Nicholson James, Christopher, Kate, James.
O'Boyle James.
O'Connell Thomas.
O'Donohoe Mary, John, Margaret.
O'Hora Kate, Ida, Willie.
Orange L.A.
Padden Thomas.
Patten James, Michael, Jane.
Peyton John.
Queenan Nellie, Annie.
Quill George, Mabel.
Quinn Mary.
Reilly Annie.
Riall P.J., Norah.
Ruddy Hugh, Celia, James, Eva.
Ruttledge Patrick.
Satchwell John, Annie.
Towey Margaret.
Townley Edmond, Angela.
Uniacke Eileen, Michael, Cecelia.
Walker William, Stella.
Walsh Bridget.
Wallace Michael, Norah.
Wilde Constance, Letetia.
Winters Joseph, Kate.
Wright John.

PRIMROSE HILL
Collins Joseph, Julia.
Kelly Thomas, Margaret.

PLUNKETT ROW
Armstrong John, Jane.
Barbour Francis, Charlotte.
Bourke H.C., Aubrey, Henry, Helena.
Burke Michael, Margaret.
Cahill James.
Costello John.
Fitzpatrick T.
Greene Margaret.
Green Thomas.
Halloran James, Mary, Michael, John.
Harrison Anthony, Ellen.

Healy Bridget.
Howley Margaret.
Hurley Thomas, May.
Jenkins Pearl, David.
Keavany Thomas.
Keaveney Ellen, Margaret, Nora, Michael.
Keavny Mary, Francis.
Kennedy Daniel, Teresa.
Kilgallon Michael, Sarah.
Landy Peter.
Leighton Maryanne, Baby.
Lyons Bridget, Thomas.
Melvin Patrick, Agnes.
Molloy Kathleen.
Murphy Mary, Thomas, Eleanor.
Murray Kate, Michael.
McCarthy Robert, Norah.
Nash Annie.
Naughton Martin, Dora.
O'Boyle Stephen, Kate.
O'Donnell Walter,Maryellen
O'Hora William.
O'Malley Mollie.
Rhattigan Margaret, Michael (garda).
Ruddy John, John T.
Rush Mary, Christine.
Ryan Harriett, Maud, Willie
Wilson Leslie.

QUIGNALECKA
Beacom Andrew, Annie.
Collins Maggie.
Cowell Patrick, Anne.
Cuffe Thomas, Annie, Patrick, Maria, Michael.
DeVere Fred V, Mrs. F.
Finnerty Tom, Sarah.
Fitzpatrick James, James, Grace.
Gallagher Agnes, Pat.
Hatley William.
Henagan Joe.
Heneghan William.
Hennigan Peter, Eveleen, Michael, Mary, Henry, Ellen, Anne.
Henry William.
Humber Annie, James, John, Joseph, Tom, William
Irwin Maggie.
Kilcullen Michael, Mary, John, Owen, Mary.
Lacken Martin, Patrick, Mark, Bridget, Pat, Agnes, Matthew, Margaret.
Langan John, Brigid.
Loughney Joseph, Patrick, Catherine, Mary, Sarah, John M., John, Catherine, Peter, William, Peter, John, Thomas, Patrick, Mary, Mary E.
McLoughlin Bridget, Anthony.
McNulty Owen, Maggie, Maryann.
Melvin Mary, John, Edward, James, Francis, Robert, Pat, Michael, Joe, Anne, Mary, Martin, Mary, Patrick.
McCleary Lizzie.
Mullan Bridget.
Munnelly James, James, Kate.
Nealon Annie, James, John, Margaret, John.
Richards Patrick.
Rolston Matthew, Hannah.
Ruddy Patrick, Maggie, John.
Rush John, Annie.
Shaw John J, Robert, Annie, Anthony, Maryanne, Robert, Bridget.
Tighe Patrick, Christopher.
Tigue Alex, Mary, Margaret.
Tighe Margaret, Michael, Patrick, Kitty, Mary,Patrick
Truman Michael, Annie.
Walsh Patrick, Thomas, Winifred, Annie.
Wynne Norman.

RATHKIP
Clarke James, Kate.
Coleman John, Mary.
Creane Edward, Mary.
Fury James.
Kennedy Anne, James.
Kilgallon Mary, Philip, John J, Patrick, Maggie.
Loftus John, Bridget, Teresa.
Melody Patrick, Mary.
Moyles Margaret, Patrick, Bertha.
Myles Thomas.

RATHNACONEEN
Finnerty Mary
Hanahoe Mary, Edward.
Judge John, Mary, Nora.
Lacken Tessie.
Langan Catherine, Martin, Kathleen.
O'Boyle Mary.
O'Hora Ellie, John, Patrick, Mary, Mary, Henry, Bessie, Michael, Mary, Edward.
Trimble John, Tilly, Frank.

RAHEEN ROW
Doyle Paddy.
Duffy William, Patrick, Bridget, Patrick, Bridget.
Durcan James.
Fulton E.J.
Gallagher Kathleen.
Garry Stephen, Beatrice.
Heron Charles B.
Jordan Patrick, Annie.
Madden Peter.
Morley Patrick.
O'Hora Thomas.
Scanlon Mary.
Shannon John.
Smith Patrick, Mary.
Watts George.

RIVERSLADE
Burke James.
Collins Maria.
Coulican Mido, Frances.
MacDonagh Maud.

RAHINS
Hopkins Edward, Mary, Mary.
Moyles Patrick.
O'Hora Thomas, Bridget.
Ruttledge Patrick, Helena.

RAISH
Moore William, Kate.

SHERIDANS LANE
Size Mary.

ST. MURDEACH'S COLLEGE
Bourke Mary.
Caffrey Rev. William.
Clarke Henry.
Gallagher Bridget, Rev. James.
Langan Katie.
Molloy Gerald.
O'Boyle Patrick Rev.
Cowley Rev. Lawrence.
Finnerty Rev. Lawrence.
Gallagher Rev. James.
Murphy Rev. John.

ST. ENDA'S COTTAGES
Bergin Patrick, Bridget.
Birrane Patrick, Mary.
Clarke James, Maryanne.
Costello James, Lilly.
Deacy John, Mary-Jane.
Frazer Harry, Margaret.
McCall Paddy.
Murphy James, Sarah.
O'Boyle Kitty, James, May.
Padden Ellen, Martin.
Scanlon Patrick, Sarah.
Wynne Michael.

ST. MARY'S TERRACE
Bell Ida, John.
Connolly John, Bridget.
Devaney James, Katie.
Duffy Eugene, Annie.
Flannery Elizabeth.
Kilgallon Joseph, Margaret.
Kirwan Emely, Thomas.
Nixon Patrick, Bridget.
O'Boyle Owen, Rosaleen.
O'Dowd Margaret.
Ruane Patrick.
Ryan James.
Sheerin Denis, Bridget.
Walshe Patrick, Mary.

ST. MARY'S VILLAS
Byron John, Margaret.

ST. MUREDACH'S TERRACE
Anderson William, Elizabeth, Michael.
Barrett John.
Brogan John, Mary, Peter, Kitty.
Browne Patrick, Sarah.
Cafferty Thomas, Margaret.
Cahill Lily, Joseph, Lizzie, Lavina, Martin.
Callaghan Mary.
Cannon Frank, Sean.
Carroll Christopher, William, Nellie.
Clarke Patrick, Kate, Edward, Mary.
Cleary Owen, Mary, Jack, Timothy.
Collins Bridget, Martin, Dan, Martin, Sarah.
Corcoran Paddy, Jerry, Patrick, Annie.
Cuffe George, Mary.
Curran Peter.
Devaney Mary, Patrick.
Deeney James.
Doherty James, Ellen.
Donnelly Patrick.
Duffy Margaret, Patrick, John J., John, Tom, Edward
Flynn Patrick, Annie, Patrick jun.
Foy John, Bridget.
Griffiths Thomas, Hannah.
Hanley Margaret.
Humber Agnes, Charles.
James Patrick, Kate, Walter.
Joyce Michael.
Keaveney Martin, Thomas, Margaret.
Kevany Margaret, Thomas.
Kelly Francis, Maria, Joseph, Annie, Daniel, Ellen, Minnie.
Kilker Alfred, John E.
Kilroy Michael, Annie.
Lavelle Mary.
Lavin Kate, Mary, Owen.
Lynam Ellen.
Marsh Mary.
Moran John, Kate.
McAvock Edward, Ellen.
McGrath Martin, Ellen.
McMahon James.
Naughton Peter.
Neill Ethel, Kathleen, Jennie
O'Brien Una, Hugh, Margaret.
Padden Harry, Patrick, Bridget.
Reape John.
Ralph Frances.
Reynolds Edward.
Sheerin John.
Sheridan Patrick, Margaret, Margaret, Michael, John.
Timlin Elizabeth, John.
Timony Anthony, Margaret.
Traynor Thomas, Bridget, Bertie.
Walsh Stephen, Mary.
Walshe Patrick, Elizabeth.
Willis Michael, Celia.

ST. PATRICKS TERRACE
Callaghan Thomas, Maryanne.
Egan Christopher, Daniel, Bridget, John J.
Forde John, Mary, Michael, Mary.
Murphy Michael, Julia.
McLoughlin Charles, Margaret, Annie, Charles.
Purcell Margaret, William.
Shannon Nellie.

Sweeney Bridget, Annie, Katie, Michael.

SLIEVENAGARK
Carr Maryanne, Bernard, Bernard, Agnes, John, Mary, Maria.
Hoban John, Michael, Mary, Catherine, Patrick,Thomas, Michael, Ellen, Michael, Agnes, James, Winifred, Sabina, Kathleen, Mary.
Moran Michael, Mary.
Murphy Thomas, Maggie.
Shea Michael, Mary,Thomas
Trainor John, Ellen.
Wynne Patrick, John, Peter.

TEELING STREET
Brogan John.
Bourke Michael.
Carroll Michael.
Caulfield Esa.
Collins Margaret.
Curley Edward.
Diamond Margaret.
Egan Martin, Bridget.
Gallagher Lizzie, William, Eileen.
Hardy John, Catherine.
Jordan Patrick.
Kelleher Mortimo.
Kerrigan Kathleen.
Kilcullen Kathleen.
Knox Douglas.
Lane John, Kathleen.
Locke Nancy, T.G.
Maloney Thomas.
Melvin Patrick, Molly.
McAndrew Mary.
McClean Joseph.
McGlade Harry, Annie.
McHale Nellie.
McLoughlin Frederick.
McNally Dan, Thomas, John, Michael, Maryellen, Michael, Annie.
Moclair Paddy.
Moloney Lily.
Mulligan John.
O'Connor Mattie.
O'Malley Mary.
O'Reilly Nellie.
Patterson Connie.
Pierce James.
Phillips Patrick, Jack.
Rowland Kate, David Dr.
Shanley Ellen.
Sweeney Bartholomew, Henrietta, Clare.
Walshe Bridget.
Ward Con.
Waters Charles, Annie.
Warde Constantine.

King St. in 1901. Now called O'Rahilly St., The names of Gaughan, Bourns, Healy, Gillespie, Jones, Browne, Bourke, Wehrly, Sheridan, O'Hora, Erskine, Heaslip, Garvin, Kelly, Garvey, Maughan, Keane and Mullen all traded here on King Street in 1901.

TONE STREET

Barrett Mary.
Beckett Teresa.
Boland Thomas.
Bourke John.
Burke Martin.
Byrne James, Norah.
Caffrey Julia, Frank.
Carroll James, Hugh, Margaret, Delia, Maria, Patrick, Daisey, Michael, Mary-Agnes, Maryanne.
Casey Patrick, Kate.
Coen Thomas, Hannah.
Connor Agnes, Thomas, Patrick, Thomas.
Coppinger Mark, Belinda, Agnes.
Courrell Gerald.
Courell Bridget, Lily, Joseph
Curry Josie.
Cronin Mary-Frances, Thomas, Mary, John.
Cunningham Annie, John, Jack.
Dever Terence, Kate, Kathleen.
Devere Vincent.
Duffy Mary, Elizabeth,Nora
Flannery Delia.
Fleming Kate.
Foy Bridget.
Frazer William, Ellen, William.
Gallagher Anthony.
Gavan Charles.
Gavin Mary.
Gawley Thomas.
Gillespie Bridget, Patrick.
Gilmartin Kathleen.
Guinan Mary, Patrick, Mary
Harrison Lizzie.
Harte Harry.
Hewson George, Florence.
Howley Edward.
Hughes William, Julia.
Keane Jeannie, Michael, Annie.
Kelly Richard, Maria.
Lee James.
Loftus Michael.
Lowther John, Ellen.
Lyons Margaret.
Marsh John.
McCawley James, Jack, Eileen.
McConn Sylvester.
McHale Thomas, Thomas, John, Margaret.
McKerracher Florence.
McLoughlin Annie.
McNamara William, James.
Melvin Maria.
Moore Robert, Bridget,Mary
Moran John, Annie.
Mulderrig Annie.
Munnelly Ellie, Annie.
Murphy Annie, J.M.
Murray John, Mary-Agnes, Teresa, Hubert,Constantine
Napier Meena.
O'Brien Peter.
O'Connor Delia.
O'Dowd Celia, Annie, John, Annie.
O'Malley Agnes.
O'Mara Joseph.
Ormsby Barbara, William, Michael.
Patterson Elizabeth.
Quinn Lizzie.
Regan Jane, Kathleen, Violet, Jeannie, John.
Reilly James, Bridget.
Ryan Norah, Thomas.
Ryder Katie, George.
Shaw Alfred.
Sherlock Margaret.
Slater Lily, Annie, Dillia, Louis, Edward.
Stephens Daniel, Mary.
Strong William, Margaret, Charles, Nan.
Sullivan Minnie, Martin.
Timlin Nuala, Martin, Bridget, Maurice, Kate, Maggie.
Walsh Patrick, Ellie.
Walshe Mary-Kate.
Wills Eliza, Edith, Mary, Netta, George, Violet.

TOLAN STREET

Bourke Patrick, Molly.
Clarke Mary, Cecilia.
Donaghy William.
Durcan M.G.
Ennis George, Norah.
English Celia, Frances, Patrick.
Garavan Charles, Joseph.
Heffernan Patrick, Bridget.
Jordan May.
Keane Kate, Nicholas.
Loftus May, William, Bridget, Thomas.
McNamara Patrick, Lizzie.
Melvin Mary.
Mullen Margaret, William.
McNulty Gerald.
O'Hara Jane.
O'Horo Ellen.
O'Sullivan Patrick, Bridie.
Swords Patrick.
Walsh Francis, Kate, Patrick, Florrie.

TOLAN STREET

Beirne Joseph.
Berry John, Mary.
Boland John, Ellen.
Cafferty Rosalie, Eileen, Maura.
Cawley Kathleen, Tessie.
Connolly Molly.
Coultry Maud.
Cosgrave William.
Doherty Margaret, Nellie, Augustine.
Egan Thomas, Lizzie.
Flannery Bridget.
Gilboy Agnes.
Kevany Delia.
Keane Kathleen.
Kelly Essie, Amelia.
Maher William, Anna.
Malone Hugh, Eleanor Dillon.
Melvin Thomas.
Murphy Annie.
McAvock Patrick.
McNamara Agnes.
Neary Bridget, Mollie, Michael.
Padden Anne, Edward, Bridgie.
Ruane Thomas, Bridget.
Sweeney Mary, Sarah, Edward, Agnes, Christopher, Bernard.
Walshe Watt.

TULLYEGAN

Coolican James, Annie.
Heneghan John.
Holmes Winifred.
McLoughlin Peter, Patrick, John, Ellen.
Murray John, Patrick, John, Thomas, Sabina, Kathleen,
Preston Kate, Annie, Thomas, Mary.
Walsh Anthony, Bridget, Edward, Martin, James.

TULLYSLEVA

Barrett Patrick, Patrick, Ellen, Mary.
Convey Peter, Kathleen.
Dowd Thomas, Patrick, Mary.
Holmes Maggie, Thomas.
Hope Michael, Patrick,Mary
Howley James, John, Margaret.
Joyce Patrick, Catherine.
Monnelly John, Bridget.
Munnelly Thomas.
Moyles Michael, John.
Quinn Michael, Nellie.
Reddington Maria, Patrick, Jack.
Reilly John.

WATER LANE

Boland Bridget.
Broderick Bridget.
Browne John, Catherine.
Carden Bridget.
Doocey Katie, John.
Hopkins Charles.
McGowan Mary.
Mangan James, Annie.
Martin William, Mary.
McGowan Owen.
Melvin Bridget, Patrick.
Reynolds James, Kate, Kate.
Walsh Michael, Mary, Patrick, Mary.

WALSH STREET

Blennerhassett R.B.
Callaghan Mary, Francis.
Carins William.
Feely Eva, James (sergt.).
Keane May.
Lewis Elizabeth, Harold, Ruth, William.
McCourt Edith.
Murphy Kathleen.
Reape Michael, Annie,Mary
Williamson Rev. Earnest, Hedwig, Christina.
Bredin James (sergt.).
Curley Thomas.
Donlon Edward.
Harkin Daniel.
Kenny Patrick.
McNamara Michael.
Ryan Thomas.